# THE GREAT HISTORY
# OF RUSSIAN BALLET

# THE GREAT HISTORY OF RUSSIAN BALLET

## its art and choreography

Parkstone
PARKSTONE PRESS

The Great Encyclopedia of Russia, Publishing House

# CONTENTS

opposite
1. A scene from
*Raymonda* at the
Bolshoi.

2. Maya Plisetskaya.

Dear friends, connoisseurs of ballet, I hope both readers and spectators who have always been enthusiastic about the performance of Russian ballet dancers on stages around the world will now be pleased to read the Great History of Russian Ballet. Formed more than two centuries ago by talented newcomers from France and Italy, the Russian ballet has acquired its unique national identity over years and decades. The encounter of two great masters, two giants, the French choreographer Marius Petipa who had spent most of his life in Russia, and the Russian composer Piotr Tchaikovsky was fortunate for the ballet stage. At the turn of the 20th century Sergei Diaghilev's Ballets Russes acquainted spectators in many countries with the artistic activities of Michel Fokine, Vaslav Nijinsky, Anna Pavlova, Tamara Karsavina, Leonid Massine, George Balanchine, Igor Stravinsky, Sergei Prokofiev, Alexandre Benois, Leon Bakst, and other talented masters, including dancers, ballet masters, composers, and stage designers. The world was overwhelmed with this discovery; its echo is still felt in the world of ballet. Russian dancers and ballerinas have always desired to express on the stage romantic beauty and profound spirituality; that is why the great Russian poet Alexander Pushkin called their art "a flight filled with spirit". The magnificent art of ballet can unite hearts, for its language is understood by everyone.

Maya Plisetskaya

left
3. Yekaterina
Maximova as Masha
and Vladimir
Vasilyev as *The
Nutcracker.*

# THE BIRTH OF RUSSIAN BALLET
From its beginnings to the early
nineteenth century

previous pages
4. A scene from *La Révolte au sérail* in a production by Titus.

5. Khorovod (circle dance): a group dance that, in ancient times, was dedicated to the god of the sun. Its pattern (the circle) represented the sun, and the khorovod usually moved from left to right. Sometimes the khorovod stretched around the entire village, moving from hut to hut in a chain-like fashion and engulfing everyone it encountered: it would begin at sunset and end at sunrise at the very spot where it began. Eighteenth-century lubok (woodcut).

Dancing has been popular in Russia from time immemorial. The Slavs had many ritual and entertainment dances, dating back as far as the pre-Christian period. Most of these dances were accompanied by songs, and this link with singing imbued Russian dance with its richness of meaning and emotion; its soft, singing "plastique"; and the smoothness and continuity of motion that later made the Russian school of ballet unique. Russian professional ballet originated in the second half of the eighteenth century, brought to Russia by dance masters from Italy, Austria, and France. Russia, with its own rich folk dancing traditions, proved to be fertile soil for the development of ballet. In addition to learning the techniques taught by foreigners, Russians introduced their own intonations to foreign dances.

On February 13, 1675 (according to most sources) the first Russian dance performance, *The Ballet of Orpheus*, was staged near Moscow in the village of Preobrazhenskoe, which belonged to Tsar Alexei Mikhailovich. It is believed that the music for this ballet was written by the German composer Heinrich Schuetz, while the ballet was staged by Nicholas Lim, a Swedish engineer who also trained the performers. Lim danced the role of Orpheus and, among other things, he performed "the dance with two moving pyramids". A strict ceremonial order was observed in the theater of that period: the Tsar sat on an armchair placed upon a piece of red cloth in the center of the hall; the most distinguished boyars sat on benches along the wall behind the Tsar's seat, and the rest of the spectators sat along the sides of the hall and, sometimes, even on the stage itself. The Tsar's wife and daughters watched the performance through a grate from a special room in the back of the hall. Subsequently, other ballets were staged, but their titles are unknown today. After Tsar Alexei Mikhailovich died, there were no ballet performances in Russia

for many years. However, the reign of Peter the Great brought new fashions in clothing and social behavior, as well as in methods of education and upbringing. An interest in forms of entertainment that were popular in Europe, such as balls and the ballet, also developed under Peter. The Tsar himself was fond of dancing, and he set the tone by dancing in public with his wife Catherine. These balls, at which dances previously unknown in Russia (such as the minuet, the polonaise, and the anglaise) were performed, paved the way for the development of stage

dance and court ballet. Specialists were needed to teach these new dances. In 1734, the French dance master Jean-Baptiste Landé was invited to teach at the Russian court. Having danced to acclaim on the stages of Paris and Dresden and having choreographed ballets in Stockholm, Landé taught the Russian nobility to dance and staged ballets at the imperial court. He highly esteemed the inherent ability of Russians to dance, and, on his initiative, professional ballet training in Russia was begun. The first dance school in Russia

6. These ceramic statuettes depict a dance for couples: the girl "attracts" her partner with grand and coquettish movements, and he tries to captivate her with his elegance and daring. These dances featured a great deal of improvisation and, therefore, demanded considerable skill and expressiveness.

7. This watercolor by Friedrich Hilferding, the set designer at Count Sheremetev's peasant theater at Kuskovo, depicts a scene from Giuseppe Solomoni's staging of *An American Ballet* or *the Vanquished Cannibals* (1798, Kuskovo). The scene is typical of eighteenth-century ballet: against a backdrop depicting a park, the female dancers (in heavy, long crinolines that did not allow graceful or free movements) pair off with the male dancers (wearing brocaded cuirasses, short tonnelets, and helmets that are luxuriantly decorated with feathers). Both male and female dancers wore high-heeled shoes.

opened in St. Petersburg on May 4, 1738: this school later became famous as the Leningrad Ballet School and is now the Vaganova St. Petersburg Academy of the Russian Ballet. Originally, the school was housed in two rooms of the old Winter Palace. The first enrollment comprised six girls and six boys from the families of court employees. Two different European schools formed the sources of ballet education in Russia. "Serious" dance (based on the minuet) was taught by Landé and, later, by his students; comic dance was taught by Antonio Rinaldi (known as Fossano) and his wife, Giulia Rinaldi. The rigid canons of the French school and the grotesque virtuosity of the Italian merged organically in Russian performance practice. Landé's students were so successful that, in 1742, his first graduates were invited to perform at court celebrations of the coronation of Empress Elizabeth, a daughter of Peter the Great. The most outstanding of Landé's students were Andrei Nesterov, who became the first Russian ballet teacher, and Aksinia Sergeyeva. A dance class was formed in Moscow in 1773 at the Moscow Orphanage, where young orphans were kept at state expense. Their first teachers were the Italian dancers Filippo Beccari and his wife, and they were later taught by the Austrian teacher and ballet master Leopold Paradisi. Graduates from his classes included a number of excellent dancers, such as Arina Sobakina, Gavrila Raikov, Vasily Balashov, and Ivan Yeropkin. This is the beginning of the Moscow Ballet School. In both the Moscow and the St. Petersburg schools, all students were obliged to study music, singing, dancing, painting, and drama. Only during the course of these studies did school authorities assign the students to particular specialties according to their professional promise. Nineteenth-century Russian dance incorporated the best stage traditions and teaching techniques of Western European ballet, having received them first hand. The

best ballet masters of the time, including Franz Hilferding, Gasparo Angiolini, Charles Le Picq, and Giuseppe Canziani, came from Europe to work in St. Petersburg. Their conceptual and creative approach was similar to that of Jean-Georges Noverre, the greatest reformer of the ballet theater. In the eighteenth and nineteenth centuries, Russian ballet passed through the same stages of

development as European ballet. In the eighteenth century, ballet was considered a part of opera. Sometimes it was used as an inserted divertissement (a set of related dances) or as an interlude (a scene between acts with its own scenario). Sometimes ballet came at the end of a performance and repeated the plot of the opera. It was only in the 1760s that ballet became an independent genre with multiact performances. From that time, on a par with the other arts, ballet developed along the general lines of the theater of Classicism.

Its aesthetic ideal was "la belle nature," and each work strove to maintain a strict proportion in the form of the three unities of place, time, and action. Within the framework of these requirements, ballet focused on the individual: it developed his or her destiny, actions, and emotions, all of which were dedicated to a single aim and inspired by reason, duty, and a single, all-absorbing

passion. The genres of heroic and tragic ballet meet the major requirements of Classicism. Usually ballet masters introduced ballets that had already become known in the West, but occasionally they used Russian subjects. For instance, in 1772, Angiolini composed *Semira* (one of his best ballets), based on a tragedy by Alexander Sumarokov, a well-known Russian playwright and classicist who was called "the Russian Boileau" by his contemporaries. The action centered around the struggle of Princes Oskold and Oleg for the Kievan throne. In

parallel with this theme, there developed the theme of the tragic love of Semira, Oskold's sister, and Rostislav, Oleg's son. It was the first ballet based on a Russian national heroic theme. In addition to the tragic ballets, there were also ballet performances modelled on anacraeontic pastorals. A special place was occupied by comic ballets, which preserved and developed folk dance traditions. These performances brought great fame to Gavrila Raikov and Ivan I. O. Yeropkin.

By the end of the eighteenth century, organized theater companies had already been formed. The history of the St. Petersburg Ballet Theater begin with court performances in which Landé's students danced. In 1742, Empress Elizabeth issued an edict that established a national Russian ballet troupe. Later, in 1779, the Bolshoi Theater, Karl Knipper's private enterprise, was founded. Its troupe consisted mainly of children from the Moscow Orphanage. In 1783, Knipper's troupe came under the authority of the Directorate of Imperial Theaters and began performing on the stage of the St. Petersburg Bolshoi (Kamenny) Theater, the first permanent theater in St. Petersburg. These are the roots of the Mariinsky Ballet. The first ballet performances in Moscow were presented on the stages of private enterpreneurs, such as the Italian Giovanni Battista Locatelli and, later, Michael Maddox, who opened the Petrovsky Theater on December 30, 1780. His ballet troupe consisted of graduates from the Moscow Orphanage. Unlike the St. Petersburg Theater, the theater in Moscow did not have to adapt to the whims of the court and the tastes of high-ranking spectators. Russian comic operas, prominently featuring Russian folk dance, were staged more often. This difference between orderly, European-styled, aristocratic St. Petersburg and patriarchal Moscow was preserved in the years to come and affected both the repertoire and the performance style of the Moscow school of ballet, which has always been more liberated

8. The Bolshoi (Kamenny) Theater in St. Petersburg was one of the largest theatrical buildings in eighteenth-century Russia. It was constructed according to a design by the theatrical painter Ludwig Tischbein (1743-1806). Until 1868 the Imperial Court Ballet Troupe performed in this theater.

and less academic than the St. Petersburg school. After the Petrovsky Theater burned down in 1805, the Moscow troupe was also subordinated to the Directorate of Imperial Theaters. A unique phenomenon of Russian art in the late eighteenth century was the serf theater. Wealthy noblemen who owned vast estates and thousands of enserfed peasants arranged their own feudal fiefdoms. In order to imitate the Russian capitals, they opened serf theaters, in which the dancers and the musicians were recruited from among the serfs and, like other peasants, continued to work in the landowner's fields or as household servants. Like other serfs, they could be sold or savagely beaten at the landowner's whim. Only very rarely were foreign teachers or stage directors invited to work at serf theaters. Instead, Russian teachers, ballet masters, and performers contributed many of their own ideas to the traditional repertoire. As a result, the performances of these theaters were more natively Russian than those presented on the court stage, and ballets on Russian subjects were staged more frequently. The most professional serf theater was owned by the Sheremetev family. Its actors were trained from early childhood: they were taken away from their parents and given family names based on the names of precious stones

9. The serf actress Tatiana Shlykova (1773-1863: stage name, Granatova) received an excellent education. She excelled equally in dramatic roles and in episodes and was considered the best dancer of her troupe. This is a portrait by the famous dance artist Nikolai Argunov, who was also a serf. In 1803, she was granted her freedom, but she continued to live with the Sheremetevs.

according to their owners' whims: among them, Mavra Biryuzova (Turquoise), Matrena Zhemchugova (Pearl), Arina Khrustaleva (Crystal) and Tatiana Granatova-Shlykova (Garnet), who was the most famous of all. Serf dancers had no legal rights, and in most cases, their lives ended badly. The serf theater disintegrated in the nineteenth century with the general decay of serfdom, which was finally abolished in 1861. However, some well-trained and talented serf artists joined the companies of the Moscow and St. Petersburg Imperial Theaters alongside ballet school graduates. At the turn of the nineteenth century, the Russian ballet fully came into its own. Native Russian composers, such as Alexei Titov and Stepan Davydov, and Russianized European composers such as Catarino Cavos and Friedrich Scholz were working in Russia. Ivan Valberg, a dancer and ballet master, began the process of synthesizing the Russian performance style with the dramatic pantomime and virtuoso technique of Italian ballet dancing, as well as with the strict forms of the French school, thus shaping a national Russian school of ballet. The principles of Sentimentalism dominated the art of this period, proclaiming virtue, preaching the moral and educational tasks of art, and condemning vice. Melodrama became the leading genre. Valberg was particularly interested in the common people and their emotions, problems, and loves, rather than in gods or heroes. Valberg's ballet *The New Werther* (with music by Sergei Titov, staged in Moscow in 1799) was the first Russian ballet to be based on a real, contemporary event that

and Adam Glushkovsky in Moscow. Generally, a simple, unsophisticated subject was chosen for a divertissement, often one connected with a popular festival, a superstition, or a historical or contemporary event. This made it possible to combine various arias, folk songs, ballet dances, and

10. A theater owner and a serf ballerina. Caricature by an unknown artist from the end of the eighteenth century.

happened in Moscow. This was a dramatic step forward in the history of choreography in Russia. The events of the Patriotic War of 1812 against Napoleon resulted in a great upsurge in the number of divertissement ballets devoted to national themes. Such ballets were staged by Valberg in St. Petersburg and by Isaac Abletz, Ivan Lobanov,

folk dances into a single performance. This interest in folklore, which yielded examples of the stage treatment of folk dance, shaped the special role of the so-called "character dance" for many years to come. Russian choreography cherished the ingenuity of national color and character and gave prominence to the folk dances of many nations in ballet performances.

In later years, this became a distinctive feature of the Russian ballet theater.

The French ballet master Charles Louis Didelot, for whom Russia became a second motherland, played an important role in the history of Russian ballet. Didelot had worked in many countries, but he believed that nowhere in the world did a stage director have such broad opportunities as in Russia. He held Russian dancers in high esteem for their lively, receptive, and natural mastery; their generous hearts; and native talent. Didelot became the all-powerful master of the St. Petersburg ballet: he composed and staged performances, danced the lead roles in them for many years, and taught in both the theater and the dance school. The staging of a production was very important for Didelot: well-established mechanical stage effects were imbued with a special artistic meaning since they were used as a continuation and development of the dance itself. Air flights were particularly expressive: in addition to solo flights, which had already become common, Didelot introduced group flights. Didelot also developed a mastery of stunts and light and scenery effects. However, Didelot emphasized dance itself in order to convey changes and nuances in characters' feelings. Didelot imbued women's dance with lightness, and it resembled a continuously changing and twisting ornament composed of living human bodies. The men danced more technically, with strong, high leaps and movements both on the floor and in the air.

Didelot's ballets were based on a wide variety of sources, including myths; fairy tales; and heroic, anachronistic, and historical subjects. However, he is primarily known in ballet history as an author of "dance dramas." Didelot contrasted the lofty and the worldly, the tragic and the comic, intertwining pantomime dialogues and monologues with mass scenes and surprising spectators with the richness of his inventiveness and the variety of his techniques. The audience was enchanted

by the swiftness of the subject development, the dramatic situations, the brilliance of the characters, and the elaboration of the plot. Maria Danilova, Avdotia Istomina, Yekaterina Teleshova, Anastasia Novitskaya, and Nikolai Goltz became famous dancing in Didelot's ballets. Didelot readily perceived and reflected the trends of the time, and sometimes he intuitively anticipated the future development

11. In Titus' production of *La Révolte au sérail*, a ballet about a group of harem girls who rebelled against their master, the corps de ballet achieved a surprising harmony and regularity. Contemporaries claimed that Nicolas I, in order to help teach the ballerinas how to move with military precision, sent several officers from his guards regiments to assist the choreographer. Watercolor by Satiro.

of his art. Didelot prepared both Russian ballet and the Russian audience for the advent of the aesthetics of Romanticism. The Moscow ballet troupe had fewer privileges than the St. Petersburg troupe; however, although it developed more slowly, it was more independent. Before 1812, a number of second-rate ballet masters had been assigned to work in Moscow. However, after the Patriotic War of 1812, Adam Glushkovsky, a student of Didelot, headed the company. His activity was crucial for the development of Russian ballet. A follower of Valberg and Didelot, he staged anacraeontic ballets and melodramas. Glushkovsky should also be credited with bringing ballet closer to Russian literature. He staged ballets written by the composer Scholtz based on works by such

Russian poets as Alexander Pushkin (*Ruslan and Ludmila, or the Overthrow of Chernomor, the Evil Sorcerer,* 1821), and Vasily Zhukovsky (*Three Girdles,* or *the Russian Cendrillon,* 1826). This rapprochement replenished the repertoire with new ballets, reinforced the traditions of the Russian school, and shaped the unique features of Russian Romantic ballet.

Glushkovsky's performances were

12. Nikolai Goltz (1800-80) was one of the most important dancers of the St. Petersburg ballet. He began to perform in the productions of Didelot and later became a famous dancer in the Romantic ballets of Filippo Taglioni and Jules Perrot. He completed his long career by dancing the roles of noble and comic old men in the productions of Arthur Saint-Léon. Goltz is shown here in the role of the Count from Perrot's *Le Diable à quatre.* Unknown nineteenth-century painter.

distinguished by pronounced national characteristics. The ballet master's interest in folklore, folk dance, and the subjects and characters of national literature corresponded to the most progressive demands of his epoch, since interest in folk legends, rites, and historical events had been stimulated throughout the world early in the nineteenth century. Glushkovsky also devoted himself to the education of his dancers. Ideally, he hoped that a dancing actor would be able to bring to life the images of heroic pantomime ballets. He wrote that a "ballerina should be clever not only with her legs." Glushkovsky developed a Romantic repertoire at the Moscow ballet company in which Alexandra Voronina-Ivanova, Tatiana Glushkovskaya, Varvara

Lopukhina and Daria Lopukhina danced. Russian ballet reached its full creative maturity by the 1830s, forming a national school characterized by sincerity, depth, and virtuoso dancing technique. Ballet became a privileged theatrical form. No other art in Russia was paid such keen attention by the ruling circles, and no other art was subsidized as heavily. In 1825, the Bolshoi Theater was opened in Moscow with a technically equipped stage. By the early 1830s, both the Moscow and the St. Petersburg ballet companies were performing in well-equipped theaters: theater school graduates regularly replenished Russia's large contingent of dancers, musicians, and stage designers. Ballet received more from the state than the other arts, but it was also ruled more closely by the state. The St. Petersburg ballet troupe depended on the court's prescripts, tastes, and fashions. After the crushing of an anti-autocratic uprising by a group of aristocrats in December, 1825 (the Decembrist Revolt), serious subjects, strong passions, and dramatic content disappeared from ballet productions, replaced by pretentious, purely entertaining spectacles. However, due to the accumulated traditions and the experience of Russian ballet workers, the Russian ballet was able to survive. The Russian ballet was regarded as one of the best ballets in Europe in terms of its professional accomplishment. It enchanted audiences with the magnificence and harmony of its performances, as well as by the skill and coordination of its corps de ballet. Although Russian ballet came to Romanticism somewhat later than ballet in other European countries, its insights were more solid, and its achievements were preserved for a longer period of time. The conflict between dream and reality, which was the cornerstone of Romantic art, reinvigorated the themes and style of artistic creation. Two forms of Romantic art became predominant in the ballet theater. The first trend proclaimed the incompatibility of dream and reality on a general lyrical plane.

Here, fantastic characters such as sylphs, will-o'-the-wisps and water-sprites predominated. The main character personified a dream, a fleeting shadow, both magic and enchanting, an unattainable ideal. Its collision with reality usually had a tragic outcome. The depiction of such a character demanded a new ballet technique from the ballerina, including leaps and prolonged standing on pointes. The other

*Le Corsaire*; and *Ondine*. Among the most important figures of the first variety of Romantic ballet, the choreographer Filippo Taglioni (*La Sylphide*) and the ballerina Marie Taglioni are particularly noteworthy; the second was represented by the choreographer Jules Perrot (*La Esmeralda*) and the ballerina Fanny Elssler. Both trends were united by a new, aesthetically promising balance of dance

stream of Romantic art borrowed subjects from great Romantic writers like Byron and Hugo. Their protagonists were often social outcasts such as bandits, gypsies, and pirates. They were typified by strong emotions and worldly passions. The dance language here was very tense and expressive. The Russian theater repertoire included all the most important Romantic ballets created in Western Europe, including *La Sylphide*; *Giselle*; *La Esmeralda*;

and pantomime. Dance occupied first place, transformed into a symbolic poetic language that was used to express specific thoughts and feelings: it became the climax of the dramatic action. Romantic art was also brilliantly manifested by such ballerinas as Yelena Andreyanova and Yekaterina Sankovskaya. Andreyanova's tours of Paris, London, and Milan were a victorious demonstration of the concepts of the new Russian school.

13. The Romantic ballet *The Naiad and the Fisherman*, (*Ondine, ou La Naïade*), the story of a water sprite whose love transforms her into a human, was particularly effective when performed in the open air on the shore of a lake in the park of Peterhof, one of the Tsar's residences near St. Petersburg. Lithograph by Borel.

14. Jules Perrot
particularly loved to
stage fantastic
ballets. In *Eoline*, ou
*La Dryade*, whose
stage design is
depicted in this
watercolor by
A. Charlemagne, the
heroine is the
beautiful Eoline, who
is engaged to Count
Edgar.
Eoline does not
suspect that she is
the daughter of a
dryad and, therefore,
a dryad herself.
She is transformed
when she attempts to
save herself from the
evil Prince of the
mountain gnomes,
who has fallen in love
with her.

# Great figures of Russian ballet

**ANDREYANOVA,**
Yelena Nikolayevna
(born July 13, 1819; died October 26, 1857, in Paris).
*Ballerina.*
In 1837, Andreyanova graduated from the St. Petersburg Theater School. She performed in the St. Petersburg Ballet Company until 1854. The most outstanding performer of Romantic ballet, she was the brightest star on the St. Petersburg stage throughout the 1840s and 1850s. Her performance combined the effective drama of Charles Didelot's ballets, the dance poetry of Filippo Taglioni's ballets, the expressiveness of pantomime, and the virtuosity of classical and character dances. She was the first Russian performer of the title roles in the ballets *Giselle*, *La Péri*, *Paquita*, and *Satanilla* (*Le Diable amoureux*). Ballet master Jules Perrot created the roles of the Black Fairy in the ballet *La Filleule des Fées* and of Countess Bertha in *Le Diable à quatre* especially for Andreyanova. Dancing in *Giselle*, Andreyanova was stunning in the madness scene, convincingly conveying "the solemn moment of a body's struggle against death." In the second act, she amazed the audience with the airy lightness of her dance. In the role of Paquita, she

expertly performed both classical and character dances. In the roles of demonic women, such as Satanilla and the Black Fairy, she demonstrated remarkable abilities of transformation, alternately presenting herself as a beautiful girl, a page, or an old woman. In 1843 and during the seasons of 1844-45 and 1848-49, she danced in Moscow, and after 1845, she toured Hamburg, London, Paris (where she was called the "Taglioni of the North"), and Milan. She was also one of the first to bring the culture of classical dance to the provinces: leading a group of dancers from Moscow and St. Petersburg, she performed in Odessa, Kharkov, Poltava, Kursk, and Voronezh in 1853-54. Her repertoire of that period included, among other ballets, *The Fountain of Bakhchisarai*, based on Alexander Pushkin's narrative poem, which she choreographed herself. Andreyanova's last performance took place in Voronezh in 1855. Seriously ill, she left for Paris, where she soon died and was buried.

**BALASHOV,**
Vasily Mikhailovich
(born 1762; died 1835).
*Dancer, ballet master, and teacher.*
A child from the Moscow Orphanage, he studied dance there under Filippo Beccari and Leopold Paradisi. In 1780, he joined the St. Petersburg Free (Volny) Russian Theater as a member of the corps de ballet. In 1783, after graduating from the St. Petersburg Theater School, where he had advanced studies under Gasparo Angiolini, Balashov became a member of the St. Petersburg Court Ballet Troupe. He was rated as the premier comic dancer of his day, and he also danced pantomime roles and character dances. He was an outstanding performer of Russian folk dances and had extraordinary dramatic talent. In 1802, Balashov was badly injured when the scenery fell during a performance

on the occasion of the opening of the Kamenny Theater in St. Petersburg, and in 1803 he applied for retirement because of that trauma. In 1804, he moved to Moscow where he staged divertissements at the Petrovsky Theater, in which he continued to perform. Later, he returned to St. Petersburg and taught at various schools until 1829.

**BERILOVA,**
Nastasia Parfentyevna
(born November 9, 1776, in St. Petersburg; died there January 24, 1804).
*Ballerina.*
She danced title roles while still a student at the St. Petersburg Theater School, where she studied under Charles Le Picq. Immediately after joining the company, Berilova became its leading dancer. She was noted for her brilliant technique, striking artistic appearance, and lively pantomime performance. Because Emperor Pavel I did not like male dancers, Berilova sometimes had to dance male roles that required much more complex technique. She appeared at the Bolshoi and Hermitage Theaters in St. Petersburg and at the Gatchina Theater. She danced primarily lyrical parts in anacreontic ballets by Le Picq, Ivan Valberg, and Chevalier Peicam de Bressole. Her dance technique and performance style anticipated the advent of a new epoch in ballet; it is quite easy to imagine Berilova's participation in Didelot's ballets. However, her untimely death interrupted her promising career.

**BUBLIKOV,**
Timofei Semenovich
(born c. 1748; died c. 1815).
*Dancer, teacher, and ballet master.*
Born in Malorossia (now Ukraine), he studied at the theater school of the Oranienbaum Theater and later at the St. Petersburg Theater School, which he graduated from in 1763.

15. Yelena Andreyanova.

He then became a dancer at the court ballet company. He was sent abroad in 1765-67 for advanced dance training. He had great success as a performer in Vienna and gained fame in Europe. After his return, he was the leading dancer of the St. Petersburg company for twenty years, receiving a court rank and the title of Court Dance Master. He enchanted his contemporaries in pastoral and hunters' ballets. He was especially known for his heroic and tragic parts, including Rostislav in *Semira*, Perseus in *Andromeda*, and Jupiter in *Jupiter and Semele*. Bublikov is credited with adapting Russian folk dances to the ballet stage. His success in this area greatly influenced the activities of later ballet masters such as Ivan Valberg, Isaac Abletz, and Adam Glushkovsky. He was often invited to train dancers and stage "Russian ballets" in private (serf) companies. In 1777, he taught at the St. Petersburg Theater School, and he worked as a teacher and ballet master at Count Nikolai Sheremetev's serf theater from 1795 to 1799.

## DANILOVA,
Maria Ivanovna
(real name, Perfilyeva)
(born 1793, in St. Petersburg; died there January 20, 1810).
*Dancer.*
Born to the impoverished family of a navy lieutenant, Danilova enrolled in the St. Petersburg Theater School at the age of eight and became a favorite student of Charles Didelot. The next year she began to play cupids and other children's parts in his ballets. Her talent was noticed by the well-known dancer Yevgenia Kolosova, who decided to train her as an actress. In 1808, she had her debut as Venus in *The Love of Venus and Adonis* and danced Rosina in *The Barber of Seville*. In 1809, she danced Eunone in *The Judgment of Paris* and Galatea in *Pygmalion*. She often danced in divertissements, and she became famous for performing Russian folk dances. Graceful in all her movements and a gifted mime noted for her serious interest in the roles she danced, Danilova gained full recognition almost immediately. Her talent was particularly evident in the role of Psyche in *Psyché et l'Amour*. In

the eight months beginning in October, 1808, Danilova danced in more than sixty different ballets. After graduation, Danilova joined the imperial company, but she soon died of tuberculosis. Danilova's natural talent was fully acknowledged by her contemporaries, and she was called "the incomparable one" and "a phenomenon." After her untimely death, several famous poets dedicated poems to her.

## DIDELOT,
Charles Louis Frederic
(born 1767, in Stockholm; died November 19,1837, in Kiev).
*French dancer, ballet master, and teacher.*
A son of ballerina Magdeleine Marechal and dancer Charles Didelot, Didelot studied under his father and under Louis Frossard in Stockholm. After 1776, he was a student of Jean-Barthelemy Lany and Jacques-François Deshayes in Paris, mastering the academic dance of the eighteenth century. Didelot

performed with the best ballet companies in Paris, Stockholm, London, and Lyon. In 1801, Didelot was appointed head of the ballet department of the St. Petersburg Theater School. Didelot became famous for his mythological and fairy-tale ballets, such as *Apollo and Daphne* (1802), *Roland and Morgana* (1803), and *Zéphire et Flore* (1804). In 1809, he staged *Psyché et l'Amour* and *Zélice et Alcindor*, or *La Forêt aux Aventures*. In 1811, he was removed from the theater and left Russia because of the war with France. From 1812 to 1814, Didelot worked in London. In 1815, he choreographed his only Paris ballet, *Zéphire et Flore*. France, which Didelot considered his homeland, refused him further hospitality, and in 1816 Didelot returned to Russia, where he spent the rest of his career. Didelot staged about forty ballets and divertissements in St. Petersburg including *Acis and Galatea* (1816); and *Theseus and Ariadne*, or *the Defeat of the Minotaur*

16. Charles Didelot. Oil painting by Vasily Baranov.

(1817), based on mythological subjects; fairy tales, such as *Ken-Si and Tao*, or *Beauty and the Beast* (1819), *Roland and Morgana*, or the *Destruction of the Enchanted Isle* (1821); and comical ballets, such as *The Young Milkmaid*, or *Nicette and Luke* (1817). He was also interested in the genres of historical and heroic ballet and staged *La Chaumière Hongroise*, or *Les lllustres Exilés* (1817) and *Raoul de Créquis*, or *Return from the Crusades* (1819). In 1823, he staged *The Prisoner of the Caucasus*, or *the Shade of the Bride,* after a narrative poem by Alexander Pushkin, who was particularly fond of Didelot's ballets. Didelot did not complete his work on *Sumbeka*, or *the Conquest of the Kazan Kingdom* because he was forced to retire in 1819 due to a conflict with the Directorate of Imperial Theaters. Didelot was famous for his poetic integrity and the dramatic clarity of his stagings. He enhanced the role of the corps de ballet, transforming it from a mere background that passively accompanied the soloists' dances into a full-fledged participant in the performance. Didelot's dance ensembles paved the way to Romantic reforms: ballet. Anticipating the poetics of Romanticism, he emphasized female dance. Yevgenia Kolosova's talent reached its prime in Didelot's ballets, as did the talents of his students Maria Danilova, Avdotia Istomina, Yekaterina Teleshova, and Anastasia Likhutina. However, he did not deprive male dance of its position either: he worked with Louis Duport, a French virtuoso, and taught the Russian dancers Adam Glushkovsky, Nikolai Goltz, and many others. Didelot's dramatic ballets represent the highest achievements of pre-Romantic ballet. Their action was developed steadily by means of dance pantomime, whose technique was very significantly enriched during this period. These ballets were characterized by a well-developed logic and a consistent dramatic plan, and the scenery and stage effects were designed to emphasize the plot. Under Didelot's leadership, the Russian ballet achieved recognition throughout Europe. Didelot's innovations were futher developed late in the nineteenth century,

particularly in the ballets of Marius Petipa.

## GLUSHKOVSKY,
Adam Pavlovich
(born 1793; died c. 1870).
*Dancer, ballet master, and teacher.*
Glushkovsky was raised in the home of Charles Didelot. In 1809, he graduated from the St. Petersburg Theater School, where he studied under Ivan Valberg and Didelot. From 1808 to 1811, he danced in St. Petersburg. In 1812, he was transferred to Moscow and was appointed the premier danseur. He immediately gained popularity dancing Zephyr in *Zephyr*, or *the Frivolous one, who Has Become Constant.* He danced this difficult part with remarkable artistry and brilliant technique. However, serious leg and back injuries compelled him to take up pantomime and character roles; later, he was forced to retire from dance performance altogether. Glushkovsky became the head of the ballet school and the chief ballet master of the Bolshoi Theater in 1812 and held this position until 1839. During the Patriotic War against Napoleon, Glushkovsky evacuated his school fron the city only two days before the Russian troops retreated from Moscow. Upon returning, he restored both the school and the companyGlushkovsky's creative activities as a ballet master were quite varied. During the war, Glushkovsky produced twenty divertissement ballets after Russian folk themes, including *The Triumph of the Russians*, or *the Battle of Krasnoye and Cossacks on the Rhine*, in which he promoted national folklore and developed stage treatments of Russian folk dances. During the same period, he produced several melodramatic ballets in the style of Gothic horror novels with music compiled by the conductor Mikhail F. Kerzelli: *The Profligate*, or *a Den of Bandits* (1814); *The Death of Roger*, *the Most Horrible Bandit Gang Leader* (1816); and others. In 1817, he staged Didelot's ballet *Zéphire et Flore* in Moscow. In all, Glushkovsky reproduced fifteen ballets by Didelot. Glushkovsky is especially noted for staging ballets based on Russian literary works. His first effort

17. Adam Glushkovsky as Raoul de Créquis in *Raoul de Créquis*, or *Return from the Crusades*. Lithograph based on a drawing by Nikolai Baranov.

was *Ruslan and Ludmila*, or the *Overthrow of Chernomor, the Evil Sorcerer* (1821) based on a poem by Alexander Pushkin, in which Glushkovsky himself danced Ruslan. Taking advantage of the traditions of the Russian fairy-tale opera, Glushkovsky used a number of typical devices of this genre, such as changes of scenery, trapdoors, and flights. He also introduced a number of new characters. Nonetheless, he preserved the main idea of Pushkin's poem, faithfulness to love and duty and a readiness for adventure. This impressive production played on the Moscow stage for ten years and was transferred to St. Petersburg in 1824. The Romantic melodrama influenced Glushkovsky's divertissement *The Harem Festival* (after *The Fountain of Bakhchisarai* by Alexander Pushkin); his ballet *The Black Shawl*, or *Punished Infidelity* (also after Pushkin); and his three-act ballet *Three Girdles*, or the *Russian Cendrillon* (after Vasily Zhukovsky's fairy tale). By turning to Russian musical and dance folklore and to the characters of Russian Romantic poetry, by developing Didelot's aesthetic tradition, and by educating Russian dancers, Glushkovsky became a central figure in ballet in the period from 1810 to 1840. Glushkovsky was the first theoretician and historian of Russian dance. His literary works contain valuable data and reflections on ballet in the first half of the nineteenth century. His wife, Tatiana Ivanovna Glushkovskaya-Ivanova (1800-57), danced in most of his performances. When young, she enchanted spectators with the fantastic lightness of her dance and, later, with her interpretation of pantomime roles, in which she was, according to her contemporaries, "beautiful, majestic, and exquisite, especially in Russian folk dances."

## ISTOMINA,
Avdotia Ilyinichna
(born January 17, 1799, in St. Petersburg; died there July 8, 1848).
*Ballerina.*
Born into the family of a police ensign, she graduated from the St. Petersburg Theater School in 1815, having been a student of Yevgenia Kolosova, Charles Didelot, and Yekaterina Sazonova. She joined the St. Petersburg ballet troupe while still a student. She had her debut in *Acis and Galatea*, staged by Didelot. Istomina's entire stage career was connected with the ballet *Zéphire et Flore*, also staged by Didelot. As a child, she played the part of Cupid; later, she danced the roles of the young nymphs Aglae and Aminthe; and finally, she danced one of her best parts in 1818 as Flore. Istomina graduated from the roles of naive nymphs to tragic characters such as Aricie in *Phèdre et Hippolyte*, and Alcestis in *Alcestis*, or *the Descent of Hercules* into the *Underworld*. According to her contemporaries, Istomina's dancing featured "tremendous leg strength, aplomb, and, with all that, grace, lightness, and swift movements." She also danced comic

19. A sketch of a costume for Avdotia Istomina as the Empress in *Sumbeka*, or *the Conquest of the Kazan Kingdom* executed by F. Serkov.

18. Avdotia Istomina as Flora in *Zéphyre et Flore* by Charles Didelot. Miniature by an unknown artist.

roles, the best one being Lise in *Lise and Colin*, or *Vain Precautions* (*La Fille Mal Gardée*; 1821). Istomina's enchanting beauty led to several scandals among her numerous admirers, and one of them ended tragically. In 1817, Staff Captain Vasily Sheremetev, Istomina's close friend and patron, was killed in a duel with Alexander Zavadovsky, a gentleman of the bedchamber. The duel was seconded by Alexander Griboyedov, a diplomat and famous poet, and by Alexander Yakubovich, who was later involved in the Decembrist Uprising. This tragedy made a great impression on Alexander Pushkin because all the participants were close acquaintances of his. In early 1830, he outlined a novel entitled *Two Dancers*, in which this duel was mentioned. Pushkin was an eyewitness to Istomina's first triumphs and immortalized her in the first chapter of his verse novel *Eugene Onegin*. In the early drafts of his historical novel *Russian Pelham*, the poet again referred to the personal destiny and artistic career of Istomina. The actress was the first to bring many of Pushkin's characters to the St. Petersburg stage, including the Circassian Girl in *The Prisoner of the Caucasus*, or the Shade of the Bride and Princess Ludmila in *Ruslan and Ludmila*, which were considered her best Romantic roles. She also participated in corps de ballet dances staged by Didelot in Alexander Shakhovskoy's trilogy *Kerim Girey, a Khan of Crimea*, based on Pushkin's poem *The fountain of Bakhchisarai*. After Didelot's retirement in 1829, a difficult period began for Istomina. The ballets in which Istomina danced so triumphantly were no longer staged. During a performance in 1829, she badly injured her right foot and was forced to limit herself to mime roles. One of her last parts was Queen Sumbeka in *Sumbeka*, or *the Conquest of the Kazan Kingdom*. During this period, Istomina's lively temperament and infallible sense of style, epoch, and nationality were manifested in divertissements, which became another popular genre. Istomina's last performance took place on the stage of the Alexandrinsky Theater, where she performed a Russian folk dance. She

retired in 1836. Having quit the theater, she married the actor Pavel Yekunin. Istomina died of cholera in 1848.

## KOLOSOVA,
Yevgenia Ivanovna
(born December 26, 1780; died April 11, 1869, in St. Petersburg).
*Ballerina and teacher.*
Kolosova's father was the corps de ballet dancer Ivan Neyelov. From early childhood, Kolosova participated in opera, ballet, and drama performances. In 1799, she graduated from the St. Petersburg Theater School, where she had studied under Ivan Valberg, and joined the St. Petersburg Imperial Theater. Her noble appearance, passionate manner and pantomime ability made her a favorite of many choreographers, including Valberg, Charles Le Picq, Chevalier Peicam de Bressoles, and Charles Didelot. Her acting was imbued with tragic power: her Juliet in *Romeo and Juliet*, Medea in *Medea and Jason*, and Phèdre in *Phèdre et Hippolyte* moved audiences to tears. Kolosova's performance in tragedies preserved some of the artificial loftiness and stylized poses of the Classicist school. However, the inner life of her characters and the power of their passions were as expressive, natural, and truthful as the theater of that epoch would permit. She was the first to perform the roles of contemporary women on the Russian stage, including the Maiden in *The*

*New Werther* and Vasilisa in *Russians in Germany*, or *a Consequence of Love to the Motherland*. She became famous as a performer of Russian folk dances, and the Russian character dance school owes much to her. She was among the first Russian actresses to replace the pompous stylized costume of the classical theater with a light tunic. She also played in drama and opera performances. Her contemporaries, including Alexander Pushkin, were delighted with Kolosova's art. Kolosova left the stage in 1826. As a teacher, she made a great contribution to the Russian school of ballet. Maria Danilova, Anastasia Likhutina, Yekaterina Teleshova, and Nikolai Goltz were greatly influenced by Kolosova. She was an attentive teacher and advisor for her junior colleagues.

## SANKOVSKAYA,
Yekaterina Alexandrovna
(born 1819 in Moscow; died there

August 28,1878).
*Ballerina.*
She was the first dancer of the Moscow stage to master the pre-Romantic and lyrical Romantic styles of Western European ballet, giving them a Russian national flavor. Sankovskaya graduated from the Moscow Theater School in 1836. She studied in Felicite Hullin-Sor's class, and Mikhail Shchepkin, a famous actor of the Maly Theater, was her drama teacher. In 1826, while studying at the School, Sankovskaya began to perform successfully both in ballet and drama on the stage of the Maly Theater along with Shchepkin and Pavel Mochalov. In 1836, she joined the Bolshoi Theater Company, and in the same year, she visited Paris with Hullin-Sor, where she saw such famous dancers as Maria Taglioni, Carlotta Grisi, and Fanny Elssler. Dancing the title role in *La Sylphide* in 1837 brought Sankovskaya great fame. She

20. Yekaterina Sankovskaya. Oil painting by Nikolai Fedorov.

made her debut as Sylphide on the same night that Maria Taglioni danced in the same ballet in St. Petersburg; while Taglioni's ethereal Sylphide never crossed the line that separated her from human beings, Sankovskaya's Sylphide was increasingly caught up by her newly experienced passion as the action progressed. Her performance and treatment of the role was highly regarded by Fanny Elssler. From that time on, Sankovskaya danced the lead in Taglioni's repertoire, including *La Fille du Danube, Robert le Diable, La Révolte au Serail, L'Ecumeur de Mer,* and *Le Dieu et La Bayadère,* while continuing to dance in pre-Romantic ballets. Later, she danced the ballets that had brought fame to Elssler and Grisi : *Giselle*; *Le Rêve du Peintre*; and *Catarina,* or *La Fille du Bandit*. Among her partners were the leading dancers of the Moscow stage of this period, including Joseph Richard, Théodore Guérinau, and Frédéric Montassu. While combining dance virtuosity with dramatic art, Sankovskaya significantly renewed dance itself, its style, expressive means, and techniques. Among other things, she was the first in Russia to use pointes. Fragile and petite, she emphasized the lightness, grace, and purity of dance rather than its grandeur. The new dance technique, ideas, and images of Romantic ballet attracted the Moscow democratic intelligentsia to Sankovskaya's performances. Her dancing enchanted a number of famous writers, including Vissarion Belinsky, Alexander Herzen, Sergei

21. Yevgenia Kolosova, presumably in *The Amazon*. Oil painting by Alexander Varnek.

Aksakov, Afanasy Fet, and Mikhail Saltykov-Schedrin. Sankovskaya was called by her contemporaries "the soul of the Moscow ballet." After Hullin-Sor left the Bolshoi Theater, Sankovskaya began to choreograph. She produced *Le Diable à quatre* by Joseph Mazilier in 1846 and *Le Rêve du Peintre* by Jules Perrot in 1853. Sankovskaya's last role as a ballerina was the title role in *La Esmeralda*, staged by Perrot in 1853. Having retired from the stage in 1854, Sankovskaya taught ballroom dancing and gave private lessons. For a time, she taught in the family of Konstantin Stanislavsky, the stage director who later reformed drama theater.

## SERGEYEVA,
Aksinia Sergeyevna
(born c. 1726; died January 27, 1756, in St. Petersburg).
*Ballerina.*
In 1738, she enrolled in the St. Petersburg Dance School, where

22. Yekaterina Teleshova as Louise in *Le Déserteur.* Oil painting by an unknown nineteenth-century artist.

she studied under Jean-Baptiste Landé. In 1739, she began to perform on the stage, becoming a Court Theater dancer in 1741. In 1742, she visited Moscow with some of Landé's students to attend the coronation of Empress Elizabeth Petrovna. She was considered the best Russian dancer of her time, and her dancing was as powerful and charming as that of any dancer in Europe. She married the dancer Thomas Le Brun and had a daughter, Natalia, who also became a dancer. She retired from the theater in 1753.

## TELESHOVA (Telesheva),
Yekaterina Alexandrovna
(born 1804; died 1857).
*Ballerina.*
She appeared for the first time on the St. Petersburg stage in the role of Hymen in *Zéphire et Flore* in 1819. Having graduated from the St. Petersburg Theater School (where she had studied with Charles Didelot),

she joined the St. Petersburg Bolshoi Theater ballet company in 1824 and soon became a leading dancer. She was the first performer of many roles in ballets staged by Didelot. The range of Teleshova's artistic activities was very broad, from the smart and sprightly Louise in *Le Déserteur* to the tragically sinful Phèdre in *Phèdre et Hippolyte*. She displayed great talent as an actress in the part of the mute girl Fenella in the opera *The Mute from Portici* by Auber. Her performance was imbued with such deep feelings that even the most impassive spectators were deeply moved. Teleshova's talent was highly esteemed by many writers and painters: Karl Brullov used her as the model for his *Italian Lady at a Fountain* and Orest Kiprensky painted her portrait. Alexander Griboyedov, the author of the famous comedy *Woe from Wit* and an outstanding diplomat, dedicated a poem to her in which he glorified her performance as the sorceress in *Ruslan and Ludmila*. Teleshova retired from the stage in 1842.

## VALBERG,
Ivan Ivanovich
(born July 14, 1766, in Moscow; died July 26, 1819, in St. Petersburg).
*Dancer, ballet master, and teacher.*
Born to the family of a theater tailor, Valberg graduated from the St. Petersburg Theater School in 1786, having studied under Gasparo Angiolini and Giuseppe Canziani. He joined the ballet company of the Imperial Theater as a solo dancer. He danced the pantomime parts of Jason in *Medea and Jason* and Romeo in *Romeo and Juliet*. Valberg was the first Russian choreographer. He was a well-educated person for his time, well-versed in ancient and contemporary literature, history, and mythology. He made translations from several European languages. In 1795, he staged the ballet *Happy Repentance*, with music written by an unknown composer. Later, he produced thirty-six original ballets and revived ten ballets by other choreographers. He also staged divertissements based on Russian folk themes and dances in dramatic

opera performances. Valberg inherited the traditions of the ballet d'action from the choreographers of the eighteenth century. However, his creative concepts were also influenced by the genre of melodrama, which was popular early in the nineteenth century. Valberg's ballets featured a combination of contrasting situations, moods, emotions, and characters. The machinations of evildoers failed before the triumph of virtuous and sentimental characters. An outstanding representative of Sentimentalism in Russian ballet, Valberg asserted the moral foundation of his art in such ballets as *Blanca*, or *Marriage Out of Revenge* (1803); *Count Costelli*, or *Trespassing Brother* (1804); *Clara, or Conversion to Virtue* (1806); and others. Valberg also staged ballets based on mythological and fairy-tale subjects (*Orpheus and Euridice* and *Cendrillon*, respectively) and divertissements on Russian themes, such as *The New Heroine*, or *a Cossack Woman* and *Russians in Germany*. His staging of *The New Werther* in 1799 was a very important development because the plot, which was similar to that of Goethe's famous novel, was connected to actual events in contemporary Moscow. By the end of his life, Valberg had become a coworker and associate of Charles Didelot. From 1794, he taught at the St. Peterburg Theater School. An advocate of the concept of dance expressiveness, Valberg trained many outstanding performers and ballet masters, including Yevgenia Kolosova, Arina Tukmanova, Isaac Abletz, and Adam Glushkovsky. Valberg stopped working as a ballet master and teacher only a few months before he died.

23. Ivan Valberg. Miniature by an unknown artist

# THE AGE OF MARIUS PETIPA
## The second half of the nineteenth century

previous pages
24. A scene from
*La Bayadère* by the
Bolshoi.

25. Matvei Shishkov
(1832-97), the
decorator of the St.
Petersburg Theater
was a leading
representative of the
historico-realistic
trend in art. His sets
were praised by
contemporaries as the
discovery of a
Russian style of stage
design.

This sketch is a set
for Arthur Saint-
Léon's *The Little
Humpbacked Horse.*

By the middle of the nineteenth century, the brilliant period of Romantic ballet had come to an end. Its ideas and discoveries, copied by numerous imitators, had become exhausted. Its profound human substance had faded away, and ballet ceased to be the drama of characters and passions, while the fantasy of ballet had lost its poetic links with life. During this period, the Russian intellectual was carried away by the lofty ideas of reforming society and of social progress. This mood was further bolstered by the long-awaited abolition of serfdom in 1861. Democratically-minded audiences longed for the theater to become a champion of progressive ideas. Russian literature, painting, and drama turned for inspiration to real life. Russian symphonic music and operas exploited and developed the concept of national identity. However, ballet failed to respond to either the struggle of ideas simmering in public life or to new currents in art. Ballet became a theater for the privileged elite and, increasingly, a gala extravaganza. Simplified plots did little to connect solo dances with divertissements. Simple music merely formed a background against which a ballerina could demonstrate her skills. Sets were sumptuous, but of little artistic value. All of this distracted spectators from the real problems seething beyond the theater walls. However, passions were aflame around individual ballerinas. Two distinct parties of balletomanes formed: one, known as the Petipists was devoted to Maria Petipa-Surovshchikova and the other, the Muravievists, consisted of Marfa Muraviova's admirers. The parties were antipathetic to one another, and their clashes occasionally ended in fierce fist fights at the back doors of theaters.

Turning to western choreography, which itself was going through hard times, failed to improve the situation. Ballet in Europe was gradually lapsing into a revue or, at best, into a dance-interspersed extravaganza dominated

by theatrical effects, the latest mechanical gadgetry, and fantastic costumes. On the Russian scene, neither sixty-six-year-old Carlo Blasis, a celebrated Italian summoned by the Bolshoi whose choreographic expertise had long lost its novelty, nor Arthur Saint-Léon, a talented Frenchman engaged by St. Petersburg's Mariinsky Theater, could help. Saint-Léon was shrewd enough to perceive the popular mood by staging a ballet based on a Russian theme. He chose Piotr Yershov's charming fairy tale *The Little Humpbacked Horse*, derived from Russian folk motifs. The magical Humpbacked Horse helps Ivanushka (nicknamed the Simpleton) to overcome the mortal dangers brought down upon him by spiteful boyars and a stupid tsar. Within Yershov's innocent fairy tale, a bitter satire on the autocracy was hidden. However, in Saint-

26. Maria Petipa-Surovshchikova (1836-82), a spectacularly gifted dancer who was a partner and first wife of Marius Petipa, was known for her charming miming and her fascinating stage presence. Petipa created "The Dance of the Little Pirate" in *Le Corsaire* especially for her. Colored photograph.

Léon's version, the tsar was transformed into a Tatar khan; the Tsar-maiden personified freedom; Ivanushka symbolized the good-natured Russian people; and the *Humpbacked Horse* represented the genius of Russia. There was virtually no plot development; a medley of scenes culminated in an immense divertissement consisting of the folk dances of the twenty-two races that populated Russia, including a chimeral Ural ethnic group. Although the choreographer succeeded in producing ingenious dances that were true to real folklore and to the achievements of both classical and character dancing, the ballet was explicitly pseudo-Russian and obsequious to the authorities. Nonetheless, the efforts of Blasis and Saint-Léon were not in vain. In reviving his old ballets and staging new ones, Saint-Léon created new possibilities for large dance ensembles, thus paving the way for Marius Petipa's accomplishments. A great authority on the classical school of the nineteenth century, Blasis helped the Moscow school retain its professionalism and identity. Even though ballets were becoming poorer in content, performers maintained the high level of the art. Although theater management spared no expense to invite the world's celebrities (remunerating them with fees unthinkable for Russian dancers), the

successors to the fame of Yevgenia Kolosova, Avdotia Istomina, Yelena Andreyanova, and Yekaterina Sankovskaya were gradually winning back what belonged to them. The St. Petersburg scene was adorned by the magnificent personalities of Nadezhda Bogdanova, Petipa-Surovshchikova, and Muraviova. In Moscow, Praskovia Lebedeva, Olga Nikolayeva, Anna Sobeshchanskaya, and Polina Karpakova maintained and augmented the fame of the Russian school, assimilated new trends in dancing from abroad, and imbued virtuoso technique with a soft, lyrical tenor. Historically, it was the Russian ballet of the last quarter of the nineteenth century that revitalized the art of ballet. In 1862, Petipa, who had already worked in St. Petersburg for fifteen years, staged his first major ballet, *The Pharaoh's Daughter*, after Théophile Gautier's *Le Roman de la Momie*. However, this production did not produce any significant breakthroughs. It was an impressive spectacle with magnificent, but rather stereotyped sets by Andrei Roller; melodic dance music by Cesare Pugni; and an exotic subject. An Englishman caught by a simoom in the desert takes refuge in a pyramid. In his sleep he turns into Ta-Hor, an Egyptian, and falls in love with the reanimated mummy of Princess Aspiccia. After numerous reversals of fortune and

27. Vasily Geltzer (1840-1908), the Moscow character dancer, who possessed a rare gift for self-transformation, danced a wide variety of roles: the majestic King of Nubia in *The Pharaoh's Daughter*, the tragic Claude Frollo in *La Esmeralda*, and women's roles such as Marceline in *La Fille Mal Gardée* and Fairy Carabosse in *The Sleeping Beauty*.

Here Vasily Geltzer is shown as Ivanushka in *The Little Humpbacked Horse*.

far right
28. The pas de six from Arthur Saint-Léon's *La Vivandière*, reconstructed from the choreographer's own miraculously preserved notes.

34

incredible adventures on the bottom of the Nile, the ballet ends with a wedding party. However, even in this ballet, Petipa demonstrated new choreographic principles that, upon further elaboration, enabled him to produce truly outstanding ballets. Petipa controlled his solo dancers and corps de ballet as a composer controls solo parts and

29a. These sketches by Adolphe Charlemagne show costumes for *A Lebanese Beauty.*

29b. In Petipa's time, the light costumes of Taglioni's period became shorter and more full. This facilitated the development of the techniques of woman's dance. The lines of this tutu recall ball dresses of the 1860s (left), but occasionally designers tried to convey, in a very approximate way, national costumes (right).

instrumental groups in an orchestra. Impressive images resulted from their interactions and contrasts. The groups might first merge and then separate again, the whole becoming a harmonious sequence. With each new ballet, Petipa delved deeper into the structure of solo and ensemble dance. Cautiously, retreating and experimenting again, he progressed to the establishment of the new. While polishing his choreographic concepts, Petipa never turned his back on the so-called diamond-studded circle, as aristocratic theater-goers referred to their place in the theater. This audience could dictate its desires and make ballet cater to its tastes. Petipa staged nearly sixty ballets, including a large number of flashy, but run-of-the-mill, productions. However, due to Petipa's efforts many of the best ballets of the past, such as *Giselle*, survived. The late 1870s saw increased interest in ballet among the theater-going public, and advance and season ticket booking systems became common.

previous pages
31. In his 1868
revival of Jules
Perrot's *Le Corsaire*,
Marius Petipa added
the beautiful dance
number *"Le Jardin
Animé"*. This dance
is shown here, being
performed by dancers
from the Mariinsky
Theater.

Louis Mérante of the Paris Théâtre National de l'Opéra, who was sent to Russia by the French government, wrote that ballet in St. Petersburg had attained a level undiscovered by Europe and that its school was exemplary. Russian ballet owed this achievement almost entirely to Petipa. However, Petipa's major accomplishments were still ahead. The choreographer regarded the multiact ballet, the "grand ballet," as an ideal vehicle for unfolding action gradually in a sequence of pantomime and dance scenes. *La Bayadère*, produced by Petipa in 1877, was crowned with an "act of shades" in which the warrior Solor discerned in his sleep the shade of his beloved bayadere, Nikia, who had been put to death by her rival. Nikia's shade appears surrounded by others: their dance chorus expressed a transparent grief that was

Below
32. Dancers from the Mariinsky Theater of Petipa's time perform the poignant scene "The Shades".

estranged from the mundane passions of the previous act. At the same time, individual parts (solo dance variations) broke from the chorus. Nikia's brilliant dance conveyed her feelings in a variety of moves changing from rigidly straight and graphically clear-cut lines to barely discernible waning dashes, to rounded patterns of rotation, to swift air-

33. This sketch by Roller relates to *A Lebanese Beauty,* or *The Mountain Spirit.*

piercing flights. Notwithstanding Ludwig Minkus' artless music, Petipa's choreography already displayed the beginnings of a ballet imagery that was characteristic of symphonic music. After *La Bayadère*, the choreographer was ready for an alliance with the great symphonist Piotr Tchaikovsky. It was Ivan Vsevolozhsky, the director of Imperial Theaters, who brought Tchaikovsky and Petipa together. A man of versatile education and fine taste, Vsevolozhsky was particularly fond of ballet. He admired French art, especially the Louis XIV style, and was also highly appreciative of Russian art and culture. The former passion accounts for his choice of a French fairy-tale plot for his new production,

*The Sleeping Beauty*; the latter explains the selection of a quintessentially Russian composer, Tchaikovsky, for the ballet. It was a happy combination of rich symphonic music, with the grandeur, ingenuity, and integrity of dance. *The Sleeping Beauty* (1890) has remained unsurpassed as a model of choreographic art. *Raymonda* (1898) became Petipa's final masterpiece. Its ingenious score, written by Alexander Glazunov, advanced that composer as a credible successor to Tchaikovsky. Petipa's *Raymonda* opened up new prospects of further symphonizing dance, both classical (as in the

case *The Sleeping Beauty*) and character dance, as well as providing the possibility for their interplay. The style of "the Classical Hungarian Pas" was classic, though tinged with elements of folk dance. Petipa also brought Tchaikovsky's first ballet, *Swan Lake*, back from oblivion. Staged in Moscow in 1877 by the mediocre Czech choreographer Wensel Reisinger, the ballet was a failure, neglected for nearly twenty years. The "swan" dances in the restaged ballet formed the apex of the creative career of yet another choreographer from the Mariinsky Theater,

ballet and helped maintain ballet as a separate art while shaping its new qualities. These qualities required a high level of professionalism from the entire company, a level that was attained as a result of the teaching talents of Christian Johanson and Enrico Cecchetti. The ballets produced by Petipa and Ivanov featured performances by Maria Petipa-Surovshchikova, Yekaterina Vazem, Yevgenia Sokolova, Varvara Nikitina, Pavel Gerdt, Platon Karsavin, Nikolai Legat, and others. By the turn of the century, foreign tours by Russian ballet dancers had become routine. The turn of the century proved to be a period of summing-up. Whatever was attainable within the aesthetic confines of the ballet spectacle had already been accomplished. The evening performance in the Mariinsky Theater on December 31, 1900, was *Swan Lake* in the version of Petipa and Ivanov. In the words of one reviewer, "the ballet of the nineteenth century ended yesterday with Swan Lake. One couldn't imagine a better ending." Russian ballet was on the threshold of new reforms.

Below
35. The inspired, poetic swan scene, created by Lev Ivanov, continues to arouse audiences to this day. This photograph shows its première in 1895.

Lev Ivanov. These scenes were imbued with a feeling of elegiac sorrow, lyrical intonations, and strains of grief and foreboding. The composer shaped this musical form in the manner of a symphonic piece following neither the choreographer's requirements nor the libretto sequence. He was able to make unprecedented poetic generalizations: Lev Ivanov's "swan" dances were a breakthrough into the future of ballet. The meeting of Petipa and Ivanov with Tchaikovsky and Glazunov yielded results that confirmed the potential of the course chosen by Russian

36. *The Sleeping Beauty*, Marius Petipa's greatest creation, continues to be performed on Russian stages. Here, dancers from the Mariinsky Theater dance a scene in which the Lilac Fairy leads the good fairies.

# Great figures of Russian ballet

## BOGDANOVA,

Nadezhda Konstantinovna.
(Born 1836 in Moscow; died Sept. 15, 1897, in St. Petersburg).
*Ballerina.*
Bogdanova was the daughter of Konstantin Bogdanov and Tatiana Karpakova, solo dancers from Moscow's Bolshoi. At the age of twelve, she had already danced leading parts in fragments from Romantic ballets while touring the Russian provinces with a company established by her father. In 1850, she began studying in Paris with Joseph Mazilier and performed on the stage of the Paris Opera. Returning to Russia in 1855, Bogdanova made her debut in St. Petersburg in *Giselle*, and, until 1864, she danced on the stages of both St. Petersburg and Moscow. Her repertoire included the leading parts in such ballets as *Gaselda*, or *Les Tziganes*; *Faust*; *Catarina*, or *La Fille du Bandit*; *La Esméralda*; and *Météora*, or *the Valley of Stars*. Lyricism was the principal distinctive feature of Bogdanova's artistic expression. Spectators admired the purity, charming naivety, and shyness of her characters. Semitones and intentionally subdued movements prevailed in Bogdanova's lyrically serene dancing. From 1857, Bogdanova toured Paris, Berlin,

Naples, and Budapest. Her last appearance was in Warsaw in 1867, after which she left the stage in the prime of her ballet career.

## GERDT,

Pavel (Paul Friedrich) Andreyevich.
(Born Dec. 4, 1844 in Volynkino near St. Petersburg; died Aug. 12 1917 in Vamaliki, Finland; buried in Petrograd (now St. Petersburg).
*Ballet dancer and teacher.*
Born to the family of a Russianized German, Gerdt graduated from the St. Petersburg Theater School in 1864. He studied there under Marius Petipa and Christian Johanson. From 1860 to the end of his life Gerdt danced with the Mariinsky Theater. His first major success came as Albert in *Giselle* in 1871. Gerdt was one of the best lyric and Romantic danseurs on the St. Petersburg stage. He was tall and well proportioned, fair haired and blue eyed, with nobly handsome features. A dramatically gifted actor, he was also an

outstanding pantomimist, who made effective use of conventional gestures. His performance style, both manly and elegant, made him a paragon for several decades. Gerdt was the first performer of the leading roles in Tchaikovsky's ballets, including Prince Désiré in *The Sleeping Beauty,* Prince Coqueluche in *The Nutcracker,* and Siegfried in *Swan Lake.* Late in his career, Gerdt danced in Alexander Glazunov's ballets, appearing as Damis in *Ruses d'Amour* (*The Trial of Damis),* Bacchus in *The Seasons,* and Abderâme in *Raymonda.* Sergei Diaghilev was so impressed with Gerdt's performance in the latter role that he invited the dancer to recreate it in a proposed production of *Raymonda* for the first "Russian Season" in Paris. A choreograher's career did not really appeal to Gerdt. In his productions of *The Imaginary Dryads, Sparks of Love,* and *Javotta,* he was strongly influenced by Petipa's experience. He completed the production of *Sylvia,* or *La Nymphe de Diane* that had been begun by Lev Ivanov. In 1880, Gerdt began teaching at the St. Petersburg Theater School. His students included Anna Pavlova, Tamara Karsavina, Agrippina Vaganova, Michel Fokine, Lidia Kyaksht, and Sergei Legat. Gerdt's teaching career ended in 1904, but he continued to appear in mime roles. He appeared on the stage for the last time in 1916. His daughter — Yelizaveta Pavlovna Gerdt (1891-1975) — was a well-known ballerina and teacher. Her art, austere and dignified, was deeply rooted in the traditions of classical ballet. Harmonious and refined in form, her dance seemed to be drawn in pastel shades, becoming a model of academicism in ballet during the 1920s. Yelizaveta Gerdt's students included Maya Plisetskaya, Yekaterina Maximova, and Alla Shelest.

37. Pavel Gerdt as Oberon in *A Midsummer Night's Dream.*

38. Nadezhda Bogdanova as Kathi in *La Vivandière.*

45

39. Lev Ivanov
as Conrad in
*Le Corsaire.*

## IVANOV,
Lev Ivanovich.
(Born Mar. 2, 1834; died Dec. 24, 1901, in St. Petersburg).
*Dancer and choreographer.*

Born out of wedlock, Ivanov stayed in the Moscow Orphanage until he was three, at which time he was brought to his parents' family. Shy and quiet, the boy grew into a man who was not much of a fighter, unable to seek favor with his superiors or to shine in public. In 1852, Ivanov graduated from the St. Petersburg Theater School, where he studied ballet under Alexander Pimenov, Frédéric (Pierre Malavergne), Émile Gredelue, and Jean Petipa senior and was enrolled in the corps de ballet of St. Petersburg ballet company. The ballerinas Yelena Andreyanova and Tatiana Smirnova noticed the gifted dancer and singled him out as a partner. In 1869, he took the position of premier danseur but soon gave it up to Pavel Gerdt Ivanov danced Phoebus and Claude Frollo in *La Esméralda*, Solor in *La Bayadère,* Colin in *La Fille Mal Gardée,* and Conrad in *Le Corsaire.* A gifted danseur and expressive pantomimist, Ivanov often gave up advantageous parts to others, while the roles he received rarely demonstrated his distinctive talents. He made his last appearance on the stage in 1893. In 1858, Ivanov began teaching the primary classes of the St. Petersburg Theater School. Such ballerinas as Yekaterina Vazem, Mathilda Kchessinska, Olga Preobrajenska, and Agrippina Vaganova began their schooling with him. In 1882, Ivanov was appointed a regisseur of St. Petersburg ballet company. In 1885, he became second choreographer in the theater. With a fabulous inborn aptitude for music, he could memorize by ear and play instantly an entire ballet. In Ivanov's understanding of choreography, music was the driving force in ballet. In 1887, Ivanov produced *The Enchanted Forest,* a ballet along Romantic lines, and, together with Marius Petipa, *The Tulip of Harlem,* which combined motifs of fantasy and folklore. He was a permanent supervisor of ballet performances in the Krasnoye Selo theater, which was something of an out-of-town branch of the imperial theaters. The choreographer's genius was revealed for the first time in his production of the Polovtsian Dances for the opening of Alexander Borodin's opera *Prince Igor* in 1890. Ivanov's exceptional musical flair resulted in an intuitive representation of Borodin's images that foreshadowed the achievements of Michel Fokine. In 1892, when Petipa suddenly fell ill,

40. "The Dance of
the Snowflakes".
After the première of
*The Nutcracker,*
by Ivanov.

Ivanov substituted for him and produced *The Nutcracker.* The choreographer scored a special success that was to influence the ballet theater of his time with his "Dance of the Snowflakes", in which sixty dancers in white tutus symbolized swirling snow in order to convey the mood of a calm, moonlit Christmas night. In 1894, Ivanov again turned to Tchaikovsky's music when he once again had to stand in for the ailing Petipa. Ivanov staged the second scene of *Swan Lake* in a concert held in the Mariinsky Theater in memory of Tchaikovsky. Though in keeping with the Romantic traditions of Russian nineteenth-century choreography, the "swan" dances also prepared the ground for the future. Ivanov devised a symphonic approach in which the swan ensembles enhanced the lyric and tragic character of the bewitched Princess Odette. The fairy-tale ballet was elevated to the level of a philosophical reflection on the dramatic fate of the beautiful Ivanov. He continued and expanded his experiments in symphonizing dance with Liszt's *Second Hungarian Rhapsody*, which was first performed in 1900 as an insertion in *The Little Humpbacked Horse.* Death prevented Ivanov from finishing his production of *Sylvia*, or *La Nymphe de Diane,* and it was completed by Pavel Gerdt. Ivanov also planned a production of *Egyptian Nights*, that was later realized by Michel Fokine.

## JOHANSON,

Christian Petrovich.
(Born May 20, 1817, in Stockholm; died Dec. 25, 1903,
in St. Petersburg).
*Dancer and teacher.*
Johanson studied dance in Stockholm, and after making his debut in 1836 on the stage of the Stockholm Royal Theater, he polished his skills in Copenhagen under Auguste Bournonville. In 1841, Johanson came to St. Petersburg for good. A brilliant classical danseur and an excellent partner, Johanson was noted for the explicit elegance of his manners and postures. At the beginning of his career, Johanson excelled primarily in virtuoso parts. His contemporaries noted that

the danseur, in performing an encore, would reproduce his act perfectly. From the late 1840s, Johanson began to appear in pantomime parts and revealed his outstanding acting talent in such roles as Pierre Gringoire in *La Esméralda* and the artist Salvator Rosa in *Catarina*, or *La Fille du Bandit*. During his forty-three years on the St. Petersburg stage, Johanson adopted a lot from his Russian fellow dancers, becoming a truly Russian performer. Yet his greatest fame came as a teacher of classical dance at the St. Petersburg Theater School. His students included Pavel Gerdt, Nikolai Legat, Mathilda Kchessinska, Olga Preobrajenska, Anna Pavlova, and Tamara Karsavina. Deeply appreciative of Johanson's teaching talent, Marius Petipa often attended his classes and borrowed material for his own ballet productions. Johanson's activities linked Russian ballet traditions with the Danish school of classical dance and, through it (since Bournonville had been a student of Auguste Vestris), with the tradition of eighteenth-century virtuoso ballet dance.

## LEBEDEVA

(married name, Shilovskaya),
Praskovia Prokhorovna.
(Born 1838; died 1917).
*Ballerina.*
In 1857, Lebedeva graduated from Moscow Theater School having studied there under Voronina and Montassu. While still a student, she danced Gitana in *La Gitana*, on the Bolshoi stage, becoming a favorite of the Moscow public who called her a "daughter of Moscow". Beginning in 1854, she danced virtually all the major parts in the ballet repertoire. What she lacked in technique was largely made up for by her natural gracefulness, subtlety, gentleness in movement, and dramatic talent. After taking part in the festivities occasioned by the coronation of Alexander II, she was invited to St. Petersburg. Having polished her skills under Huguet and Christian Johanson, she was enrolled in St. Petersburg's ballet troupe in 1867. The ballerina's major success came with roles that required emphatic dramatics, such as the title parts in *Giselle* and *Paquita* and Marguerite

41. Praskovia Lebedeva in the title role of *La Esméralda.*

in *Faust.* After choreographer Arthur Saint-Léon joined the company, she danced only those leading parts requiring virtuoso technique rather than those demanding expressive playing, thus failing to develop all her talents. As a protest against the triviality of her new repertoire, Lebedeva retired from the stage in 1867. Her resignation marked the end of an era of outstanding ballerinas representing the Romantic school of Russian ballet.

## MURAVIOVA,

Marfa Nikolayevna.
(Born July 11, 1838, in Moscow; died Apr. 27, 1879,
in St. Petersburg).
*Ballerina.*
The daughter of an emancipated serf, Muraviova studied in the St. Petersburg Theater School under Frédéric (Pierre Malavergne), Eugène Huguet, and Marius Petipa Displaying an exceptional flair for dancing at early age, she made her debut in 1848 as Cupid in *Le Rêve du Peintre*. In 1857, Muraviova graduated from the school and danced in St. Petersburg until 1865, except for the period from 1860 to 1862 when she performed in Moscow. Muraviova's artistry had a specific quality. She was not much of a mime, but her body was expressive, her lines were harmoniously perfect, and she had a subtle sensitivity to music Muraviova's jetés were not particularly high, but her dance, because of its delicately transparent gracefulness, nevertheless produced the impression

42. Marfa Muraviova as the Tsar-Maiden in *The Little Humpbacked Horse.*

of flight. Her brilliant technique of dancing sur les pointes prompted ballet critics to compare her pas to choreographic lacework. Her movements, discreetly reserved at times, were charged at dramatic moments with wholehearted candor and intimate lyricism. Muraviova excelled in the leading parts in *The Naiad and the Fisherman* (*Ondine*, or *la Naiade*), *La Péri*, and *The Little Humpbacked Horse.* The part of *Giselle* was the apex of Muraviova's ballet career. In 1863, her Giselle electrified Paris, while her next tour confirmed her performing art as an exceptional phenomenon. At the age of twenty-seven, Muraviova married Nikolai Seifert, a nobleman, and resigned from the stage in the prime of her talent.

**PETIPA,**
Marius (Alphonse Victor Marius) Ivanovich.
(Born Mar. 11, 1818, in Marseille; died July 14, 1910, in Gurzuf; buried in St. Petersburg).
*Dancer, choreographer, and teacher.*
Petipa's parents were French, and his family was associated with the theater as far back as the eighteenth century. His father, Jean Antoine Petipa, was a ballet dancer and choreographer. His mother, Victorine Grassau, was a tragic actress. Petipa first studied under his father and then polished his skills with Auguste Vestris. From 1838 until 1846, he appeared both as a dancer and ballet master in the theaters of Bordeaux, Nantes, New York, and Madrid. In

1847, he was invited to St. Petersburg as a danseur mime. Until 1869, he appeared in such parts as Phoebus in *La Esméralda* and Conrad in *Le Corsaire.* Between 1855 and 1857, Petipa taught at the St. Petersburg Theater School. Right after his arrival in Russia, he also began to choreograph, reproducing Joseph Mazilier's *Paquita* on the stage of St. Petersburg's Bolshoi Theater, as well as staging his own ballets. After sucessfully producing *The Pharaoh's Daughter* (1862), Petipa became a full-time choreographer. After Saint-Léon's departure in 1869, Petipa took over as the head of St. Petersburg's ballet company, remaining in that capacity until 1903. All his life, Petipa was driven by a thirst for creative activity. In all, he staged over sixty ballets, including more than forty-six original ones. In his multiact ballets, such as *The Pharaoh's Daughter, Le Roi Candaule* (1869), *Don Quixote* (1869, Moscow; 1871, St. Petersburg), and *La Bayadère* (1877), Petipa gradually defined a code of rules for academic ballets. These productions were notable for their masterful compositions, their solo parts. Petipa's memory stored vast amounts of information regarding numerous combinations in classical (primarily female) dance. Blending simple and complex movements and inventing new ones, he developed ways to convey moods, characters, and feelings, gaining in the process a level of craftsmanship that remains, to some extent, unsurpassed even to the present. Without violating the rigid patterns of classical dance, Petipa strove to fill it with poetic content and images. He possessed the exceptional talent of hearing and seeing an entire ballet in his imagination. His work with the music of the great Russian symphonic composers Tchaikovsky and Alexander Glazunov culminated in the ballet master's creative work. Experiments in symphonizing ballet were firmly substantiated in the scores of *The Sleeping Beauty* (1890) and *Raymonda* (1898). In *The Sleeping Beauty,* the ballet's musical and choreographic heights (the four adagios of each act) provided unparalleled examples of poetic expression. In the three musical suites of *Raymonda* Petipa innovatively

combined classical and character dance. His pas de deux of Odile and Siegfried in *Swan Lake* is a real masterpiece of Russian choreography. Petipa's ballets have been staged throughout the world as models of nineteenth-century ballet. Petipa's wife, Maria Sergeyevna Petipa-Surovshchikova (1836- 82), a St. Petersburg Theater School graduate, was a ballerina with the St. Petersburg ballet theater. A gifted mime, lively, lithe, and attractive, she enjoyed great succes with the public. Marius Petipa staged a number of ballets and character dances especially for her, and in 1861-82, he toured with her in Riga, Berlin, and Paris.

**VAZEM,**
Yekaterina Ottovna.
(Born Jan. 25,1848, in Moscow; died Dec. 14, 1937, in Leningrad (now St. Petersburg).
*Ballerina and teacher.*
Vazem was the daughter of a Russianized German teacher. From 1857 to 1867, Vazem studied in the

43. A scene from Marius Petipa's *Paquita* performed by the dancers of the Leningrad Maly Opera Theater.

St. Petersburg Theater School under Lev Ivanov, Alexei Bogdanov, and Eugène Huguet. She danced with the Imperial Ballet Company of St. Petersburg until 1884. Fair-haired, blue-eyed, and shapely, Vazem was nobly reserved in her manner, though her mime was not particularly impressive and her acting was rather cool. At the same time, her perfected technique was compared to the fioritura of virtuoso flautists. Her repertoire included *La Fille du Danube; Le Corsaire; Giselle; Catarina, or La Fille du Bandit;* and others. Marius Petipa staged *Two Stars, The Butterfly, La Bayadère, The Brigands, The Daughter of Snows,* and *Zoraya* especially for Vazem. She seemed to have no difficulty adapting to any of the whims of Petipa choreographic imagination and bringing them to perfection. From 1886 to 1896, Vazem taught in the St. Petersburg Theater School, instilling in her students (including Agrippina Vaganova, Olga Preobrajenska, Mathilda Kchessinska and Anna Pavlova) a sensitivity to music and a flexibility that added expressiveness to dance. Disapproving of machine-like training, she tried to foster an intelligent attitude toward performance in her disciples. Her methods influenced the shaping of the Russian school of dance. After 1917, she continued teaching privately and wrote a book of memoirs.

44. Yekaterina Vazem as Zoraya in *Zoraya.*

49

# THE REFORMS OF FOKINE AND GORSKY

The early twentieth century

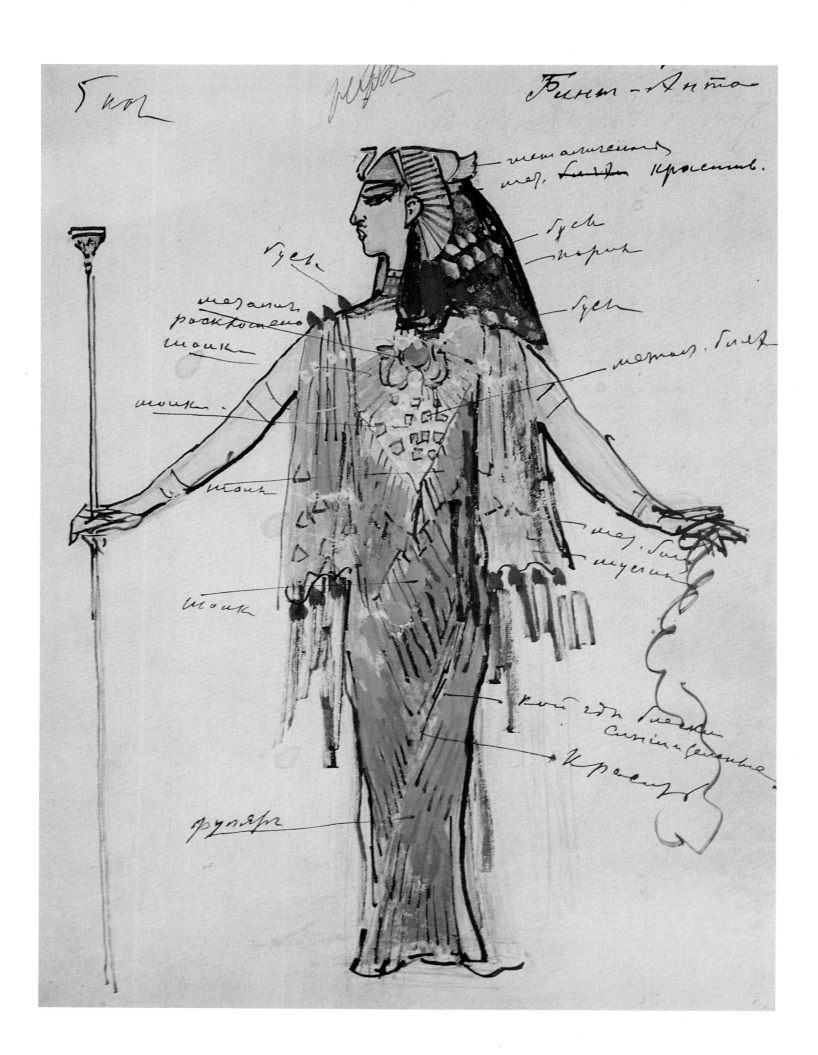

At the turn of the twentieth century, a political turbulence and a longing to remake Russian society led to a need for changes in art. It was a time for summing up in Russian ballet and the beginning of a period of innovation. Petipa's ballet theater had been perfected; in order to avoid stagnation, new paths had to be found. After Petipa left the theater, many dancers tried their hand at choreography, but their ballets were largely modeled on time-tested patterns.

renovation of the ballet. Gorsky came to the Bolshoi in 1898 to produce *The Sleeping Beauty*, a ballet which he had already staged in St. Petersburg. The theatrical life of Moscow greatly impressed Gorsky. The recently opened Art Theater amazed him with the novelty of its approach to staging, the veracity of its acting, its detailed crowd scenes, and its harmonious combination of all the components of a production Performances staged by the Moscow Private Russian Opera

previous pages
45. Sketch by L. Lelong for Fokine's *Shéhérazade*

46. This sketch by Korovin shows a costume for Gorsky's *The Pharaoh's Daughter.*

47. The magnificent painter Konstantin Korovin (1861-1939) created a new type of painted theater design that reflected the idea and the mood of the production. One of Korovin's favorite themes was Spain, and this theme was spectacularly developed in his sketches for Alexander Gorsky's *Don Quixote.*

Valuable as these models were, they lacked finesse and vitality. The academic tenor in ballet, which had been a yardstick of artistic harmony in Petipa's productions, gravitated toward stereotypes. By the early twentieth century, it had become obvious that ballet was approaching a turning point in its history. Two choreographers — Alexander Gorsky in Moscow and Michel Fokine in St. Petersburg — emerged as ballet reformers. However, they each took a different approach to the

(which was founded by Savva Mamontov, a well-known art patron and industrialist) stunned Gorsky with the producer's conceptions, the brilliance of the settings and costumes, and the talent of the opera singers (especially, that of the young Fedor Chaliapin). After taking charge of the Bolshoi, Gorsky selected *Don Quixote* for his choreographic debut. He decided to create his own version of the ballet rather than to simply copy Petipa's production. To design the ballet, Gorsky

53

invited Konstantin Korovin and Alexander Golovin from Mamontov's Private Opera, because they were noted for their keen sense of color and style. In his work with the dancers, Gorsky used the principles elaborated by the Art Theater, and he sought to embellish orthodox dance forms with elements of folklore. In mise-en-scènes, the corps de ballet was no longer confined to a conventional routine, and the corps de ballet dancers no longer arranged themselves in symmetrical groups. Each dancer had his or her own function in the context of the general movement of the crowd. The crowd itself functioned according to the laws of the drama,

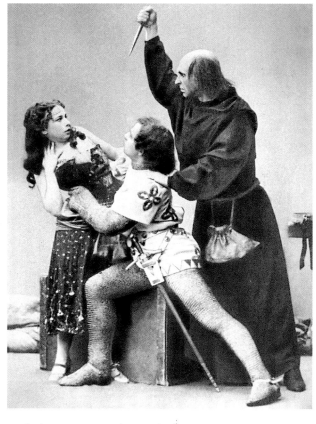

48. Alexander Gorsky chose to base his new ballet, *Gudula's Daughter* on Victor Hugo's novel *Notre-Dame de Paris,* which had already been interpreted by Jules Perrot. Gorsky's production was fundamentally different in style from other ballets of the time and from Gorsky's own earlier works because he stressed its dramatic content.

and dancing — both by the corps de ballet and by soloists — sprung directly from the elements of popular festivity. As a result, the conduct of the protagonists also changed. They became characters from the crowd who moved through the plot, interfering in the events and contributing to their happy resolution. Gorsky could not claim to have succeeded in everything he strove to achieve in that production; however, he continued to

develop the general principles he had outlined in *Don Quixote*. In 1902, Gorsky presented *Gudula's Daughter,* a multiact ballet that he considered his most serious accomplishment. It was not for the first time that Victor Hugo's novel had been made into a ballet. But, in contrast to *La Esméralda* (staged by the French choreographer Jules Perrot in 1844), Gorsky's production was conceived not as a Romantic ballet, but as a pantomime drama with realistic characters shown in their natural environment. Gorsky preferred pantomime because it could convey the development of a dramatic conflict with great verisimilitude. However, the pantomime drama was less effective in depicting the inner world of the characters. There were quite a few dances in the ballet, but they were secondary to the pantomime dialogues and monologues in advancing the plot. In his last grand ballet, Gorsky once again returned to these principles to produce *Salammbô*, based on Gustave Flaubert's novel. One critic referred to the production as a "symphony of color and movement." Korovin's scenery conveyed the austere splendor of ancient Carthage. The sets dazzled the audience with their scope and historical accuracy. The outlandishly picturesque crowds brought to the stage a cruel people that was dominated by a tyrant: this image was very important to Gorsky. In *Salammbô*, Gorsky used both classical dance (for the part of the goddess Tanit) and free movement (for Salammbô's dances in soft sandals). In arranging the duets of Salammbô and Mâtho, Gorsky not only rejected classical dance, but he also discarded the very structure of traditional dance patterns. The prescribed adagio and variations used in the classical pas de deux were replaced by a free dialogue that blended dance and pantomime. This dialogue signified an encounter of two equally strong wills with different tempers and their gradual, mutual submission. This psychologism was an essentially new characteristic in choreographic images, and it promised good prospects for

the future. In spite of its eclecticism, *Salammbô* made a profound impression as an ingenious attempt to reform the ballet theater. In St. Petersburg, the search for new forms took a quite different direction. Early in his career, Michel Fokine became disenchanted with the 42 garish vestiges of the ballet, including many unjustified stunts (such as a ballerina's 32 fouettés), the absurd costumes worn by female dancers (always short tutus, regardless of the period of the ballet or the dancer's nationality), stereotyped sets, and the general eclecticism of ballet performance. Fokine studied paintings and sculpture from various epochs, modern music, and the theater. Later, these studies had a marked effect on his choreographic productions. Two events in particular inspired him to begin his search for innovation. In 1904, the American dancer Isadora Duncan toured Russia with her "free dance," which proclaimed the natural essence in man and strove for movement inspired by

49. "I wanted to provoke the audience with the unexpectedness of the forms and a fountain of colors emanating from the stage", Korovin said.

This sketch shows his set for *Salammbô*.

50. Alexandre Benois (1870-1960) was not only the set designer for Michel Fokine's *Le Pavillon d'Armide* but the librettist as well. He took the plot from Théophile Gautier's *Omphale*. The novel's subtitle, "A Roccoco Story", became the key to Benois stage designs.

This sketch shows a costume for the same ballet.

the soul. She defied the stereotypes of the old ballet and assumed an attitude that was akin to Fokine's beliefs. In her impromptu performances, Duncan danced to the music of Chopin, Beethoven, Gluck, and Tchaikovsky. She saw her ideal of art in the world of classical Greece. An even more important would emphasize the development of storylines and the evolution of characters. Based on Benois' scenarios, Fokine produced *Le Pavillon d'Armide* (a stylistically refined masquerade ballet of the period of Louis XIV) and the famous *Petrushka*. On the initiative of Benois, the World of Art group established

51. Michel Fokine considered *Petrushka* to be the most successful of all his ballets. Petrushka's room is shown here. In this production, he was able to most fully realize his reform of the ballet theater. Moreover, Fokine considered this ballet to be one of the finest achievements of Alexandre Benois, who was both the librettist and the designer for the ballet.

influence on Fokine was his acquaintance with Alexandre Benois. As early as 1898, Benois and Sergei Diaghilev set up the World of Art association for painters who had broken with the academic routine. They addressed themselves to the art of many countries and epochs. They were attracted by ancient Egypt; classical Greece; the Orient; France of the seventeenth, eighteenth, and nineteenth centuries; and the folklore genres of the Russian theater. Like Gorsky, Benois sought to turn ballet into a theater of active logic that closer contacts with the ballet theater. Benois strove to exert a broad influence on ballet: he was engaged in stage design, wrote scenarios, and published critical articles and theoretical essays. This alliance with the painters was very productive for the ballet. Highly artistic sets emerged from this collaboration, and scenery and costumes were noted for their historical authenticity and immaculate artistic taste. Fokine's searching took a number of paths. His early ballets, *Eunice* and *Chopiniana* (*Les Sylphides*) (both produced in 1907), already displayed all the principle features of the choreographer's mature work and defined the two basic lines in Fokine's repertoire. The first can be defined as the line of plastic drama, while the other is the line of stylized presentation that characterized bygone epochs. These two lines crossed, intertwined, and were

as the pas de deux and the pas de trois and, generally, demanded new music written specifically for the dances. Therefore, Fokine (and later Gorsky) often resorted to music that was not originally written for ballet. This was undoubtedly beneficial because it helped expand the repertoire and the genre potential

52. According to Fokine's idea for *Petrushka*, each character in this tragic puppet theater had his own theme. The ballerina personified the eternal feminine; Petrushka was "the spiritual and suffering part of humanity"; and Arap was "everything that is inexplicably attractive, powerfully masculine and undeservedly triumphant".

transformed; however, their essence remained unchanged. In Fokine's ballets, pantomime flowed freely into the dance, and the dance dissolved back into pantomime. Fokine used a variety of expressive means. When he was producing *Eunice*, he focused on the art of ancient Greece. In *Egyptian Nights*, Fokine simulated the profile positions of ancient Egyptian bas-reliefs; in *Les Sylphides*, he exploited the classical dance of the epoch of Romanticism. This tendency to rely on illustration denied such structural ballet forms

of ballet and set higher standards for the quality of music. As a result, Fokine established a type of a performance that was entirely new for the ballet theater. It was a one-act ballet that was completely subordinated to the action, in which the content was revealed through the unity of music, choreography, and stage design. The reforms of Fokine and Gorsky were not all completely successful. In the course of the generally constructive contest between the old and the new, productive notions (for instance, symphonism as a system of musical and choreographic generalizations) were rejected together with obsolete conceptions. As a result, artistic disagreements sprang up within ballet companies. In Moscow, the classical heritage was advocated by Yekaterina Geltzer and Vasily Tikhomirov; in St. Petersburg, its adherents included Olga Preobrajenska, Mathilda Kchessinska, Agrippina Vaganova, and Nikolai Legat. Sophia Fedorova and Mikhail Mordkin sided with Gorsky, while the principal dancers who implemented Fokine's ideas included Anna Pavlova, Tamara Karsavina, and Vaslav Nijinsky. The aesthetic findings of the reformers brought Russian ballet to the center of modern art and expanded the sphere of its impact on the world's ballet theater. The first "Russian Season" that included ballet took place in Paris in 1909. It was a significant event in the history of world art. The "Seasons" were organized by Sergei Diaghilev, an art critic and an official with the Directorate of Theaters. The ballet presentation was preceded by exhibitions of Russian paintings and by concerts of Russian music. Prior to the

53. This famous poster for the first "Russian Season" in Paris was designed by Valentin Serov (1865-1911).

54. The great artist
and portrait painter,
Valentin Serov, did
not only design the
poster for the
"Russian Seasons",
but he also created
the curtain for
Michel Fokine's
*Shéhérazade,* which
was produced by
Diaghilev's troupe.

festival, Diaghilev presented a Russian opera on the stage of the Paris Opera.

The ballet act from Alexander Borodin's opera *Prince Igor*, known as the *Polovtsian Dances* (staged by Fokine and featuring sets by Nikolai Roerich) made a real hit at the first festival. *Les Sylphides* also scored a huge success. The performing art of such Russian dancers as Pavlova, Karsavina, and Nijinsky, as well as the harmony, exactitude, and inspiration of the entire company, provoked the unrestrained admiration of the audience. The first "Season" was a trailblazer: together with the ones that followed, it made a profound impact on world art and affected stylistics and subjects in literature, painting, music, and theater. From the moment that Diaghilev set up his Opéra touring company in 1911, Russian ballet began to exist as two parallel entities — one in Russia and the other in Europe.

far left
55. Perhaps the most distinct artist of the "Russian Seasons" was Leon Bakst (1866-1924). The refinement, brilliant colors, and emotion that are unique to his art are most clearly expressed in his sketches of costumes. A relentless innovator, he remade the ballet costume and exercised considerable influence on contemporary theater and fashion designers. This sketch shows a costume for *Shéhérazade*.

56. This sketch by L. Lelong brings to life the rare exotic flavor of Fokine's *Shéhérazade*.

# Great figures of Russian ballet

57. This watercolor by Mikhail Bobyshev shows Vera and Michel Fokine in the ballet *Le Carnaval*.

**FEDOROVA,**
Sofia Vasilyevna.
(Born Sept. 28, 1879, in Moscow;
died Jan. 3, 1963, in Neuilly-sur-Seine near Paris).
*Ballerina.*
Upon graduation from the Moscow Theater School, Fedorova danced from 1899 with the Bolshoi Ballet. Initially, she performed character dances, such as the czardas in *Coppélia*, the Spanish dance in *Swan Lake*, panaderos in *Raymonda*, and Ukrainian and Gypsy dances in *The Little Humpbacked Horse*. Her first major part was that of Mercedes in *Don Quixote*. She was a devoted associate and follower of Alexander Gorsky in his protest against academicism in ballet. She danced her best parts, including the Khan's Wife in *The Little Humpbacked Horse*, Esmeralda in *Gudula's Daughter*, Moloch's Priestess in *Salammbô*, Lisa in *La Fille Mal Gardée*, Celestine in *Robert and Bertram*, or *Two Thieves*, Bacchanal in *The Seasons* in Gorsky's productions. She also performed in *Anitra's Dance*. Noted for her expressiveness as a dramatic actress, eloquence of movement, and

58. Sophia Fedorova perfoms the gypsy dance from *The Little Humpbacked Horse.*

unconstrained emotion (reaching at times the point of ecstatic frenzy), Fedorova created images overwhelmed by inward tragedy. One of her contemporaries observed that the dark mystique of the soul was her realm. From 1909 to 1913, Fedorova took part in the Russian seasons abroad, dancing in Fokine's productions including *Polovtsian Dances, Cleopatra* (Tahor), *Shéhérazade* (Almea), and *Bacchanale*. In 1919, she left the Bolshoi and she settled in Paris in 1922, where she taught and appeared in concerts. She danced with Anna Pavlova's company in 1925 and 1926. Fedorova left the stage in 1928.

## FOKINE,

Michel (Mikhail Mikhailovich).
(Born May 5, 1880,
in St. Petersburg; died Aug. 22,
1942, in New York).

*Dancer, choreographer, and teacher.*
In 1898, Fokine graduated from the St. Petersburg Theater School in Nikolai Legat's class and was invited to the Mariinsky Theater. A slim and well-proportioned dancer with high elevation and a virtuoso foot technique, Fokine had an inherent gift for dancing and stage manner that let him always look handsome and elegant. His style of performance absorbed the best of the academic tradition. He tended toward gallant elation and was capable of setting off specific features in his characters. He danced the principal parts in the classical repertoire, including Basil in *Don Quixote*, Prince Désiré in *The Sleeping Beauty*, Siegfried in *Swan Lake*, and Jean de Brienne in *Raymonda*. He also appeared in character dances and, later, in his own productions, including Amoun in *Egyptian Nights*, Tsarevich Ivan in *Firebird*, Daphnis in *Daphnis and Chloe*, and the Poet in *Chopiniana* (*Les Sylphides*). He made his debut as a choreographer with *Acis and Galatea*, performed by the St. Petersburg Theater School. He also produced *A Midsummer Night's Dream* for the students of the school and *The Vine and Eunice* at the theater. In 1910, he was made choreographer of the Mariinsky Theater. True to the spirit of his time, Fokine rejected abstractions and the division of expressive means into dance and pantomime that had been characteristic of ballet in the past. One of Fokine's basic concepts — "not to combine ready-made and established dance movements, but to create in each case a new form corresponding to the story" — suggested the necessity of looking for unique choreography in each ballet. Rejecting the conventional gesture, he combined in dance the plastic wealth found in the world around him, in fine arts, in the folklore of various nations, and in classical dance. The latter was only used as one means, rather than as a universal system. Story ballets, dramatically tense and action-packed, prevailed in Fokine's artistic work. His outstanding musical sensitivity enabled him to produce dances based on music not originally intended for ballet. He continued the trend started by Marius Petipa and Lev Ivanov in the field of symphonic dance and developed the abstract, plotless ballet into a genre of its own. Such ballet was structured according to the rules of music and choreography and used both classical and character dance. In contrast to Petipa's ballets, relationships between good and evil in Fokine's productions were not governed by fairy-tale laws. In his ballets, life was presented as a bacchanalia in which the themes of loneliness, disillusionment, and doomed passions struck a discordant note. Reality turned out to be infernal and destructrive, while beauty was deceptive and unattainable. However, the pursuit of a dream signified the moment of the human spirit's predominance over the transience of existence. When working on a production, Fokine would cooperate with such artists as Alexandre Benois, Leon Bakst, Nikolai Roerich, Alexander Golovin, Mstislav Dobujinsky, Boris Anisfeld, Natalia Goncharova, and Sergei Sudeikin, as well as with such composers as Igor Stravinsky, Nikolai Cherepnin, Alexander Glazunov, and Sergei Rachmaninoff. From 1901 to 1911, Fokine taught at the St. Petersburg Theater School. His students included Yelizaveta Gerdt, Lidia Lopukhova, Yelena Smirnova, Yelena Lukom, Lubov Chernysheva, Piotr Vladimirov.

59. A scene from Michel Fokine's *Les Sylphides*.

60. A scene from Alexander Gorsky's *The Little Humpbacked Horse.*

Ida Rubinstein took private lessons from him. From 1909 to 1912 and in 1914, Fokine was art director, choreographer, and dancer at the "Russian Seasons" and with Diaghilev's Ballets Russes. In 1918, he went on tour in Sweden. He moved to the United States in 1921, and there he danced until 1933. In 1931, he worked with the Colon Theater in Buenos Aires; in 1934-35, in the Paris Opera; in 1936, with Les Ballets Russes de Monte Carlo; and from 1937 to 1939, with the Ballet Russe du Colonel de Basil. From 1923 to 1942, he managed a studio in New York. His foreign students included Jean Borlin, Lincoln Kirstein, and Helen Tamiris. In addition to such world-famous productions as *The Dying Swan, Chopiniana (Les Sylphides), Polovtsian Dances, Le Carnaval, Shéhérazade, Firebird, Le Spectre de la Rose,* and *Petrushka*, which remain in international theater repertoires, Fokine staged many ballets that were remarkable events in the ballet life of the time. They were *Islamey, Le Dieu Bleu, Thamar, Daphnis and Chloe, Les Préludes, La Légende de Joseph, Le Coq d'Or, Eros, Jota Aragonesa, L'Apprenti Sorcier,* and *Don Juan.* Fokine wrote a book of memoirs, *Against the Current,* and a number of articles on

ballet. His wife, Vera Petrovna Fokine (1886-1958), was a character dancer with the Mariinsky Theater. The new expressive means developed by Michel Fokine enabled her to appear in parts that were based on free movements, Chiarina in *Le Carnaval,* the Tsarevna in *Firebird.* She participated in the "Russian Seasons" and in performances of Diaghilev's troupe. She also taught in Fokine's studio in New York.

## GORSKY,

Alexander Alexeyevich.
Born Aug. 18, 1871,
in St. Petersburg; died Oct. 20, 1924, in Moscow).
*Choreographer, dancer, and teacher.*
After graduating from the St. Petersburg Theater School (where he had studied under Platon Karsavin and Marius Petipa), Gorsky danced in the Mariinsky company from 1889 to 1900. He appeared in classical, character, and grotesque parts. His first experience in choreography came with the production of Clorinda, *Queen of the Mountain Fairies,* a fantastic ballet staged in the Mikhailovsky Theater in 1899 as a graduation performance of the St. Petersburg Theater School. Becoming a ballet regisseur in 1901, Gorsky remained with the

Bolshoi from 1902 to 1924 as a choreographer. Having taken charge of the Moscow ballet troupe, he set about introducing reforms to ballet. He sought to overcome the conventions of nineteenth-century academic ballet which were quite numerous and included, among others, a rigid structure and a strict separation between dance and pantomime. An authority on Petipa's ballets, Gorsky evolved from the mere duplication of his productions on the Moscow stage (such works as *The Sleeping Beauty* in 1899 and *Raymonda* in 1900) to their ingenious reinterpretation. He replaced corps de ballet ensembles with dances that were justified by the action and strove for historical and national authenticity. He invited Konstantin Korovin to work as a stage designer. Gorsky's work was greatly influenced by the Moscow Art Theater. His productions of *Don Quixote* at the Bolshoi in 1900 and at the Mariinsky Theater in 1902 were significant events in his career. This ballet was imbued with the passionate spontaneity of dance that sprang naturally from the action and reflected it emotionally. Gorsky also produced his own versions of classical ballets such as *Swan Lake, The Little Humpbacked Horse, Coppélia, The Pharaoh's Daughter, Giselle, La*

*Bayadère,* and *Le Corsaire.* Some of these he staged several times. In these productions, dance was subordinated to the logic of particular actions or situations, and it sometimes lost its generalizing characteristics. Gorsky realized his creative aspirations most fully in his original productions, including *Gudula's Daughter, Salammbô, Love Is Swift!* and *Eunice* and *Petronius.* In 1916, Gorsky first attempted to produce a ballet set to the music of Alexander Glazunov's Fifth Symphony, translating it into the images of a Greek pastorale. In 1918, he tried to capture the spirit of a popular revolt in Stenka Razin. In the same year, he supervised a summer ballet festival at the Aquarium Garden Theater, presenting *En Blanc* and *Night on Bald Mountain* for the first time. In 1919, he staged *The Nutcracker,* followed by *Salomé's Dance, Les Petits Riens,* and *Venus' Grotto.* In 1923, he staged a contemporary ballet for children called *Ever Fresh Flowers.* The significance of Gorsky for the Bolshoi is extremely great. Under his management, the company nearly equaled the prestige of the St. Petersburg troupe. Moscow's interest in ballet grew considerably. These accomplishments can be accounted for by the fact that Gorsky always considered the specific features of the Moscow theater in his reforms. Moreover, Gorsky's experiments were in the mainstream of the development of Russian ballet in the early twentieth century. Gorsky succeeded in implementing only part of his designs within the framework of the Imperial theaters. Not all dancers in his company approved of his reforms; still, he had quite a few followers and disciples. In the final analysis, his twenty-five-year tenure as the Bolshoi's ballet manager was quite remarkable. Gorsky profoundly influenced the artistic careers of a number of major dancers, including Geltzer, Fedorova, Vera Karalli, Alexandra Balashova, Mordkin, and Vladimir Riabtsev. He taught at the St. Petersburg Theater School from 1896 to 1900 and in Moscow starting in 1902. His students included Asaf Messerer, Mikhail Gabovich, Anastasia Abramova, and Lubov Bank.

# KARSAVINA,
Tamara Platonovna.
(Born Mar. 9, 1885,
in St. Petersburg; died May 26,
1978, in London).
*Ballerina.*
Daughter of Platon Karsavin (1854-1922), a dancer of the Mariinsky Theater who was noted for his appearances in grotesque and character parts; goddaughter of Pavel Gerdt; grandniece of Alexei Khomiakov, a philosopher and essayist of the first half of the 19th century; and sister of Lev Karsavin, another well-known philosopher. Karsavina graduated from the St. Petersburg Theater School in 1902 after studying with Gerdt and Alexander Gorsky. While still a student, she danced the part of Cupid at the premiere of Gorsky's *Don Quixote* and appeared in an old pas de deux called "The Pearl and the Fisherman" that Gerdt incorporated into his revival of *Javotte.* Karsavina's artistic skill was shaped by the context of the crisis of academic art. As a result, she never became a truly academic dancer. Critics who clung stubbornly to the tenets of academic art constantly found flaws in Karsavina's dancing. She later studied under Christian Johanson and Yevgenia Sokolova, trained in Italy with Caterina Beretta, and worked with Sergei Legat. Karsavina gradually progressed from small solo parts to lead roles, including Flora in *Le Reveil de Flore* and the Tsar-maiden in *The Little Humpbacked Horse.* However, her unique qualities were not revealed until Fokine's new productions. Karsavina's intelligence

added a constructive basis to Fokine's impressionistic choreography. The play of colors and shades that characterized impressionism never became an end in itself, and in Karsavina's interpretation, it contributed to the embodiment of eternal truths. She did not trust the spontaneity of temper and emotion, although she did not lack passion. Karsavina became the founder of a new trend in twentieth-century ballet performance called "intellectual art." Fokine choreographed a number of parts for Karsavina: the waltz in *Les Sylphides,* the title parts in *Firebird* and *Thamar,* and the parts of the Slave Girl in *Egyptian Nights,* Columbine in *Le Carnaval,* the Girl in *Le Spectre de la Rose,* the Ballerina in *Petrushka,* Chloe in *Daphnis and Chloe,* and the Queen of Shemakhan in *Le Coq d'Or.* Karsavina's two best roles — the Girl in *Le Spectre de la Rose* and the Ballerina in *Petrushka* — were performed as duets with Vaslav Nijinsky. Karsavina's refined intelligence was isolated and amplified by Nijinsky's subconscious brilliance. Karsavina acquired a taste for stylistic ornamentation during her work with Fokine, and it affected her performance in the academic repertoire, where she danced in ballets such as *Giselle, Swan Lake, Raymonda, The Sleeping Beauty, Don Quixote,* and *Paquita.* Her last appearance on the Mariinsky stage was in *La Bayadère* in 1918. Karsavina went on tour with Georgy Kyaksht's company in 1906. Her subsequent tours included Prague in 1908; Milan and London in 1909; and Berlin, Brussels, and again London in 1910. In 1909, she jouned Diaghilev's company. Karsavina married Henry J. Bruce, a British diplomat, and from July 1918, she lived in London. Until 1929, she continued to dance with Diaghilev's company, and in addition to her standard roles, she appeared in Leonide Massine's ballets: she danced the Miller's Wife in *Le Tricorne (The Three-Cornered Hat),* Rossignol in *Le Rossignol,* and Pimpinella in *Pulcinella.* In 1930-31, she danced with Ballet Rambert. She left the stage in 1931 but returned to revive *Le Spectre de la Rose* for Sadler's Wells Ballet in 1943 and *Le Carnaval* for the Western Theater Ballet in 1961.

61. Tamara Karsavina
in *Chopiniana*
(Les Sylphides).

She also helped Frederick Ashton produce *La Fille Mal Gardée* and coached Margot Fonteyn for her part as the *Firebird*. An author of many articles, reminiscences, and manuals on classical dance, Karsavina held the position of vice president of the Royal Academy of Dance from 1930 to 1955.

## KCHESSINSKA,
Mathilda-Maria Felixovna.
(Born Aug. 31, 1872, in Ligovo, near St. Petersburg; died Dec. 6, 1971, in Paris).
*Ballerina.*

62. Mathilda Kchessinska in *La Esméralda.*

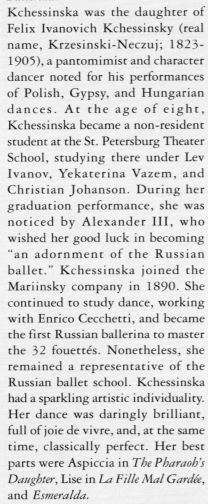

Kchessinska was the daughter of Felix Ivanovich Kchessinsky (real name, Krzesinski-Neczuj; 1823-1905), a pantomimist and character dancer noted for his performances of Polish, Gypsy, and Hungarian dances. At the age of eight, Kchessinska became a non-resident student at the St. Petersburg Theater School, studying there under Lev Ivanov, Yekaterina Vazem, and Christian Johanson. During her graduation performance, she was noticed by Alexander III, who wished her good luck in becoming "an adornment of the Russian ballet." Kchessinska joined the Mariinsky company in 1890. She continued to study dance, working with Enrico Cecchetti, and became the first Russian ballerina to master the 32 fouettés. Nonetheless, she remained a representative of the Russian ballet school. Kchessinska had a sparkling artistic individuality. Her dance was daringly brilliant, full of joie de vivre, and, at the same time, classically perfect. Her best parts were Aspiccia in *The Pharaoh's Daughter*, Lise in *La Fille Mal Gardée*, and *Esmeralda*.

Kchessinska's artistic career was closely linked with that of Marius Petipa. She danced in many of his ballets, appearing as Aurora in *The Sleeping Beauty*, Columbine in *Les Millions d'Arlequin*, Nikia in *La Bayadère*, and Niriti in *The Talisman*. She also danced in *The Fairy Doll*, a ballet staged by Nikolai Legat, her partner for many years. In Michel Fokine's productions, such as *Eunice*, *Les Papillons*, and *Eros*, she

danced the leading parts, but she was indifferent to the choreographer's innovations. Kchessinska excelled on St. Petersburg's stage and even superseded touring foreign dancers. Enjoying the patronage of the royal family and being on intimate terms with some of them, including Crown Prince Nicholas (later Tsar Nicholas II), Kchessinska maintained her influence on the repertoire and her monopoly on her favorite parts. In 1904, she left the theater "for family reasons" (without a pension) but returned to the company the same year as a danseuse on contract. She successfully toured Monte Carlo, Warsaw, Vienna, and Paris between 1903 and 1909 and danced with Sergei Diaghilev's troupe in 1911 and 1912. The last time she danced in Russia was 1917 on the stage of the Petrograd Conservatory. After the October Revolution, she rejected all offers. In 1920, she emigrated to France. In 1921, she married Grand Duke Andrew, a cousin of Nicholas II, thus legitimizing their long-term relationship. She received the title of Duchess Romanovska-Krasinska. In 1929, she opened a ballet studio in Paris. Her students included Tatiana Riabushinskaya, Boris Kniazev, and André Eglevsky. Kchessinska gave lessons to a number of noted foreign dancers, including Yvette Chauviré and Margot Fonteyn. She also wrote a book of memoirs.

## LEGAT,
Nikolai Gustavovich.
(Born Dec. 27,1869, in Moscow; died Jan. 24, 1937, in London).
*Dancer, teacher, and choreographer.*
Trained initially by his father, Gustav Legat (1837-95), Legat studied at the St. Petersburg Theater School under Marius Petipa and Pavel Gerdt. After graduating, he joined the Mariinsky company in 1888, and he took advanced training with Christian Johanson. A leading man in classical dance, Legat was noted for his perfect technique, elegance, and refined plastique. He was a physically strong and deft partner, maintaining a noble bearing in the most spectacular lifts. Appearing as a partner of Pavlova, Kchessinska, Karsavina, and Preobrajenska, Legat danced many parts in the classical repertoire including Siegfried in *Swan Lake*, Prince Désiré in *The Sleeping Beauty*, Albert in *Giselle*, and Jean de Brienne in *Raymonda*. Although he looked perfect in these roles, demi-caractère, jeune premier roles, like Colin in *La Fille Mal Gardée*, were more to Legat's taste. In 1910, Legat became the chief choreographer of the Mariinsky Theater. There he staged several of his own ballets and revived a number of Petipa's productions. The main thing that makes Nikolai Legat a remarkable figure in the history of Russian and world ballet is his safeguarding of the traditions of the Russian school of classical dance. From 1896 to 1914, he taught at the St. Petersburg Theater School and there he struggled to maintain the rules of classical dance. His basic teaching principle was a combination of a stubborn insistence on the purity of dance and an individual approach to each student. Among Legat's students were Anna Pavlova, Michel Fokine, Tamara Karsavina, Lidia Kyaksht, Vaslav Nijinsky, Bronislava Nijinska, Agrippina Vaganova, and Fedor Lopukhov. In 1922, he went abroad, and he taught in Diaghilev's *Ballet Russe* from 1925 to 1926. In the late 1920s, he opened a school in London that was headed after his death by his wife, Nadezhda Nikolayeva-Legat. The school became, citing an English critic, "an academic center of Russian ballet" abroad, attended by students

from all over the world. Legat's students included Ninette de Valois, Alicia Markova, Margot Fonteyn, and Frederick Ashton. He wrote a book entitled *The Story of the Russian School*. His brother, Sergei Gustavovich Legat (1875-1905), was also a dancer at the Mariinsky Theater. His career began promisingly. He gradually took over the aging Pavel Gerdt's parts, including Tahor in *The Pharaoh's Daughter*, Lucien in *Paquita*, and Jean de Brienne in *Raymonda*. Together with his brother, Nikolai Legat, he produced *The Fairy Doll* in 1903. From 1896, he taught pantomime and partnering at the St. Petersburg Theater School. In 1898, he became a coach with the ballet troupe of the Mariinsky Theater. In 1905, he committed suicide.

## MORDKIN,
Mikhail Mikhailovich.
(Born Dec. 21, 1880, in Moscow; died July 15, 1944, in Millbrook, N.J., USA).
*Dancer, choreographer, and teacher.*
After his graduation from the Moscow Theater School (where he had studied under Vasily Tikhomirov), Mordkin worked at the Bolshoi Theater from 1900 to 1910 and then again from 1912 to 1918. While still a student, Mordkin made appearances on the Bolshoi stage in major parts. In 1899, he danced Colin in Gorsky's revival of *La Fille Mal Gardée*, and this part was to become one of the best in his repertoire. An inclination to natural and unrestrained plastique determined his approach to classical parts: this was manifest in Siegfried in *Swan Lake*, Albert in *Giselle* and Prince Désiré in *The Sleeping Beauty*. Among the numerous parts that he danced in Gorsky's ballets — his Matho, the savage leader in *Salammbô*, proved to be the most remarkable. Dramatic actors, as well as Fedor Chaliapin, would come to the theater specially to see the scene of Mâtho's death. In addition to an outstanding physical expressiveness, Mordkin possessed great dramatic talent, and his creative dance was distinguished by strong emotion, manliness, and forceful energy. Mordkin significantly influenced the development of male dance. In 1909, Mordkin took part in the first Russian art season abroad, dancing René de Beaugency in Michel Fokine's *Le Pavillon d'Armide*. In 1910-11, he toured the United States

and Great Britain with great success with Anna Pavlova and his own company. In 1914, he began concentrating on pantomime parts such as the Khan in Gorsky's production of *The Little Humpbacked Horse*. In 1904, Mordkin became a coach and in 1905, he was promoted to deputy choreographer at the Bolshoi Theater. Hrs best concert dances, all staged by Mordkin himself, included *Bow and Arrow Dance, Bacchanale* (which he danced in duet with Anna Pavlova), *Pas Comique*, and *Italian Beggar* (Gypsy). He also produced *Azyadé*, a ballet that he included in the repertoire of his US tour under the title of *The Legend of Azyadé*, and a number of ballets in the Tbilisi theater (*The Carnival, Flowers of Granada, A Pearl of Seville*, and others). In 1924, he moved to the United States and set up a school in New York. In 1926, he organized the company that, in 1927, became the Mordkin ballet. In 1937, he reappeared on the stage, but this time in purely pantomime parts such as the Old Fisherman in his own production of *Goldfish*, Mother Simone in *La Fille Mal Gardée*, the General in *Voices of Spring*, and the Devil in *Trepak*. His company's repertoire also included The *Carnival, Swan Lake*, and *Giselle*. In 1939, the Ballet Theater emerged from this company, but without Mordkin's participation.

## NIJINSKY,
Vaslav Fomich.
(Born Dec. 1889 (according to other sources, Mar. 12, 1890), in Kiev; died Apr. 8, 1950, in

63. A caricature of Sergei Legat. Artists: the Legat brothers.

64. A caricature of Nikolai Legat. Artists: the Legat brothers.

65. Mikhail Mordkin as Mâtho in *Salammbô*. By P. Mak.

67

London).

*Dancer and choreographer.*

His parents, Eleonora and Tomasz (Foma) Nijinsky, were natives of Warsaw, and they first danced in the Warsaw Imperial Theater. In 1898, Nijinsky entered the St. Petersburg Theater School, where he studied under Sergei Legat. The boy's remarkable talents quickly became apparent. While still at school, he appeared frequently on the stage of the Mariinsky Theater At the age of fifteen, he put on an amazing performance as the Faun in *Acis and Galatea*. After he graduated in 1907, he joined the Mariinsky Theater. His outstanding talent as a dancer and an actor immediately brought Nijinsky the status of premier danseur, even though he did not outwardly look like one. He was not tall; his muscular legs were not wellproportioned; his pale face featured high cheekbones and Mongolian eyes. But the stage transformed him. There came a deftness and a refined, but unobtrusive, grace. His unique, fabulous leaps and his ability to virtually hover in the air were amazing. His perfect grasp of dancing styles won all hearts. He became a partner for such ballerinas as Mathilda Kchessinska, Olga Preobrajenska, Anna Pavlova, and Tamara Karsavina. Nijinsky danced lead parts in Fokine's productions, including the Slave of Armide in *Egyptian Nights*, and the Poet in *Les Sylphides.* He was discharged from the Mariinsky Theater for putting on, without approval, a new costume based on a fifteenth-century German outfit that Alexandre Benois designed for *Giselle*. Having neglected to wear a pair of shorts over his tights, he shocked the audience, including those seated in the imperial box. Nijinsky's appearance in the first Russian season in Paris brought him great fame. From 1909 to 1913, Nijinsky was a leading man in the Russian seasons and he danced in Fokine's repertoire including *Le Carnaval, Shéhérazade, Le Spectre de la Rose, Petrushka, Narcissus, Le Dieu Bleu* and *Daphnis and Chloe*. In 1912 Nijinsky staged *The Afternoon of a Faun* for Sergei

66. Vaslav Nijinsky in *Shéhérazade*.

Diaghilev's company dancing the principal part. In 1913 he followed this with *Jeux* and *Le Sacre du Printemps*. Nijinsky's productions received controversial press and excited heated debates among the public and critics. In 1914 Nijinsky set up his own company in London. In 1916 he returned to Diaghilev's company and produced *Till Eulenspiegel* for the company's American tour. As a dancer Nijinsky breathed new life

into male dance, combining refined techniques of elevation and tours with the expressiveness of plastique and pantomine. In his choreography, Nijinsky was ahead of his time. A mental disease forced Nijinsky to leave the stage prematurely. In 1919, he wrote his diary, which was published in Paris in 1958. Many ballets, dramas, television programs, and motion pictures were produced about Nijinsky.

Nijinsky was active on the stage for only ten years, but his extraordinary talent brought him immortal fame.

**PAVLOVA,**
Anna Pavlovna (Matveyevna).
(Born Feb. 12, 1881, in St. Petersburg; died Jan. 23, 1931, in The Hague).
*Ballerina.*
Upon graduation from the St. Petersburg Theater School in 1899, Pavlova was invited to the Mariinsky ballet troupe. Her teachers included Andrei Oblakov, Yekaterina Vazem, and Pavel Gerdt. Despite her frailty, Pavlova's natural endowments – a delicate head set on a dainty torso; an elongated body; shapely legs with an instep of rare exquisiteness; a long, swanlike neck; expressive, slender arms; beauty of movement; and an innate grace

67. Vaslav Nijinsky
as the Faun in *The
Afternoon of a Faun*.
By Leon Bakst.

and musicality – helped her advance to the rank of a leading lady in the company. Pavlova gave new meaning to classical roles but preserved the academic traditions of the nineteenth century as the basis of her artistic work. Her roles, while staying within the traditional framework, were psychologically enhanced, absorbed additional dramatic stresses, and revealed new expressive capacities. The productions of Marius Petipa and Lev Ivanov made it possible for Pavlova to realize her versatile potential. Thus, she treated the part of Nikia in *La Bayadère* in a new manner, along the lines of a classical tragedy; her psychological interpretation of the title role of *Giselle* led to a poetically radiant finale. The ballerina was brilliant in parts that combined classical dance with folk or character dances, as was illustrated by her panaderos in *Raymonda*, her Urals dance in *The Little Humpbacked Horse*, her Spanish dance in *The Nutcracker*, and her fandango in the dance scene from *Carmen*. Pavlova's contacts with Alexander Gorsky, a choreographer who aspired to renew and dramatize ballet, helped her find new approaches to the parts of Kitri in *Don Quixote* and Bint-Anta in *The Pharaoh's Daughter* and prepared her to meet Michel Fokine, another reformer of the Russian ballet. Fokine's experiments were close to Pavlova's own ideas and made a great impact on her subsequent evolution. Pavlova danced lead parts in his ballets *The Vine, Eunice, Chopiniana* (*Les Sylphides*)*, Le Pavillon d'Armide,* and *Egyptian Nights*. The essence of their artistic alliance was the subjection of dance to spiritually expressive tasks. In 1907, at a charity concert at the Mariinsky Theater, Pavlova danced *Le Cygne* (subsequently known as *The Dying Swan*) for the first time. Fokine had choreographed this dance especially for her, and it was to become a poetic symbol of Russian choreography of the early twentieth century. In 1910, Pavlova changed her status to that of a touring dancer. Her last performance at the Mariinsky Theater took place in

1913, and the Russian public saw her perform for the last time in 1914. In 1909, Pavlova began to participate in the "Russian Seasons" in Paris, and this paved the way for her worldwide renown. Pavlova's silhouette on a poster designed by Valentin Serov will forever remain a symbol of the "Russian Seasons". In 1910, Pavlova set up her own company in London. She made triumphant tours in many countries, dancing in ballets by Tchaikovsky and Alexander Glazunov, as well as in *La Fille Mal Gardée, Giselle,* and *Coppélia.* A number of dances were staged especially for Pavlova, including *La Nuit, Valse Caprice, Dragonfly* and *Rondo,* in which the dancer kept up the traditions of

Russian ballet. Fokine choreographed *Seven Daughters of the Mountain King* and staged Franz Liszt's *Les Préludes* for her company. Pavlova became a living legend. Her life was entirely devoted to dance. "A true artist," Pavlova wrote, "should sacrifice herself for her art. Just like a nun, she has no right to live the life longed for by most women." Pavlova died in the Hague while on tour. Her last words were: "Prepare my Swan costume..."

## PREOBRAJENSKA,
Olga Iosifovna (Osipovna).
(Born Feb. 2, 1871,
in St. Petersburg; died Dec. 27,
1962, in Paris).

*Ballerina and teacher*
Although she had taken the entrance examination three times before being accepted, Preobrajenska graduated from the St. Petersburg Theater School in 1889, after studying with Marius Petipa, Lev Ivanov, and Christian Johanson Upon graduation, she was invited to join the corps de ballet of the Mariinsky Theater. She did not have a beautiful face; her complexion was wan and her legs were definitely not shapely. "I exercised literally day and night... until I gradually changed from a frail weakling into an iron girl," she later wrote. Beginning with small parts, Preobrajenska expanded her repertoire to such an extent that it became difficult to name a ballet in which she had not danced. After she performed the part of Isora in *Bluebeard* in 1900, she became a lead in the troupe. Preobrajenska polished her skills continuously and tirelessly. She took lessons with Petipa, Joseph Hansen, Enrico Cecchetti, and Caterina Baretta. Her talent was most clearly manifested in classical dance, where she rose to the heights of poetry. She danced the most difficult variations of the Italian school with immaculate brilliance. She sought to add a fresh tenor to each old repertoire part that she danced and was not afraid to improvise, as was especially clear in her *Javotte* and *Paquita*. In lyrical adagios, the ballerina was particularly tender and graceful — for instance, as Swanilda in *Coppélia* and the Butterfly in *The Butterfly's Whims*. Her exceptional sensitivity to music helped her become one of the best performers of ballets by Tchaikovsky (Aurora in *The Sleeping Beauty* and Fée Dragée in *The Nutcracker*) and Alexander Glazunov (the title part in *Raymonda* and Isabelle in *Ruses d'Amour*). Michel Fokine staged a prelude in *Chopiniana* (*Les Sylphides*) and the part of the Slave Girl in *Egyptian Nights* especially for her. Preobrajenska began touring in Monte Carlo and then in the cities of Europe and South America before the "Russian Seasons" came into fashion. In 1909 she changed her

status to that of a touring dancer, preserving her renown as a Russian stage star of the first decade of the twentieth century. She left the stage in 1920. Her teaching career began in 1914. From 1917 to 1920, she trained opera performers at the Mariinsky Theater in "plastique" and held classes of classical dance at the Petrograd Ballet School and at Akim Volynsky's School of Russian Ballet. In 1921, she emigrated and continued her teaching career in Milan, London, Buenos Aires, and Berlin. In 1923, she settled in Paris. Preobrajenska trained several generations of the best European dancers including Agrippina Vaganova, Tamara Toumanova, Georges Skibine, Nadia Nerina, and Nina Vyroubova.

69. Anna Pavlova and Mikhail Mordkin.

70. Olga Preobrajenska as Berenice in *Egyptian Nights*.

RUSSIAN BALLET ABROAD

Sergei Diaghilev's project, begun in 1909, opened a new aesthetics in the art of choreography to the West. Diaghilev chose the one-act ballet as the principal vehicle of his performances; in them, dance and pantomime formed an integral whole. The choreographer, together with the designer and the composer, created a spectacle of striking emotional and visual intensity, with intricate dance and plastique. Some time later, however, Diaghilev and those who were to help him create the first "Russian Seasons" disagreed in their views on performance: Michel Fokine's picturesque productions began to seem obsolete to Diaghilev. Gradually, a withdrawal from the principles of Mir Iskusstva (the World of Art) and from traditionalist aesthetics began. In 1911, Diaghilev quarreled with Alexandre Benois. After 1912, Fokine was no longer the only choreographer of the Ballets Russes: Vaslav Nijinsky made his debut as a choreographer, staging *L'Après-midi d'un Faune* (1912), *Jeux* and *Le Sacre du Printemps (The Rite of Spring*; both in 1913). Nijinsky, captivated by the new French painting (specifically by Paul Gauguin), sought a new, tentative means of dance movement. He broke with the usual ideas of dance, and expressionist tendencies manifested themselves in his productions, evoking a stormy reaction from the public and critics. These tendencies became firmly established in the art of the subsequent decade. The First World War gave an outside impetus to the break between Diaghilev and Fokine. Changes that made their further cooperation impossible occurred in the Ballets Russes during the war years (1914-18). Diaghilev dramatically dismissed Nijinsky in 1913, and Leonide Massine replaced him in the company. However, to a certain extent, the stylistic development of the Ballets Russes continued in the direction anticipated by Nijinsky. In 1914, Diaghilev's company temporarily disintegrated. Diaghilev, Massine, and the artists Natalia Goncharova and Mikhail Larionov (who had settled in Switzerland) were

working on new productions, and Igor Stravinsky was composing music for new ballets. The company, composed anew of Russian, British, and Polish dancers, held performances in Spain, Switzerland, and America in the season of 1915-16. The dancers spent the autumn of 1916 and the winter of 1917 on their second tour in the United States under Nijinsky, who had been invited especially for this tour. At the same time, a production of *Parade*, with music by Erik Satie, was being prepared in Europe. It was devised by the poet and playwright Jean Cocteau and the artist Pablo Picasso, who was the designer of the production; Leonide Massine was the choreographer. The production of *Parade* was a crucial moment for Diaghilev's company: from that time, it opted for a western orientation, while Diaghilev strove to be in the vanguard of Western European theater art, rather than to popularize the achievement of Russian ballet abroad. For the first time ever, the company turned to a French artist, the head of a leading trend in contemporary painting. Also for the first time, cubism broke into ballet, and the "futuristic" methods of épatage were used. The boundary between academic theater and buffoonery was erased. A new stage in Diaghilev's endeavor was linked with the work of the artists of the Paris school and the young French composers of the "Six" group. Among Massine's comedy ballets, André Derain was the designer of *La Boutique Fantasque* and Picasso of *Le Tricorne (The Three-Cornered Hat)*

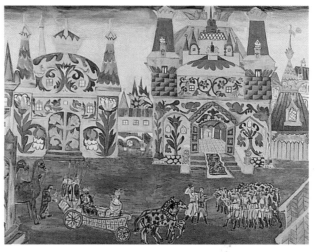

previous pages
71. This sketch shows a set that Anisfeld designed for *Seven Daughters of the Mountain King.*

far left
72. The premiere of *Le Sacre du Printemps (The Rite of Spring)* ended in a scandal. The general dissatisfaction with Igor Stravinsky's music evolved into shouts and catcalls. Surprised by the constrained, angular movements of the dancers, the audience quickly divided into two camps. However, even those who hated Nijinsky's choreographic attempt to convey the original essence of an ancient Slavite acknowledged the beauty of Nikolai Roerich's sets and costumes, which consisted of spring landscapes and patterned peasant tunics and long shirts.

73. One of Michel Fokine's last productions was Nikolai Rimsky-Korsakov's opera *The Golden Cockerel,* which the Ballets Russes presented as an opera-ballet in 1914. This ballet was unusual for Fokine because of its neoprimitivist motifs. Both Fokine and Natalia Goncharova, who was invited by Diaghilev to serve as artist for the production, were inspired by Russian folk woodcuts (luhki), embroidery, and toys.

This sketch by Goncharova shows a set for *The Golden Cockerel.*

74. Massine's debut as a choreographer came with *Le Soleil de Nuit* (*The Midnight Sun*) (1915), based on Nikolai Rimsky-Korsakov's opera *The Snow Maiden*. Following Nijinsky, Massine also filled the dance with the forms of folk rituals of spring, but his production was clear and transparent, largely due to the work of the designer Mikhail Larionov (1881-1964). An admirer of Russian folklore, Larionov was invited by Diaghilev not only to work on the sets and costumes but to advise and assist the choreographer as well.

This sketch by Larionov shows a set for *Le Soleil de Nuit* (*The Midnight Sun*).

77

and *Pulcinella*. In 1921, Bronislava Nijinska, who had recently joined the company, staged, along with two "Russian" productions based on Stravinsky's music, a refined and frivolous ballet called *Les Biches* (*The House Party*), with music by Francis Poulenc and scenery by Marie Laurencin. She also presented a "choreographic operetta" entitled *Le Train Bleu* with music by Darius Milhaud and scenery by Henri Laurens, Coco Chanel, and Pablo Picasso. Nijinska's extravagant, "urbanistic" productions expressed the epoch's interest in "light", variety, and circus genres, including sports and popular dance. Dances based on machines were presented in Massine's *Le Pas d'Acier*, staged in Paris. At the same time, the awareness of the impossibility of returning to Russia cast a different light on Russian themes : with the participation of Goncharova and Larionov, the company created a number of "neoprimitivist" productions: *Le Soleil de Nuit* (*The Midnight Sun*) and *Les Contes Russes* by Massine, *Le Renard* and *Les Noces* by Nijinska, and *Chout* by Thadée Slavinsky and Mikhail Larionov. In their search for a synthesis of their national outlook of the world, the authors gave up on the theme of exotic locales or historic pieces. Instead, the company's productions affirmed the daring strength and vitality of Russian folklore and the internal profundity of the "savage" ancient rite. Diaghilev's attempt in 1921 to present Petipa's ballet in all its splendor to Europe did not win financial success for the company. Despite Bakst's fantastic and luxurious scenery, the London production of *The Sleeping Princess* (*The Sleeping Beauty*), a multi-act ballet with alternating

variations and ensembles punctuated by pantomime episodes, was reproached for its monotony. The significance of this production was only comprehended much later: contemporaries regarded it as a deviation from Diaghilev's innovations. On the brink of financial ruin, Diaghilev began to demand new, unusual contributions from his collaborators. However, his disregard for classical dance and its expressive potential gave rise to criticism. George Balanchine, a choreographer who viewed tradition as a foundation for innovation in art, was Diaghilev's last discovery. For the Ballets Russes, he began to create compositions based on choreographic neoclassicism. In *Apollon Musagète*, Balanchine found new opportunities for exploiting and developing the classic forms inherited from the nineteenth century, in particular from the choreography of Marius Petipa.

Strong, new dancers of the classical school continually joined the company: Lubov Tchernicheva, Vera Nemchinova, Alexandra Danilova, Alicia Markova, Alice Nikitina, Anatole Vilzak, Ludmila Schollar, Anton Dolin, Serge Lifar, Lydia Sokolova, Leon Woizikovsky, Stanislav Idzikowsky, and Olga Spessivtseva were all regular performers there by the mid-1920s. *The Prodigal Son*, staged in 1929, was the last premiere of Diaghilev's Ballets Russes. This dramatic ballet by Balanchine was very much in the spirit of the time and was a distillation of the choreographer's impressions from the Petrograd constructivism of the 1920s and

75. *Parade* was presented as a performance consisting of several numbers. Managers, dressed in cubistic costumes by Pablo Picasso (rigid constructions that made them look like giant puppets) presented the artists to the public. Massine himself played the role of a Chinese conjurer, and his number was considered one of the best in the program. For many years later, it was performed as a divertissement.

Leonide Massine as the Chinese Conjurer.

from the productions of Kasyan Goleizovsky, Nicolai Foregger, and Vsevolod Meyerhold. In August 1929, Diaghilev died in Venice from blood poisoning, and the activity of the company, which had been fueled largely by his talent, ceased. The name of Diaghilev had become legendary throughout Europe. His glory could be compared only with the fame of Anna Pavlova, whose company in Great Britain toured all over the world between 1911 and 1931, performing abridged versions of ballets from the academic repertoire and the productions of Fokine (*Les Préludes* and *Seven Daughters of the Mountain King*), Ivan Clustine (*Les Fresques d'Adjanta* and *Dionysos*), Laurent Novikov (*Les Contes Russes*), and others. But Pavlova, who opened the lofty beauty of classic ballet to the general public,

was no innovator. By contrast, Diaghilev managed to present in Europe what ballet in Russia was only striving for. He gave an impetus to the further development of choreography and of theater as a whole. Almost all of the Russian companies that worked abroad were linked with the Diaghilev enterprise in one way or another. They were set up by people who had worked with Diaghilev and had been influenced by him. They developed the ideas advanced by the Ballets Russes, but could not rival it. The productions of Ida Rubinstein, who had become famous for her performance of pantomime roles in Fokine's early ballets, figured prominently in the artistic life of Paris. Being very rich and striving to outdo Diaghilev in the scale of her enterprises, Rubinstein collaborated with many

famous choreographers, artists, and talented dancers: Fokine, Massine, Nijinska, Bakst, and Benois worked with her. Ravel's *Bolero* (1928), *Le Baiser de la Fée* and *Perséphone* by Igor Stravinsky (1929, 1934) were composed on her commissions and were staged for the first time with her participation. Anatole Vilzak, Ludmila Schollar, Frederick Ashton, David Lichine, and others performed in her company, which worked periodically after 1910 and then in 1928-29, 1931 and 1934. Even critics who disapproved of Rubinstein as a person showed interest in her productions. Some of the dancers of Rubinstein's company later joined Nijinska's Dance Theatre (1933-34), whose repertoire also included ballets staged for Rubinstein. In Berlin, the choreographer Boris Romanov, who was influenced by Fokine and had cooperated with Diaghilev, established the Russian Romantic Theater (1922-25). Yelena Smirnova and Anatole Oboukhov, dancers from the Mariinsky Theater, held the leading positions in it. The company's repertoire included Romanov's versions of classical ballets, his pre-revolutionary productions, and new ballets that were permeated with romantic inspiration or were in the spirit of theater play or witty stylization. The companies of Adolph Bolm (the Ballet Intime, created in 1916, and others) and of Mikhail Mordkin (the Mordkin Ballet, founded in 1926; then a company with the same name that worked in 1937 and, on the basis of which, the American Ballet Theater was founded) worked in the United States. Fokine, Vera Fokina, and a group of

76. Diaghilev believed that the participation of Mikhail Larionov guaranteed the success of any production on Russian themes and often engaged him as a consultant for beginning choreographers. Having assisted Massine with *Le Soleil de Nuit* (*The Midnight Sun*) in 1915, Larionov went on to help Serge Lifar with his production of *Le Renard*. The poster for *Chout* indicates that Larionov was, along with the dancer Tadeusz Slavinsky, one of the choreographers for that production.

This is a scene from the ballet *Chout*.

their students also established themselves in America. In 1924, their company was named the Fokine American Ballet, but it never became a permanent company and gave performances periodically until the end of 1930. The two ballet companies that were created after Diaghilev's death, the Ballets de l'Opera de Monte Carlo (headed by the French ballet and art critic René Blum) and the Ballets de l'Opéra Russe à Paris (with Vasily Voskresensky, also known as Colonel de Basil, as one of its directors), fused in 1932 and formed the Ballet Russe de Monte Carlo with de Basil as its director and Blum as artistic director. It included many former members of Diaghilev's company : Lubov Tchernicheva, Sergei Grigoriev, Felia Doubrovska, Alexandra Danilova, Leon Woizikovsky, and others. It also included Tamara Toumanova, Irina Baronova, and Tatiana Riabouchinska, who had been trained by Russian teachers in France (they were known as the "baby-ballerinas", because they were between 14 and 16 years old), Nina Vershinina, Andre Eglevsky, David Lichine, and others. In addition to ballets taken from the repertoire of Diaghilev's company and the Ballet de l'Opéra Russe à Paris, and productions by Romanov, Nijinska, and Fokine, this company performed new ballets by Balanchine (who became the company's first choreographer) and Massine (who replaced him in 1933). The company broke up in 1935, and de Basil and Blum parted. Two new companies were created: the Ballet Russe du Colonel de Basil (the Original

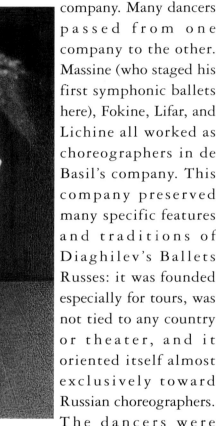

Ballet Russe after 1939) and the Ballet de Monte Carlo with Blum as director (later, the Ballets Russes de Monte Carlo). Dmitry Rostov, Roman Jasinsky, Sono Osato, Tatiana Leskova, Igor Schwezov, and others performed in de Basil's company, while Vera Nemtchinova, Anatole Vilzak, Anatole Oboukhov, André Eglevsky, Alexandra Danilova, Alicia Markova, Tamara Toumanova, Georges Skibine, and others starred in Blum's company. Many dancers passed from one company to the other. Massine (who staged his first symphonic ballets here), Fokine, Lifar, and Lichine all worked as choreographers in de Basil's company. This company preserved many specific features and traditions of Diaghilev's Ballets Russes: it was founded especially for tours, was not tied to any country or theater, and it oriented itself almost exclusively toward Russian choreographers. The dancers were trained and rehearsed by the Russian teachers Sergei Grigoriev and Lubov Tchernicheva. The performances of the Ballet Russe du Colonel de Basil usually consisted of several one-act ballets, and its repertoire was based on the productions of the Ballets Russes. However, while Diaghilev had been a reformer who inspired creativity in his dancers and developed new talent, de Basil was known primarly as an administrator. He preserved what had been created before. Massine's symphonic ballets were the only contribution to the development of ballet that his company made. The Original Ballet Russe toured not only in Europe and the United States, but also in Australia and the small

*77. The last star of the Russian Ballet and the Diaghilev's last discovery was the young Serge Lifar, who was born in Ukraine, studied under Bronislava Nijinska, and who later became one of the leading figures of twentieth-century French ballet. He became the artistic director of the Grand Opéra in Pans and taught many of the best French dancers. Among his greatest creations was the title role of The Prodigal Son.*

countries in Latin America. In Cuba, the company helped lay the foundation for the further development of national choreography. Blum's Ballet Russe de Monte Carlo proved to be the most long-lived among the Russian companies that emerged abroad. Having begun its activity in France, it moved to the United States in 1939, and it worked there until 1962. Alexandra Danilova, who danced with Britain's Frederic Franklin, was the prima ballerina of the company from 1938 to 1952. The repertoire of the Ballet Russe de Monte Carlo comprised several nineteenth-century ballets and a number of productions that Fokine and Massine had created for other companies. The most fruitful period of the company's activity is associated with Massine's name: he was its chief choreographer from 1938 to 1942. Here, he staged performances in cooperation with the surrealist artist Salvador Dalì, as well as comic and symphonic ballets and ballets on American themes. Nijinska and Balanchine also worked in the company: Balanchine staged a number of new ballets there and transfered some of his best old productions. With the passing of time, productions by the American choreographers Agnes de Mille, Ruth Page, and Valerie Bettis appeared in the company's repertoire. Since the Ballet Russe de Monte Carlo did not have an innovative director, it gradually found itself pushed into the background of American artistic life, which came to be dominated by the New York City Ballet (founded by Balanchine in the 1930s) and the Ballet Theater (based on Mordkin's company and

established in the 1940s). The company, which was originally headed by Blum and then by Serge Denham (Sergei Dokutchaev) and which became almost completely Americanized by the beginning of the 1960s, failed to move into the foreground as an American company. However, it greatly influenced the development of ballet in the United States. Many American dancers rose to prominence in this company, and it presented the Russian repertoire to American spectators. Moreover, when Russian dancers of the older generation left the stage, they opened schools in many American states. Among the other Russian companies that worked abroad in the middle of the twentieth century were Les Ballets (created in 1933 under the direction of Balanchine and Boris Kochno) and Lévitov-Dandré's Ballet Russe (headed by Alexander Lévitov and Victor Dandré, with Paul Petrov as choreographer in 1934-35). Russian companies generally did not assimilate the culture of the countries in which they worked. Influencing national choreographic art and, in turn, experiencing the impact of the national schools of these countries, they still retained their original character and were regarded as a particular phenomenon — "the Russian ballet." The companies of many national theaters were essentially Russian during the initial years of their work. For instance, Paul Petrov and Nicholas Zverev worked in the Lithuanian National Ballet; Nicholas Sergeyev and Alexandra Fedorova worked in the ballet company of the Opera

78. The ballet *La Chatte* was a daring experiment for the young George Balanchine. For this ballet, whose plot followed Aesop's fable about a cat who was turned into a girl by the goddess Aphrodite, Naum Gabo and Antoine Pevsner created a number of abstract sets out of metal and plexiglass (one of the constructions depicted Aphrodite). The choreography was also rather abstract: Balanchine concentrated on the exactness and technical perfection of the composition and hardly even hinted at the plot of the story.

Alice Nikitina and Serge Lifar in *La Chatte*.

Theater in Riga, etc. Russian dancers made a great contribution in shaping national ballets in several Latin American countries: Tatiana Leskova, Igor Schwezov, Nina Vershinina, and others in Brazil; Georgy Kyasht, Boris Romanov, Paul Petrov, and Leonide Massine in Argentina; Dmitry Rostov in Peru, etc. The idea of the "Russian ballet abroad" also includes the ballet schools that were opened by Russian dancers and teachers in various

79. For his production of *The Sleeping Princess*, Diaghilev turned to the choreography of Marius Petipa with all of its imperial splendor in order to show Europe classical Russian ballet of the nineteenth century. The magnificence and excess of the production also entered into its artistic arrangement: Leon Bakst created literally hundreds of costumes that were noted for their complexity and detail.

This sketch shows one of the costumes Bakst created for *The Sleeping Princess*.

countries. The first of them emerged even before the First World War (the schools of Anna Pavlova and Serafima Astafieva opened in London in 1912 and 1914, respectively; Fedor Kozlov's school worked in New York in the early 1910s). After the Russian Revolution in 1917, when many dancers emigrated from Russia, the number of such schools increased rapidly. Olga Preobrajenska and Lubov Egorova taught in Paris from 1923; Mathilda Kchessinska, from 1929; Boris Kniasev, from 1937; among others. Their schools originally trained the children

Lincoln Kirsten in 1934. Beginning in 1941, Novikov taught at the school at the Metropolitan Opera and, later, in Chicago. Bolm taught in Chicago and, during the 1920s, in San Francisco. Schwezov, Alexander Volinin, Novikov, and others were also well-known teachers. A number of less famous Russian dancers also opened schools and studios. After the Second World War, many dancers who had been trained by these teachers and, therefore, upheld and promoted the traditions of the Russian ballet school, also opened training schools. As a rule, the

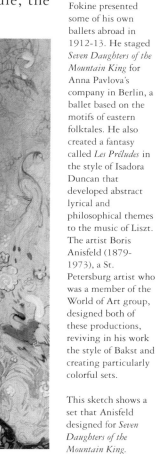

80. After leaving Diaghilev's Ballets Russes, Michel Fokine presented some of his own ballets abroad in 1912-13. He staged *Seven Daughters of the Mountain King* for Anna Pavlova's company in Berlin, a ballet based on the motifs of eastern folktales. He also created a fantasy called *Les Préludes* in the style of Isadora Duncan that developed abstract lyrical and philosophical themes to the music of Liszt. The artist Boris Anisfeld (1879-1973), a St. Petersburg artist who was a member of the World of Art group, designed both of these productions, reviving in his work the style of Bakst and creating particularly colorful sets.

This sketch shows a set that Anisfeld designed for *Seven Daughters of the Mountain King*.

of Russian émigrés, many of whom became popular members of Russian companies. The school of Nikolai Legat and Nadezhda Nikolayeva-Legat was among the best known in London (from 1926). Fokine opened his school in New York in 1921; Mordkin, in 1924. Anatole Vilzak and Ludmila Schollar (who also had their own school in 1940), Felia Doubrovska, and Alexandra Danilova worked at the School of American Ballet, which was organized by Balanchine and

people who organized companies in Latin American countries, in Australia, and in other countries where ballet was not yet know began by training at these schools. Russian ballet abroad has had a great influence on the education and professional training of dancers and choreographers from every corner of the globe.

# Great figures of Russian ballet

**BALANCHINE,**
George (originally Georgy)
Melitonovich Balanchivadze;
(born January 22, 1904, in St.
Petersburg; died April 30,1983,
in New York).
*Dancer and choreographer.*
Balanchine was the son of a
Georgian composer, Meliton
Balanchivadze. He studied at the
Petrograd Theater School under
Pavel Gerdt and Samuel
Andrianov from 1914 to 1921
and at the Petrograd Conservatory
from 1920 to 1923. In 1921,
Balanchine joined the Petrograd
Opera and Ballet Theater
(formerly, the Mariinsky Theater).
He was a soloist in Fedor
Lopukhov's dance symphony *The
Greatness of the Universe* in 1923.
His career as a choreographer
began with performances for the
students at the Petrograd Theater
School. In 1922, under the
influence of the Petrograd tour of
Kasyan Goleizovsky's "Chamber
Ballet," Balanchine founded the
Young Ballet Company in
Petrograd with a group of young
dancers of the former Mariinsky
Theater. He staged *La Marche
Funèbre* by Frédéric Chopin,
*La Valse Triste* by Jean Sibelius,
and *The Twelve* (a pantomime
performance while a chorus read
Alexander Blok's poem) for the
Young Ballet. Balanchine was one
of the first in Russia to use
acrobatic elements in ballet. In
1923, Balanchine staged the
dances in the opera The Golden
Cockerel by Nikolai Rimsky-
Korsakov at the Maly Opera
Theater, as well as those in Shaw's
*Caesar and Cleopatra* and Ernst
Toller's *Hinkemann* (*Eugene the
Unfortunate*) (Alexandrinsky
Theater). In 1924, Balanchine
went abroad with three dancers
from the Young Ballet: Tamara

81. Portrait of
George Balanchine
by Zinaïda
Serebriakova.

Gevergeyeva, Alexandra Danilova,
and Nikolai Efimov. They toured
Germany and then, a year later,
were brought into the company of
Diaghilev's Ballets Russes. It did
not take long for Balanchine to
determine the general tendency of
the company's activity. In Diaghilev's company, he staged the
ballets *Le Chant du Rossignol* and
*Barabau* (both 1924), *La Chatte*
(1927), *Apollon Musagète* (1928),
*Le Bal* and *The Prodigal Son*, which
illustrated the Biblical tale in a

series of episodes and combined
the lofty pathetic with
blasphemous irony and
sophisticated stylized movements
with elements of buffoonery. It
was the last production of
Diaghilev's life.
In 1932-33, Balanchine worked in
the Ballet Russe de Monte Carlo,
producing *La Concurrence*, *Cotillon*,
and other ballets. In 1933, he
organized the 1933 Ballet Company
in Paris, with which he staged *The
Seven Deadly Sins* and *Mozartiana*.

The American period of his career began in late 1933. Invited to the United States by Lincoln Kirstein (a writer, ballet director, and the author of several books on ballet), Balanchine (together with Kirstein) organized the School of the American Ballet and the American Ballet Company, as well as the New York City Ballet in 1948. In the 1920s and the early 1930s, Balanchine primarily staged dramatic and comic farces on simple subjects, using both dance and pantomime. Later, he abandoned the idea of a synthetic production. Turning to the academic tradition and the heritage of Marius Petipa and enriching them with intonations and rhythms of the twentieth century, Balanchine founded a new school of classical dance. As Balanchine put it while working on *Apollon Musagète* in cooperation with the composer Igor Stravinsky: "Here was the beginning of the direct conversion of sound into visible movement." This plotless ballet was a new expression of the beauty of classical dance. After 1934, this trend predominated in Balanchine's choreography. His ballets usually did not have any plot: they were often staged to music that was not designed for dance (suites, concerts, symphonies, etc.), and their content was developed by musical, choreographic images and "in the rhythmic movement of the dancers and the motions of the dancers and groups." Balanchine, a refined lyric choreographer, avoided open emotions, giving the audience a chance to enjoy the perfection of form and the integrity of music and dance. He created "a world of mastery and immaculately strict lines." Among Balanchine's "neoclassical" ballets are *Sérénade* (1934), based on Tchaikovsky's *Serenade for String Orchestra; Concerto Barocco* (1940) based on music by Johann Sebastian Bach; *Ballet Imperial* (1941), based on Tchaikovsky's Second Piano Concerto; *Symphony in C (Le Palais de Cristal)* (1947), based on Bizet's First Symphony; and Tchaikovsky's, *Suite No 3* (1970). Balanchine's long collaboration with

Stravinsky was of immense importance for him. Stravinsky's music helped Balanchine design dance deriving from academic structures and, at the same time, differing from them in principle. Balanchine created twenty-seven ballets to Stravinsky's music, including *Le Baiser de la Fée* and *Jeu de cartes* (1937), *Orpheus* (1948), *Firebird* (1949 and 1970), *Agon* (1957), *Pulcinella* (1972, together with Jerome Robbins), and *Circus Polka* for fifty elephants from the Barnum and Bailey Circus. Balanchine also interpreted some of Stravinsky's music that was not designed for the theater (*Danses Concertantes*, 1944; *Elégie*, 1945; *Movements for Piano and Orchestra*, 1963; *Rubies* (second part of ballet *Jewels*; sometimes retitled *Capriccio*), 1967; *Violin Concerto*, 1972; and others). Classical dance was the principal means of expression for Balanchine, even in ballets in which the characters were in a specific ethnic setting, such as *The Scotch Symphony* (1952), *Western Symphony* (1954), *Who Cares?* (1970), and others. Balanchine preferred the one-act ballet, but he also staged *A Midsummer Night's Dream* in two acts and *Don Quixote* (music by Nicholas

Nabokov) in three acts (1965). Balanchine created new versions of old ballets (*The Nutcracker*, 1954; a one-act version of *Swan Lake*, 1951; etc.). In the 1930s and 1940s, Balanchine choreographed dance scenes in musicals, operettas, and operas. Among those, *The Rake's Progress* by Stravinsky (Metropolitan Opera, 1953), is the most famous. Balanchine founded a new school in choreography; the choreographers William Dollar, John Taras, Todd Bolender, and Jerome Robbins are among his followers. Most of the members of the New York City Ballet were his students.

## BOLM,
Adolph (Emile) Rudolfovich (born September 25,1894, in St. Petersburg; died July 16, 1951, in Hollywood, USA).
*Dancer, choreographer, and teacher.*
Bolm was the son of the first violin and assistant conductor of the St. Petersburg Mikhailovsky Theater. He studied at the St. Petersburg Theater School under Platon Karsavin. Upon graduating in 1903, he entered the corps de ballet of the Mariinsky Theater where he also danced as a soloist. Although he did not receive any major roles, Bolm

82. A scene from *Apollon Musagète* performed by dancers from the Kirov Theater in Leningrad, created by Balanchine in 1928.

was a success among the public and the critics. He was Anna Pavlova's partner for her first foreign tour (1908). In 1909, he participated in Diaghilev's first "Russian Season" in Paris and brilliantly performed the part of the Chief Warrior, which had been specially designed for him by Michel Fokine. The expressiveness of his leap, the daring fantasy of his pirouettes, and his suppleness and storming power produced an immense effect on critics, who viewed him as a match for Pavlova, Tamara Karsavina, and Vaslav Nijinsky. Nonetheless, at the Mariinsky Theater he remained in the shadows; therefore, in 1911 he became a permanent member of Diaghilev's Ballets Russes. He was the first character dancer in the company and became its chief coach in 1912. He performed as the Prince in *Thamar*, as Amoun in *Cléopatre*, and in other roles. He also staged the "Dance of the Persian Women" in the opera *Khovanshchina* (1913). After a tour of America in 1916, Bolm decided to remain in New York, where he organized a company of his own called the Ballet Intime. He also staged productions at the Metropolitan Opera (Le Coq d'Or, 1918 and Petrushka, 1919). Bolm later worked in the Chicago Opera, the San Francisco Ballet, in Buenos Aires, and in Washington D.C. Adolph Bolm greatly influenced the development of American ballet. He staged Stravinsky's *Apollon Musagète*

on commission from the Library of Congress (1928). One of Bolm's most popular productions was *The Iron Foundry*, in which the dancers acted as dynamos, switches, gears, pistons, etc. This production was based on music by Alexander Mossolov, a Russian constructivist composer of the 1920s. This dance was created for the film *The Mad Genius*, and its stage version was a success at the Hollywood Bowl (1932). During the last years of his life, Bolm worked in Hollywood as a teacher and continued to stage dances for films.

## DANILOVA,
Alexandra Dionysievna
(born November 20,1904, in Peterhoff).
*Dancer and teacher.*
Danilova studied at the Petrograd Theater School under Olga Preobrajenska and Agrippina Vaganova. Upon graduating in 1921, she joined the Petrograd Opera and Ballet Theater (formerly, the Mariinsky Theater). It did not take her long to master a vast repertoire, including the parts of Myrtha in *Giselle*, the Queen of the Dryads in *Don Quixote*, Princess Florine and the Lilac Fairy in *The Sleeping Beauty*, and Berenice in *Egyptian Nights*, and others. She was also a soloist in Fedor Lopukhov's dance symphony *The Greatness of the Universe* (1923). In 1924, Danilova received the principal role in Lopukhov's production of *Firebird*. The critics noted her virtuoso technique, her "noble elegance," the restraint in her dance (which the critics regarded as "rather cool"), and the accuracy and clarity of her style. In short, they predicted a brilliant future for the ballerina. Their forecasts came true, but Danilova's talent did not find full expression on the Leningrad academic stage. Graduating together with George Balanchine in 1922, she joined his Young Ballet. In 1924, Danilova went on tour abroad with Balanchine and two other dancers of the Young Ballet, Tamara Gevergeyeva (Geva), and Nikolai Efimov. None of them ever returned to Russia; they all joined Sergei

Diaghilev's Ballets Russes in 1925. Danilova became a leading ballerina and was the first performer of the principal parts in Balanchine's productions: *Pastorale* and *The Triumph of Neptune* (1926), and *Le Bal* (1929). She also starred in Leonide Massine's *Le Pas d' Acier* (1927). Beginning in 1933, Danilova worked with the Ballets Russes du Colonel de Basil, as well as with other companies. Massine preferred her for demi-caractère parts (the Street Dancer in *Le Beau Danube* and the Gloveseller in *La Galeté Parisienne*). He admired the brilliance, elegance, and charm of her performance: as he put it, the ballerina "sparkled like champagne." In 1938, Danilova became the leading ballerina of the Ballet Russe of Monte Carlo, and she worked there until 1952. At that time, she also danced with two British companies, Sadler's Wells Ballet (1949) and the London Festival Ballet (1952, 1955). Between 1954 and 1956, Danilova headed her own company in the United States. Danilova danced in classical ballets (*Swan Lake*, *Giselle*, *Coppélia*, and *Raymonda*) and in the productions of Fokine (*Firebird* and *Les Sylphides*) and Balanchine (*Danses Concertantes*, *Night Shadow*, and others). A prima ballerina, a star of the middle of the twentieth century, Danilova brought the traditions of the Russian school of classical dance to American ballet. In 1957, Danilova gave her farewell performance, but she repeatedly revived classical ballets in American and European companies (including *Raymonda* and *Coppélia*). From 1959 to 1961, she staged dances in operas at the Metropolitan Opera. She taught at the American Ballet School in the 1970s and 1980s. She also published a volume of memoirs entitled *Choura. The Memoirs of Alexandra Danilova* (New York, 1986).

## MASSINE,
Leonide Fedorovich
(born August 8, 1895, in Moscow; died March 15, 1979, in Borken, Westphalie).
*Dancer and choreographer.*
Massine studied at the Moscow Theater School and, in addition to ballet, he also took up drama and participated in the productions of the Moscow Maly Theater. Upon graduating in 1912, Massine joined the company of the Bolshoi Theater. Massine's destiny was shaped by a meeting with Diaghilev, who had come to Russia after breaking with Vaslav Nijinsky and was seeking a replacement for him. Diaghilev decided to groom Massine as the principal dancer and choreographer of his company and brought him to Paris in 1914. Massine began to train under Enrico Cecchetti and, shortly afterwards, performed the main role in Michel Fokine's new ballet *La Légende de Joseph*. In 1915, Massine staged his first ballet, *Le Soleil de Nuit* (*The Midnight Sun*). From 1914 to 1920 and from 1924 to 1928, Massine worked in Diaghilev's Ballets Russes. Of great importance for him were his creative contacts with the painters Mikhail Larionov, Natalia Goncharova, Pablo Picasso, and others. Accepting the aesthetics of the latest artistic trends, Massine boldly brought it to ballet. *Parade*, "the first cubistic ballet," which he staged in cooperation with Picasso in 1917 (its plan and libretto were by the French poet and playwright Jean Cocteau), marked the beginning of a new stage in the activity of Diaghilev's enterprise, which had opted for an orientation toward the modern West. This merry and blasphemously daring spectacle, aimed at shocking the public, destroyed the system of values that Fokine and the World of Art artists had established in the Ballets Russes. Massine's works were infused by his wit and bright temperament. He often staged genre ballets in a burlesque style in which he usually performed the leading parts himself. He preferred dynamically developing action and theatrical folk dances (Spanish and Italian), and he used the methods of the commedia dell'arte and others. These productions included *Les Femmes de Bonne Humeur* (*The Good-Humored Ladies*, 1917), *La Boutique Fantasque* and *Le Tricorne* (*The Three-Cornered Hat*, 1919), *Pulcinella* (1920), etc. In 1927, Massine paid homage to constructivism by staging *Le Pas d'Acier* (libretto and scenery by Georgy Yakulov) with sketches from Soviet life of the 1920s and featuring "The Dance of the Machines." Surrealistic tendencies manifested themselves in Massine's ballet *Ode* (with scenery by Pavel Tchelitchev), which was based on an ode by Mikhail Lomonosov, a Russian poet of the eighteenth century. After he left Diaghilev's Ballets Russes, Massine worked with Ida Rubinstein's company. In 1932, he began to choreograph for the Ballet Russe de Monte Carlo and, in 1933, he became its chief ballet master. At first, Massine specialized

85. Leonide Massine as Joseph (*The Legend of Joseph*).

86. A scene from *Les Femmes de Bonne Humeur* (The Good-Humored Ladies) created by Leonide Massine in 1917.

in comic ballets, but later a different line prevailed in his work. Massine was the first in the west to stage symphonic ballets: *Les Présages*, to the music of Tchaikovsky's Fifth Symphony; *Choréartium*, to the music of Brahms's Fourth Symphony (both, 1933); *La Symphonie Fantastique*, to the music of Hector Berlioz (1936); and others. Thanks to Massine, ballet created a new use for classical music. Massine's symphonic ballets differed from Balanchine's "plotless" productions in that they projected not only the purely musical content but some extra-musical message as well. They manifested Massine's tendency toward allegoric thinking, and the action was frequently built on the clash of such abstract ideas as fate, passion, temptation, etc. When the Ballet Russe de Monte Carlo broke up, Massine first became the principal ballet master of the company of Colonel de Basil and, in 1938, joined René Blum's company. Among the productions staged there were *La Gaité Parisienne* and *Nobilissima Visione* (both in 1938), *Beethoven's Seventh Symphony* (1938), and *Le Rouge et le Noir* (*L'Etrange Farandole*) with the music of Shostakovich's First Symphony (1939). In the ballets *New Yorker* (1940) and *Saratoga* (1941), as in his earlier production of *Union Pacific* (1934), Massine turned to American themes. In the 1940s, Massine collaborated with the surrealist artist Salvador Dali, who was the author

of the scenarios and designed the scenery for the ballets *Bacchanale* (1939), *Labyrinth* (1941), and *Mad Tristan* (1944, Ballet International Company). In 1945-46, Massine toured with his own company. In 1947, he staged productions in various (primarily European) companies, including l'Opera Comique (France), the Ballet Theater (USA), La Scala (Italy), etc. He revived his famous productions and worked as a choreographer in cinema, including such films as *The Red Shoes* (1946), *Tales of Hoffmann* (1951), and *Carosello Napoletano* (1954). He was the author of *My Life in Ballet* (London, 1960) and *Theory and Exercise in Composition* (London, 1976). Massine's son Lorca (Leonide) Massine is an American dancer and ballet master, and his daughter Tatiana is a ballerina.

## NIJINSKA,

Bronislava Fominitshna
(born January 8, 1891, in Minsk; died February 22, 1972, in Los Angeles).
*Ballerina, choreographer, and teacher.*
Nijinska was the daughter of the Polish dancers Tomasz (Foma) Nijinsky and Eleonora Bereda and the sister of Vaslav Nijinsky. She studied at the St. Petersburg Theater School under Enrico Cecchetti, Michel Fokine, Klavdia Koulitchevskaya, and Nikolai Legat. During summer vacation Nijinska was trained by her brother. Upon

graduating in 1908, she joined the company of the Mariinsky Theater, but she left in 1911 in protest against the dismissal of Vaslav Nijinsky. In 1909, she performed in Diaghilev's Russian Seasons and became a regular dancer of Diaghilev's Ballets Russes. She left it in 1913, once again in protest against the dismissal of her brother. In those years, Nijinska performed the parts of Papillon in *Le Carnaval*, the Street Dancer in *Petrushka*, and the Nymphe in *L'Après-midi d'un Faune*. Her contemporaries noted her virtuoso technique, high and light elevation, and rare aplomb and strength. In 1914, Nijinska participated in her brother's London enterprise; she then returned to Russia, and from 1915 to 1921, she performed and taught in Kiev (Serge Lifar was among her pupils). In the 1920s, Nijinska began to work as a choreographer. Having emigrated in 1921, she rejoined Diaghilev's company and participated in the London production of *The Sleeping Princess* (*The Sleeping Beauty*), restaging some of the scenes and parts and composing the "Three Ivans" dance for the final act. Next, she produced ballets to the music of Igor Stravinsky, including *Le Renard* (1922) and *Les Noces* (1923). The latter earned Nijinska a reputation as a reformer of the choreography of the twentieth century. Nijinska's composition in *Les Noces* did not "describe" the rite but focused on its essence: it had tremendous concentration and intensity and a keen penetration into a solemn mystery. The ballet was expressed in the movement of many figures: human bodies formed garlands and pyramids as a living ornament; the immobility of the stiff "wooden sculptures" of the Bride, the Bridegroom, and their parents was markedly expressive. Nijinska's ballets were stunning in the uniqueness and diversity of their choreography. After the deeply tragic *Les Noces*, Nijinska produced the ironic *Les Biches* (*The House Party*), a picture of contemporary high society life (1924): in this ballet, the forms of classical dance were accented by new movements, poses, and jazz rhythms. Dances depicted the frivolous atmosphere of salon flirtation. *Le Train Bleu*, a "choreographic operetta" (1924), featured elements of acrobatics and of the variety show and the "cinemographic" effect of slow motion to depict games on the beach of a fashionable resort. In 1926-27 and in 1932, Nijinska worked at the Teatro Colon in Buenos Aires. In 1928, she became a choreographer of Ida Rubinstein's company in Paris, where she staged *La Princesse Cygne*, *La Bien Aimée*, and *Le Baiser de la Fée*. She also choreographed two compositions by Maurice Ravel, Bolero and La Valse. At that time, she headed the ballet company of Opéra Russe à Paris. Nijinska, a vigorous and authoritarian woman with a strong and rather difficult character, inspired great respect in those who worked with her. According to dancer Nina Tikhonova's memoirs, Nijinska "could not cooperate with indifferent people and, probably for this reason, preferred the young to more experienced dancers, who were not always prepared to respond to her endeavor." From 1931 to 1935, Nijinska headed her own company, Nijinska's Dance Theater (Bronislava Nijinska's Ballet) in which she combined her old productions with new ones of *Les Variations*, *Etude*, *Les Comédiens Jaloux* (all in 1932), and *Hamlet* (1934). She continued to perform the leading parts in her productions. She later cooperated with a number of companies, including Ballet Russe du Colonel de Basil (1935, 1936) and Ballet

Russe de Monte Carlo (1942-43). Nijinska also worked in Berlin with director Max Reinhardt; in particular, she staged the dances in the film *A Midsummer Night's Dream*. In 1938, Nijinska founded a ballet school in Los Angeles, and from 1952 she headed the Ballet Theater School New York. Maria and Marjorie Tallc and Allegra Kent were her pupils. Bronislava Nijinska continued to produce ballets in many theaters of the world and to revive her most famous productions until 1966. She is the author of the book *Early Memories* (New York, 1981).

**ROMANOV**, Boris Georgievich (born March 22, 1891, in St. Petersburg; died January 30, 1957, in New York).
*Dancer, choreographer, and teacher.*
Romanov was the son of the chief costumier of the Mariinsky Theater. He studied at the St. Petersburg Theater School under Mikhail Oboukhov and joined Mariinsky Theater in 1909. A highly temperamental dancer, Romanov was a success in a series of typical grotesque roles (the Jester in *The Nutcracker*, the Archer in *Polovtsian Dances* (Prince Igor), the Negro in *The Pharaoh's Daughter*). He also performed in *Le Roi Candaule*, *Eunice* and *Islamey*, etc While still a member of the Emperor's company, Romanov also took charge of the choreography at the Liteiny Theater in St. Petersburg: there he staged dances using stylization and grotesque methods. His fantasy *Les Chevrepieds*, a frantic Dionysian orgy set to the music of Ilia Satz, a modern Russian composer, became the most popular of Romanov's productions. The

dancer was a habitué of the famous St. Petersburg literary and artistic cabaret "The Stray Dog." His aesthetic views were formed under the influence of the World of Art group and the acmeist poets, specifically Mikhail Kuzmin. As a choreographer, Romanov was greatly influenced by Michel Fokine, and he adhered to the aesthetic of traditionalism and admired the commedia dell'arte of the eighteenth century, the exotic East, and Spain. In the mid-1910s, Romanov staged two productions for Sergei Diaghilev's Ballets Russes (*La Tragédie de Salomé* 1913, and the dances in Stravinsky's opera *La Rossignol*, 1914). In 1914, he became a choreographer of the Mariinsky Theater, producing mainly the dances

in operas and divertissements in ballet productions. The expressiveness and nervous strain of Romanov's productions horrified advocates of the academic traditions. In his pantomime ballet *Pierrot et les Masques of Pierrot*, (1914; second version in 1917), the traditional characters of the commedia dell'arte were plunged into a nightmare atmosphere. A bloody drama of rivalry, jealousy, and death was staged in the suite of Spanish dances in

*Andalusiana*, the most significant of the choreographer's pre-revolutionary works. However, this exaggerated passion was fraught with irony. In 1918-19, Romanov collaborated with a group from the Drama Theater, who organized the Tragedy Theater, the Theater of Artistic Drama in Petrograd, and, eventually, the Bolshoi Drama Theater. For the first anniversary of the October revolution, Romanov and composer Boris Asafiev staged the ballet *La Carmagnole*, which was shown only on the stage of a worker's club to piano accompaniment. In the spring of 1919, Romanov was elected to the Directorate of the former Mariinsky Theater, but he left Petrograd with his wife, the ballerina

Yelena Smirnova, in 1920. In 1922, Romanov organized his own company in Berlin, the Russian Romantic Theater, which existed until 1926. The high emotions of the productions of the 1910s did not lead the choreographer to pure expressionism. He continued to affirm the romantic outlook in his productions abroad and relied heavily on classical traditions. The repertoire of his company was diverse and included *Giselle* (reduced version), *Les Millions d'Arlequin*, the ethnographic performance *Les Noces de Boyards*, the opera-ballet *La Reine du Mai*, several of Romanov's old St. Petersburg productions, etc. Elements of acrobatics and athletic movements were used in Romanov's productions *Trapèze* and *Schubertiade* (both 1925). Romanov was later a choreographer for Anna Pavlova's company. He lived in Argentina and staged ballets on Argentine subjects at the Teatro Colon in Buenos Aires (1928-34). He worked in the theaters of Paris, Monte Carlo, Belgrade, Rome, and Chicago. Between 1934 and 1938, Romanov worked in La Scala in Milan and, from 1938 to 1942 and from 1945 to 1950, in the Metropolitan Opera in New York. Romanov taught in Buenos Aires and at the School of Ballet Repertory in New York. He staged new productions and revived the ballets of other choreographers. *El Amor Brujo* (*Love, the Magician*, 1929), *The Nutcracker* (1936), and *Pulcinella* (1950) were among his last productions.

## SPESSIVTSEVA,

Olga Alexandrovna (also performed abroad as O. Spessiva)
(born July 18, 1895, in Rostov-on-Don; died September 16, 1991, in Newark, New Jersey, USA).
*Ballerina.*
At the age of six, after the death of her father, Spessivtseva was put into the orphanage for the children of actors at the St. Petersburg Home of Theater Veterans. In 1906, she was admitted to the St. Petersburg Theater School and was trained by Klavdia Kulichevskaya. Upon graduating in 1913, she joined the Mariinsky Theater, and she was immediately a success in

solo variations in classical ballets. She perfected her skill under Anna Johansson, Yevgenia Sokolova, and Agrippina Vaganova. In the 1910s, her friendship with Akim Volynsky (a writer, critic, and ballet theorist) contributed to Spessivtseva's development. He devoted a series of articles to her, viewing her as the embodiment of his ideas in art. In 1916, Spessivtseva participated in the performances of Sergei Diaghilev's Ballets Russes. She danced with Vaslav Nijinsky in America in *Le Spectre de la Rose*, *Les Sylphides*, and the pas de deux of Princesse Florine and the Blue Bird from *The Sleeping Beauty*. From 1918, she performed the leading parts of the academic repertoire at the Petrograd Opera and Ballet Theater (formerly, the Mariinsky Theater), including Giselle, Esmeralda, Nikia, and others. Shortly afterwards, Spessivtseva became a star of the Petrograd company. In 1921, she danced Aurora in the premiere of the London production of *The Sleeping Princess* (*The Sleeping Beauty*) with Diaghilev's Ballets Russes. In 1923, she performed in the Teatro Colon in Buenos Aires. In 1924, she went on a long tour abroad and did not return to Russia. The elegant, slim beauty of the pale-faced ballerina "with the features of a romantic peri," and the suffering glance of her black eyes imparted a unique character to her performance. Spessivtseva's dance was marked by graphic accuracy

and the perfection of her subtle lines. As a contemporary noted, "her elevation was almost unbelievable." The theme of frustration and the inevitable ruin of beauty permeated her art. Almost all of her characters were enigmatic and unreal. They were doomed, and anxiety prevailed in their souls regardless of whether this accorded with the nature of the role. Spessivtseva's tragic gift found its utmost expression in *Giselle*; her performance was built on contrasts and dissonances, which were in accord with the epoch in which she performed. The ballerina's expressionism manifested itself in her interpretation of this role and exerted an immense influence on later performances of *Giselle*. Between 1924 and 1932, Spessivtseva starred at the Paris Opera, and she was deemed the greatest ballerina of the twentieth century. She danced in *Giselle* and the ballets of Leo Staats (*Soir de Fête* and *La Péri*) and Serge Lifar (*Creatures of Prometheus* and *Bacchus and Ariadne*). As a guest ballerina in Diaghilev's Ballets Russes, she performed the leading parts in the productions of Michel Fokine. But modern choreography was alien to her. She danced only once in the ballet *La Chatte*, staged for her by George Balanchine (1927, Diaghilev's Ballets Russes). According to her, she stayed a week at home to avoid this engagement, pretending to have sprained her ankle during rehearsal. On the other hand, Spessivtseva imparted the acuteness of the modern outlook to classical "white ballet." From 1932 to 1937, Spessivtseva toured with a number of companies, including those of Fokine (Buenos Aires) and Victor Dandré (formerly Anna Pavlova's company). She also danced in Australia. In her everyday life, she felt defenseless and strove to be with strong people in whom she hoped to find support. In 1937, Spessivtseva left the stage as the result of a nervous breakdown. For a time, she taught classical dance. In 1939, she moved to the United States, where she spent twenty years (1943-63) in a mental hospital. After her recovery, Spessivtseva lived in a Russian community organized by Countess A. Tolstoy near New York.

**VILZAK,**
Anatole Josifovich
(born September 10, 1896, in Vilno).
*Dancer and teacher.*
Vilzak was born into a circus family: his brother, Nikolai Vilzak, is known in Russia as the clown Bim-Bom. In his childhood, Anatole Vilzak performed as a dancer and a juggler. He studied at the St. Petersburg Theater School under Leonid Leontiev and Michel Fokine and entered the company of the Mariinsky Theater upon graduating in 1915. In the post-revolutionary years, when few male dancers remained in the Petrograd company, Vilzak, who had mastered "many of the most responsible roles," shouldered almost the entire repertoire. Vilzak was an excellent partner, and his noble bearing, elegance and his softness of movement enabled him to successfully perform the parts of princes. He often danced in Fokine's productions. In 1921, Vilzak went abroad with his wife, the ballerina Ludmila Schollar. From 1921 to 1925, he worked in Diaghilev's Ballets Russes. At the end of the 1920s and in the first half of the 1930s, Vilzak danced noble danseur roles in the companies of Ida Rubinstein and Bronislava Nijinska and performed in the Riga Theater, the Ballet Russe de Monte Carlo, and other companies He starred in productions of *Les Biches* (*The House Party*, 1924) and *Boléro* (1928) by Nijinska. He also danced in Fokine's *Don Juan* and Kurt Jooss's *Perséphone*. He began to work as a teacher in Riga in 1932. At the end of the 1930s, Vilzak and Schollar settled in the United States, where they taught at the American Ballet School (1937). Later, they ran their own school in New York (1940-46). Still later, they worked in the Ballet Russe de Monte Carlo School in Washington, D.C, and from 1965, at the San Francisco Ballet School. Alicia Alonso, Svetlana Beriosova, and Nora Kaye were among their students.

91. Anatole Vilzak and Ludmila Schollar dancing at the Mariinsky Theater.

THE 1920s

previous pages 92. Sketches of Mikhail Kurilko's scenery for *The Red Poppy*.

Many artists welcomed the fall of the Russian autocracy in February 1917; however, the October Socialist Revolution plunged them into confusion. Performances on the former imperial stages came to a halt. In the Mariinsky and Bolshoi Theaters, most of the company members refused to cooperate with the Bolsheviks. However, it soon became evident that any attempts to act

economic collapse, and general chaos. The actors were undernourished and often fell ill; there were shortages of fuel in the winter, and spectators sat in fur overcoats and felt boots while dancers in transparent tunics became numb from the cold. Theaters were repeatedly threatened with complete closure. One by one, the leading ballet figures and talented young dancers emigrated. The Mariinsky Theater opened the season of

93. Lopukhov's *Nutcracker* was staged at a time when the government was fighting against "religious prejudices." The Christmas tree, which serves as the pivot of Hoffmann's tale and Petipa's ballet, was thrown off the stage as a vestige of the past that was "intolerable both in everyday life and art" (the idea of the New Year's tree had not yet occured to the leaders of the Soviet state). Stage designer Vladimir Dmitriev (1900-48) developed the principle of movable colored planes that easily transformed the stage to form walls, partitions in toy boxes, etc. These sets imbued the performance with elegance and festivity.

Here is a sketch of Vladimir Dmitriev's scenery for *The Nutcracker*.

independently were doomed to failure. Initially, the government was cautious in establishing contacts with theaters, and it was only in the late 1920s that ideological pressure, which had been gradually increasing, ended in open dictate. Performances were resumed in Moscow as early as November 1917 and in St. Petersburg, in January 1918. Ballet companies continued to work even though it was nearly impossible to maintain a high artistic level in the face of the Civil War,

1918-19 without Michel Fokine, who had been intended for the post of company director. Boris Romanov left Russia in 1920 together with his wife, ballerina Yelena Smirnova. Mathilda Kchessinska, Olga Preobrajenska, Tamara Karsavina, Olga Spessivtseva, Nikolai Legat, Anatole Vilzak, Georgy Balanchivadze (George Balanchine), and Alexandra Danilova were also among those who emigrated. The Bolshoi Theater lost Mikhail Mordkin, Sophia Fedorova, and Vera Karalli. In the first year after the

Revolution, ballet was usually labeled a "bourgeois heritage" and was attacked for obscurity, archaic symbolism, and affectedness. The survival of the Russian school of ballet and the preservation of its academic tradition became a critical issue. The choreographers of state-owned (formerly Imperial) theaters affirmed the eternal value of the ballet classics, but they had to confront the fact that their theaters were now filled with a new audience of workers, soldiers, and sailors. Proponents of a new repertoire believed, on one hand, that it was their duty to familiarize the general public with the best examples of the "grand ballet" of the nineteenth century. On the other hand, they understood that their new audience was unprepared to appreciate the

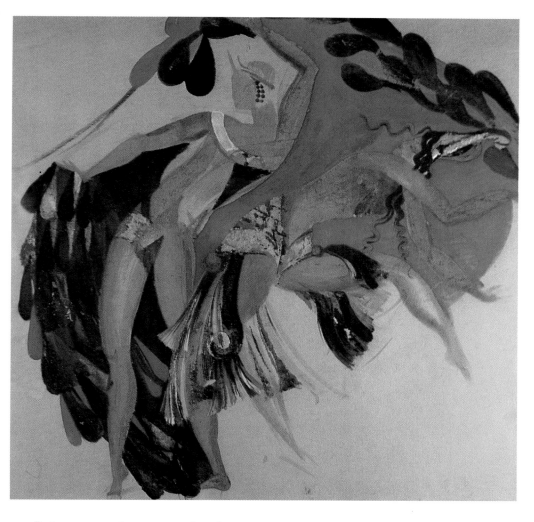

symbolic language of choreographic art and strove to make their performances more dynamic and exciting by bringing the main conflicts to the foreground. The repertoire was reviewed, and ballets were updated. In spite of the protests of academically minded dancers (grouped around Vasily Tikhomirov and including Yekaterina Geltzer, the leading ballerina of the company), Alexander Gorsky at the Bolshoi Theater modernized the classics, assigning the main parts to

young performers such as Yelena Ilyushchenko, Maria Reizen, and Anastasia Abramova. In his work on *The Nutcracker* in 1919, *Swan Lake* in 1920 (together with art director Vladimir Nemirovich-Danchenko, a founder of the Moscow Art Theater), and *Giselle* in 1922, Gorsky rejected virtuoso dance elements that were not sufficiently justified by the logic of stage events and combined classical dance with elements of free plastic and pantomime. Petrograd ballet master Fedor Lopukhov, who became the director of the ballet company of the former Mariinsky Theater in the early 1920s, was more careful about the classics. He studied the choreography of his predecessors and restored the masterpieces of Marius Petipa and Lev Ivanov (including *The Sleeping Beauty* in 1922 and *The Nutcracker* in 1923), rejecting all irrelevant accretions, restoring deletions that had been made earlier, and

94. Studio members tried to find a new correlation between dance and music. They learned to listen to musical rhythms with their whole body and they required "musical vision" from the stage designers who worked with them.

A sketch for the ballet *Bacchanale* executed for the studio of Viktorina Krieger. Stage designer Fedor Fedorovskis strove to find the color equivalents of the sounds in the music.

maintaining the integrity and the emotional power of the action. In addition to the nineteenth-century classics, the repertoire of academic theater during the 1910s and 1920s consisted of Gorsky's original productions, as well as of stagings by Fokine and his followers that reflected the aesthetic standards of the early twentieth century. However, as the position of theater became more stable and the problems of everyday life were gradually overcome, theaters began to demand more insistently that ballet be "revolutionized" and that artistic forms be found that would conform to the spirit of the language of symbols and allegories, the producers of mass shows and pageants depicted the proletarian revolution on a cosmic scale, as the culmination of world history. The first attempts to apply propaganda theater techniques to ballet were rather naive. The 1920s saw a number of ballet scenarii that were never actually produced and that followed the pattern of the symbolic and romantic plays staged in workers' clubs. These techniques were also applied occasionally to the classics: in 1924, it was proposed in Petrograd to remake *The Sleeping Beauty* into a ballet called *The*

95. In the staging of *Swan Lake* by Gorsky and Nemirovich-Danchenko, episodes featuring the corps de ballet were worked into the ballet in the manner of mass scenes in a dramatic production. The peasant scene in the first act therefore lost its character as a divertissement.

times. It became clear that the stylistic renewal of ballet was both necessary and inevitable. Leftist trends had already dominated in painting, music, and poetry for several years: the passion of the destroyers of the old world echoed that of the Futurists, who dreamed of an art of the future based on the ruins of bourgeois civilization. Spectacles were characterized by poster-like garishness and brightness, generalized forms, and bold spatial arrangements. Using a conventional

*Sun Commune.* The libretto would have contained three scenes of popular exultation, and in the place of Prince Désiré , the Leader of the Workers would use a torch to blow up a red coffin, in which the chained Aurora (i.e. "the Red Dawn of World Revolution") was sleeping. In his choreographic performance for children, *Ever Fresh Flowers* (1922), Gorsky attempted to combine the forms of fairy-tale ballet with those of revolutionary pageants. Initially a fairy-tale similar to

Maurice Maeterlink's *Blue Bird*, the ballet culminated in an apotheosis in which emblems of the Revolution, such as the rising sun or the hammer and sickle, were shown, and the "Internationale" was played. Later, the techniques of poster- and rally-styled theater were reflected in *Red Whirlwind* by Lopukhov (1924), *The Whirlwind* by Kasyan Goleizovsky (1927), and other ballets. However, these choreographers had already developed new devices and were moving away from Gorsky, who hesitated in his choreographic constructions between impressionism and a

studios increased dramatically in the 1920s. Moscow had become the most important center of the studio movement. Duncan herself, who came to Soviet Russia upon the invitation of the Soviet Government, opened a school in Moscow in 1921. Duncan's idea that dance is a means of creating a free, harmoniously developed, and creative personality were in the spirit of the utopian thinking of the period. In concerts with her students, Duncan interpreted the "Marche Slave" and "Symphonie Pathétique" by Tchaikovsky and danced to the music of "Marseillaise" and the "Internationale." Her

96. *The Red Whirlwind*, a ballet in which the whirlwind of the revolution wipes out everything obsolete, was, according to one critic, "the embodiment of political ideas in dance forms." The program included such episodes as "the gathering of the elements of a socialist world outlook untainted by nationalism" and a "a classical choreographic adagio that characterized socialism." Allegoric scenes in which "the forces of revolution" and "forces of counterrevolution" danced in uniforms were interspersed with more specific scenes depicting the class struggle in cities and villages.

purely classical style. Changes in the language of dance had to precede the creation of an integrated performance conforming to the spirit of the times. "Laboratory" searches for new dance forms in the 1920s were conducted in a number of schools, studios, and plastic and rhythmo-plastic workshops, many of which had appeared as far back as the 1910s in the wake of enthusiasm for Isadora Duncan's performances in Moscow and St. Petersburg. The number of these

compositions, however, contain few unexpected discoveries. Nonetheless, her followers gradually made her "natural" dance more sophisticated. Propagating the ideas of Duncan, Emile Jacques-Dalcroze and François Delsarte, leaders of the Moscow and Petrograd studios, simultaneously developed a new choreographic vocabulary, trying to combine free plastics with classical and folk dance, as well as with elements of variety and circus shows. If futuristic expressiveness in

97. Studio directors developed original systems of training dancers. Studying anatomy and the mechanics of human body movements, Vera Maya invented special exercises for muscles that were normally poorly developed and demanded a mastery of acrobatics from her students.

Here, Vera Maya's student Olga Semenyak performs the composition *Skriabin, Prelude No. 20*. A sketch by the artist Dani.

general proved to be alien to the Russian ballet, the urbanistic aesthetics of constructivism and the "industrial utopia" style, with its tendency toward laconism, geometrical strictness, and the functional justification of forms, influenced it greatly. The rapid acceptance of athletic dance and acrobatics was connected with the new aesthetic ideals: in the 1920s, choreographers were attracted by the power and agility of a well-trained body, rather than by the natural grace of a liberated human form. Constructivism and urbanism were uniquely represented in ballet in the form of "machine dances," which were first presented in variety shows in 1922 by Valentin Parnakh and, in 1923, by Nikolai Foregger. These dances reproduced the movements of various parts of machine tools; the human being was likened to a smoothly operating mechanism and was incorporated into a production process. Later, Lopukhov introduced machine dances to ballet, and in 1931, he based an episode of

his ballet *The Bolt* on them. Moving ever further from Duncanesque lyrical improvisations, studio choreographers tried to absorb the rhythm of the new epoch and to saturate ballet with new content. Sometimes, expressionist motifs were evident in performances. Productions by Inna Chernetskaya (which were often tragic and philosophical); tart, voluptuous, and somewhat erotic compositions by Lew Lukin (Saks); as well as stylized national dances, propaganda études and genre scenes by Vera Maya broadened the contemporary understanding of the possibilities of choreography. The founders of the Drama-Ballet studio regarded dance as just one means of revealing a dramatic theme and attributed primary importance to psychologically specific pantomime, which was developed by a director anticipating the flourishing of dramatic ballet in the 1930s and 1940s. Goleizovsky's studio experiments were especially important for the further

98. Costumes in Goleizovsky's ballets also "came to life" only during the dance. Narrow bands and strips of cloth were applied to the body, leaving it nearly naked, and short panties and skirts together with long scarfs accompanied the dancer's movements and emphasized the unique choreographic pattern. In *Joseph The Beautiful*, the costume was reduced to a fillet or an Egyptian pinafore. In imitation of Egyptian paintings, makeup was applied not only to faces: men's bodies were painted brown, while women's bodies (except that of Queen Tayakh) were orange.

Nikolai Erdman's sketch of a costume for the ballet *Joseph the Beautiful.*

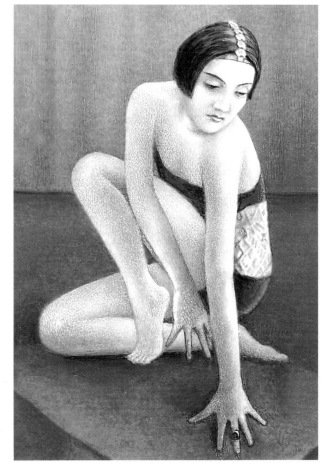

99. Lyubov Bank, who danced the part of Queen Tayakh in the ballet, was distinctly different from the crowd that surrounded her. Her body, which was densely powdered and nearly naked, was blindingly white. The choreography of the part was based on capers and deep bends, expressing the Queen's voluptuous, imperious, and cruel nature.

development of Russian ballet. The choreographer strove for the revolutionary transformation of ballet and venomously criticized the academic repertoire which, from his point of view, was hopelessly obsolete. Recognizing classical dance as the basis of choreographic art, he interpreted its movements in his own way, putting them together in unprecedented sequences and combining them with other means of bodily expression. A new type of impressionist dance and short ballet emerged from

choreographer to reach the stage of the Bolshoi Theater in the 1920s. The ballets that he created in this theater in cooperation with young dancers such as Lubov Bank, Nina Podgoretskaya, and Vasily Yefimov (particularly *Joseph the Beautiful* in 1925) marked the culmination of his studio experiments and elevated them to a new level. Influenced by Goleizovsky's activities, Georgy Balanchivadze (Balanchine), who had been a beginning dancer at the former Mariinsky Theater in the early 1920s,

100. Dance incorporated the entire stage space in mass scenes: performers moved up and down landings located at different heights. In the "bucolic" round dance in the first act, the dancers streamed from landing to landing: some crept on the floor, while others stretched high or were tangled in garlands. Here is a scene from the first act of the ballet *Joseph the Beautiful*

Goleizovsky's Moscow Chamber Theater, including such works as *Harlequinade*, *Visions Fugitives*, *Faun*, and *Salomé*. The images in these productions were determined by Goleizovsky's emotional and poetic perception of the world. In his dynamic compositions, human bodies were interlaced into a complex pattern; the dance was either based on a series of extravagant, winding, and tense poses, or it consisted of the interplay of wavelike movements. Goleizovsky was the only innovative

decided to devote himself to choreography. The tour of the Moscow Chamber Theater to Petrograd in 1922 was a seminal experience for him. Having headed a group of Mariinsky dancers who had recently graduated from the Petrograd Ballet School, including Alexandra Danilova, Lidia Ivanova, Olga Mungalova, Piotr Gusev, Nikolai Yefimov, Leonid Lavrovsky, and Tamara Gevergeyeva, Balanchivadze organized an association called the Young Ballet. Concerts of the Young Ballet were arranged in and around

Petrograd and, occasionally, in Moscow. Their programs included pas de deux from Petipa's ballets, Fokine's productions, and Balanchivadze's own compositions and were badly received by his venerable colleagues. The Young Ballet was a remarkable phenomenon in the artistic life of Petrograd at least until Ivanova's tragic death and the emigration of Balanchivadze, Gevergeyeva, Danilova, and Yefimov in 1924. There were fewer studios and dance schools in Petrograd than in Moscow. The principal experimental

*of the Universe*, based on music of Beethoven's Fourth Symphony (1923). The philosophical content of this ballet, which praised the universe as beautiful in its eternal movement, was expressed by means of pure dance. Subsequently, the idea of symphonic ballet was successfully developed by other choreographers, mainly abroad. However, Lopukhov's contemporaries did not accept his work, and he was forced to modify his ideas. For several years, he developed the idea of a synthetic performance, in which

101. Here is a scene from the first act of the ballet *Joseph the Beautiful*. Having rejected illusory scenery, Goleizovsky used neutral structures that "came to life" only in interaction with dancers. This sketch by designer Alexandra Ekster shows the possibilities for structuring vertical groupings offered by the landings and stairs of a functional stage installation.

A sketch of scenery by Alexandra Exter for a production by Kasyan Goleizovsky based on music by Alexander Skriabin.

site remained the academic stage, and the period of experimenting began approximately in 1921 with Lopukhov's first independent activities. Lopukhov produced a variety of different ballets, in which classical traditions and the innovations of drama theater and the stage were combined. His bold experiments were misunderstood, but many subsequent trends are reflected in them. A special place in the history of ballet is occupied by the first dance symphony staged by Lopukhov in Russia, *The Greatness*

dance was combined with singing, verbal text, buffoonery, circus tricks, etc. Stravinsky's *Le Renard* (1927) was interpreted by Lopukhov as "a buffoon performance." In *Pulcinella* (1926), forms of the Italian commedia dell' arte were used. Many approaches reflected in the new staging of *The Nutcracker* in 1929 dated to the works of avant-garde stage directors such as Vsevolod Meyerhold and Sergei Eisenstein. The principles of the "grand ballet" of the nineteenth century were

102. The idea of Nordic ballet, based on the music of Grieg and Norwegian fairy tales, appeared as far back as 1917 and belonged, according to the composer and music critic Boris Asafyev, to the painter Alexander Golovin, who took Scandinavian themes close to heart. The staging was originally to be done by Boris Romanov; after his emigration the work was entrusted to Paul Petrov. His ballet *Solveig* was a failure, however, and was quickly removed from the stage. Lopukhov returned to the original concept and once again used the magnificent scenery and costumes designed and made by Golovin in 1920.

Here is a sketch of Alexander Golovin's scenery for the ballet *The Ice Maiden (Solveig).*

103. In *The Red Poppy*
which was designed
and had a libretto by
Mikhail Kurilko
(1880-1969),
revolutionary ideas
were represented in a
very exotic setting,
which irritated many
critics of the 1920s.
Choreographers were
warned against
turning the Red
Army soldier into "a
statue made of
whipped cream."
However, a
melodramatic subject
and a variety of
spectacular effects
ensured the success of
*The Red Poppy*.
Spectators were
delighted to watch
Chinese coolies and
Soviet sailors unload
a huge ship and to
watch guests at the
Chinese banker's
fancy ball dance,
fashionable foxtrots
and the Boston
waltz...

Sketches of Mikhail
Kurilko's scenery for
*The Red Poppy*.

further developed in *The Ice Maiden*. Lopukhov imbued classical dance with modern dynamic traits, making it more complex and "acrobatized." His leading dancers, including Olga Mungalova, Piotr Gusev, and Boris Shavrov, were renowned as athletic dance performers. The choreographer experimented with different ways of developing the plot through dance. He was the first to produce dramatic ballet which was to dominate the ballet stage in the 1930s and 1940s. However, in the late 1920s, Lopukhov (like all other experimenters) was repeatedly reproached for formalism. The theater was dominated by adherents of dance drama who felt that pantomime should be the main technique for relating content in ballet. On the other hand, they felt that classical, or acrobatic, dance was "void of meaning." The ballets of the late 1920s that developed satirical topics

and characters (such as *The Golden Age* by Vasily Vainonen, Vladimir Chesnakov, and Leonid Jakobson (1939), *The Footballer* by Lev Lashchilin and Victor Oransky (1930), and *The Bolt* by Fedor Lopukhov) marked the end of a historical period in the development of Russian ballet. Instead of the innovative productions of Goleizovsky and Lopukhov, the choreographers of the 1930s and 1940s took their cue from *The Red Poppy*, which was staged in 1927 at the Bolshoi Theater by the academist Tikhomirov. In this production, the forms of the "grand ballet" of the nineteenth century were combined with revolutionary content: Soviet sailors danced "Yablochko" alongside Zephyr variations, and characters expressed their feelings in pantomime. However, choreographers returned to the innovations of the 1920s several decades later in the 1960s.

104

104. Lidia Ivanova (1903-24), a young graduate from the Petrograd Ballet School and soloist with the former Mariinsky Theater and the Young Ballet, was a favorite with the Petrograd public. Impressing critics with "the beauty of the free flight and the impetuous span of her movements", she charmed even the most unsophisticated spectators with her childlike spontaneity and love of life. She was planning to emigrate in July, 1924, together with Balanchine and his companions, but she died mysteriously in June, drowning during an outing on the Gulf of Finland.

Portrait of Lidia Ivanova by Zinaida Serebryakova.

# Great figures of Russian ballet

## GELTZER,
Yekaterina Vasilyevna
(born November 14, 1876,
Moscow; died there December 12,
1962).
*Ballerina.*
Geltzer's father was Vasily Geltzer
(1841-1909), an outstanding
character dancer and pantomime actor
of the Moscow Bolshoi Theater, and
her uncle was Anatoly Geltzer, a
famous stage designer. She studied
under Ivan Nikitin and José Mendès
at the Moscow Theater School.
After graduating in 1894, she joined
the Bolshoi Theater as a coryphée and
was soon promoted to the rank of
second dancer. Upon her own request,
she was transferred to St. Petersburg
and worked in the Mariinsky Theater
for two seasons, taking advanced
studies from Marius Petipa and
Christian Johanson. Soon after
returning to Moscow in 1898, Geltzer
became the prima ballerina. She
toured a number of Russian cities and
foreign countries. In 1910, she visited
Brussels, Berlin, and Paris where
she participated in Diaghilev's
Russian Seasons. In 1911, she visited
London with a group of Bolshoi
dancers and the United States with
Mikhail Mordkin. Having mastered

virtuoso dance technique, Geltzer
impressed the audience with her
particular elegance in performing
such parts, as Aurora in *The Sleeping
Beauty*, Kitri in *Don Quixote*, and
others. Geltzer's dance was brilliant
and energetic; her movements, which
were sometimes frenzied and dashing
and sometimes grand and flowing,
manifested a genuinely Russian
nature. It was quite natural that
the Russian dance from *The Little
Humphacked Horse* was to become one
of her most popular concert
performances. In her aesthetic
inclinations, Geltzer was an
academist, unconditionally devoted
to Petipa's authority. This served as
the basis for her artistic partnership
with the dancer Vasily Tikhomirov,
also a dedicated adherent of the
academic school, and brought
about inevitable conflicts with
Alexander Gorsky, an innovative
choreographer. Nevertheless, it was
in Gorsky's dramatic ballets that
Geltzer's talent was most clearly
manifested. The part of Salammbô
in the ballet of the same name staged
by Gorsky in 1910 after the novel by
Flaubert was of particular importance
for Geltzer. Her finest roles include
Medora in Gorsky's version of
*Le Corsaire* and Undine in
*Schubertiana*. Geltzer often treated her
characters in the style of Romantic
drama or high melodrama; she was
prone to heroic and pathetic
interpretations. While her
performance was true to life, she
reached, according to her
contemporaries, "hyperbolic plastic
expressiveness."
Unexpected dimensions of Geltzer's
talent were revealed in her demi-
caractère role in *Love is Swift!*, "a
choreographic scene from Norway's
folk culture." After the revolution,
Geltzer continued to dance. Geltzer's
last two important roles were in
ballets staged by her husband Tikho-

mirov: the title role of *Esmeralda* in
1926 and Tao Hoa in *The Red Poppy*
in 1927. Having retired from the
Bolshoi Theater, she toured the Soviet
Union from 1935 until the early
1940s.

## GOLEIZOVSKY,
Kasyan Yaroslavich
(born March 5, 1892, in Moscow;
died there May 4, 1970).
*Dancer and choreographer.*
Goleizovsky's mother was a Bolshoi
Theater dancer, and his father was an

opera singer. He began to study at
the Moscow Theater School and then
continued at the St. Petersburg
Theater School, where he was tutored
by Mikhail Obukhov and Samuil
Andrianov. After graduating,
Goleizovsky joined the Mariinsky
Theater, but he soon moved to the
Bolshoi. Goleizovsky danced the parts
of Kamon in *Salammbô*, Blue Bird
in *The Sleeping Beauty*, Alain in
*La Fille Mal Gardée*, etc. From the
beginning of his artistic career,
Goleizovsky participated in the
innovative experiments of Michel
Fokine and Alexander Gorsky and
was interested in choreography. His
first productions were at so-called
"miniature theaters." He left the

105. A sketch of
Harlequin's costume
for the ballet *A
Tragedy of Masks*.
Designer: Kasyan
Goleizovsky.

106. Yekaterina
Geltzer in the
Russian dance from
*The Little Humphacked
Horse*.

107. A scene from *Leili and Medjnun.* The last great ballet presented by Goleizovsky.

Bolshoi Theater in 1918 and established the Children's Ballet Studio, where he staged a number of ballets including *Max and Moritz* (based on a popular book by Wilhelm Busch, a German poet and painter), *Snow White*, and others. He headed the studio from 1919 to 1925 (it was renamed the Moscow Chamber Ballet in 1922), and there he staged most of his innovative productions including *Harlequinade, Salomé, Faun*, and *The Tragedy of Masks*. Goleizovsky's taste for romantic characters, who were deprived of any descriptive and illustrative nature, was reflected in his compositions based on the music of Claude Debussy, Alexander Skriabin, Franz Liszt, and Frédéric Chopin. He strove to reveal the most subtle nuances of an emotional condition by means of dance rather than develop content or character. Protesting against the dogmatic interpretation of the classical dance system as something unchangeable and against the clichés of ballet, Goleizovsky began to renovate ballet's means of expression. His choreography was characterized by a rich musicality and imagination. However, his innovations, unlike most of the choreographic experiments of

107

the 1920s, were based on a thorough understanding of classical choreography. Many of the supports, poses, and dance techniques that Goleizovsky invented have since been further developed. Many choreographers, including George Balanchine, were influenced by him. Goleizovskywasthefirst choreographer to use constructivist sets that enabled him to present human figures on different stage levels and in various, sometimes unexpected, aspects. He also reformed stage costumes: the ones he introduced were as revealing as possible, had no specific link with a particular style or period, and were primarily intended to demonstrate the expressiveness of a dancing body. In the 1920s, Goleizovsky created a wide range of ballets and dances, including some for dramatic productions. After collaborating with the famous stage director Vsevolod Meyerhold, Goleizovsky began to use grotesque forms in allegorical, but contemporary ballets such as *The City* and *The Whirlwind*, as well as in concert programs such as *Excentric Dances*. His most important production during this period was *Joseph the Beautiful*, based on a biblical story. This ballet was staged at the Experimental Theater, an affiliate of the Bolshoi, and the choreographer developed the theme of Eternal Beauty which is untouched by violence. Goleizovsky's innovations

provoked opposition on the part of the management of the Bolshoi Theater and strictly academic dancers. As a result, he had to leave the theater. Nonetheless, young dancers remained interested in Goleizovsky's experiments, and he was able to work fruitfully with them in concerts. However, having been deprived of his own company and of any opportunity to stage ballets at the Bolshoi Theater, Goleizovsky had to cooperate with the music hall, demonstrating his inventiveness by developing new movements in evolutions for forty precision dancers and other genres. He also staged sports parades in Red Square and worked on films. In the mid-1930s, Goleizovsky began to work at theaters in various republics of the Soviet Union. His productions included his own versions of *The Sleeping Beauty* in Kharkov, Ukraine; *The Fountain of Bakhchisarai* in Minsk, Byelorussia; and *Du Gul* (*Two Roses*) in Dushanbe, Tadjikistan. He staged *Charda* (*Dances of Danube Peoples*), *Dyonisus* (*Ancient Greek Dances*), *Chopin* in 1933, and *Polovtsian Dances* in 1944 at the Bolshoi Theater. He also collaborated with the Leningrad and Moscow Ballet Schools. In 1960-61, he choreographed concert programs after music by Skriabin and Liszt and in 1964, he staged *Leili and Medjnun*, his last big ballet, at the Bolshoi Theater. In 1968, he produced the choreographic suite *Visions Fugitives*

at the Moscow Young Ballet. Throughout his life, Goleizovsky wrote extensively: he was the author of a number of controversial articles on ballet and a book entitled *The Images of Russian Dance Folklore*.

## GUSEV,
Piotr Andreevich
(born December 23, 1904, in St. Petersburg; died March 31, 1987, in Leningrad).
*Dancer, teacher, and ballet master.*
A student of Vladimir Ponomarev and Alexander Shiryaev at the Petrograd Theater School, Gusev joined the Petrograd Opera and Ballet Theater upon graduation in 1922. He helped establish the Young Ballet and danced with Olga Mungalova in dances staged by Georgy Balanchivadze. He was one of the participants in Fedor Lopukhov's dance symphony *The Greatness of the Universe* (1923). Becoming Lopukhov's faithful adherent, Gusev created the roles of Asak in *The Ice Maiden* (1927) and the title role of *The Nutcracker* (1929), both of which were specially choreographed for him by Lopukhov. His dance greatly influenced the technique of men's performance generally. Gusev was able to master the acrobatic technique and complex combinations that Lopukhov composed. An outstanding performer of duet dances (according to Lopukhov, he was "the king of support"), Gusev performed adages with Mungalova in variety shows during the 1920s, affirming boldness, dynamics, and energy as traits of contemporary art. From 1932 to 1935, Gusev participated in Lopukhov's productions at the Leningrad Maly Theater, where he danced the part of Piotr in *The Bright Stream*. When it was decided to transfer *The Bright Stream* to the Moscow stage in 1935, Gusev was invited to perform this role at the Bolshoi Theater, where he decided to stay permanently. He gradually took up pantomime roles, and the role of Girey in *The Fountain of Bakhchisarai* was regarded as one of his most successful achievements. During the Second World War, Gusev performed in

108. Olga Mungalova and Piotr Gusev in the ballet *The Ice Maiden*.

many concerts with Olga Lepeshinskaya. In 1945, he retired from the stage. In the late 1940s, Gusev began to work as a choreographer. One of his most important works was *Seven Beauties* (Baku, 1952), a ballet after a narrative poem by Nizami Gyanjevi, a major Azeri writer. This ballet was later transferred to the Leningrad Maly Theater, to Kiev, and to Novosibirsk. In his productions of classic ballets, Gusev strove to restore them accurately, but he did not always succeed. He was the art director of the Kirov Ballet from 1945 to 1950, the Bolshoi Theater from 1950 to 1956, and the

Leningrad Maly Theater from 1960 to 1962. Between 1962 and 1966, he headed the ballet company of the Novosibirsk Theater. Oleg Vinogradov and Nikita Dolgushin began their artistic careers there during those years. Gusev established the company of the Chamber Ballet in Leningrad in the late 1960s. From 1922 on, Gusev was involved in teaching at various educational institutions and theaters in Leningrad and Moscow. From 1935 to 1941, he was the art director of the Moscow Ballet School. In 1962, he organized (together with Lopukhov) the training of choreographers at the Leningrad Conservatory, where he taught until 1983. Between 1958 and 1960, he taught choreography courses in China and helped establish the Ballet Theater in Beijing, as well as ballet schools in Shanghai and Canton.

## LUKOM,
Yelena Mikhailovna
(born May 5, 1891,
in St. Petersburg; died February 27, 1968, in Leningrad).
*Ballerina and teacher.*
Lukom was a student of Michel Fokine at the St. Petersburg Theater School. After graduating in 1909, she was enrolled in the corps de ballet of the Mariinsky Theater. As a corps de ballet dancer, she participated in Diaghilev's "Russian Seasons" in 1910. She began by dancing solo lyrical and comic parties such as the Little White Cat in *The Sleeping Beauty* and began to dance starring roles only in the late 1910s. Lukom reached her artistic prime in the 1920s. She was especially attracted to lyrical and poetic parts in classical ballets and Fokine's productions. Lukom's dance could be taken for an improvisation: each movement was psychologically justified and emotionally tinted. Pretty, delicate, and "light as a feather," the ballerina created fascinating and touching characters. Her Giselle and Esmeralda were trusting, impressionable, mischievous, coquettish, and capricious; they enjoyed life sincerely and ingenuously. Boris Shavrov was Lukom's permanent partner both on the theater stage and in variety shows. He and Lukom experimented together, creating new technical devices in classical duet dance and interlacing it with elements of acrobatics. She toured widely, including a tour of western Europe in 1922-23. Lukom's last major success was as Tao Hoa in *The Red Poppy* in 1929. Her repertoire began to shrink during the 1930s. Lukom turned to teaching and became increasingly involved in it. In 1941, the ballerina retired from the stage. She was a teacher and coach at the Kirov Theater and conducted advanced study classes there from 1953 to 1965.

## LOPUKHOV,
Fedor Vasilyevich
(born October 20, 1886,
in St. Petersburg; died January 28, 1973, in Leningrad).
*Dancer, choreographer, and teacher.*

Born to the family of an usher of the Alexandrinsky (Drama) Theater, Lopukhov graduated from the St. Petersburg Theater School, where he had been a student of Nikolai Legat. He was an actor at the Mariinsky Theater from 1905 to 1909; then, he worked at the Bolshoi Theater in 1909-10, where he became acquainted with Alexander Gorsky's reforms. In 1910-11, Lopukhov toured Europe and the United States. From 1911 to 1922, he again worked at the Mariinsky Theater, where he performed minor character parts. He was attracted by choreography at an early stage: in 1906, he began producing dances for himself and, later, for his sister, Yevgenia Lopukhova. In 1918, he created his first ballets, *The Dream* and *The Mexican Tavern*. Between 1922 and 1930, in 1944-45, and from 1951 to 1956, Lopukhov was the art director of the Leningrad Kirov Theater ballet company. Lopukhov was among the first to renovate and restore classical ballets such as *The Sleeping Beauty*, *Raymonda*, *Swan Lake*, *Don Quixote*, and *The Little Humpbacked Horse*; thus, he helped preserve ballets created by great choreographers for future generations. Lopukhov was able to combine, develop, and enrich the traditions of both Petipa and Fokine in his unique creative work. While his love of classical dance and traditional dance structures was rooted in Petipa's concepts, Lopukhov's interest in ballets that used dance to advance the plot and in the development of new expressive means reflected Fokine's influence. Lopukhov enriched classical dance by means of acrobatic elements. He proclaimed the idea of ballet as an independent art that can do without the support of other theatrical components, such as plot, scenery, etc. This idea was embodied in *The Greatness of the Universe*, a ballet based on Beethoven's Fourth Symphony that Lopukhov described as a "dance symphony." This production laid the foundation of the genre of the ballet symphony, and this genre later became popular throughout the world. In addition, keeping up with the times, Lopukhov

109. Yelena Lukom as the Girl and Anatole Vilzak as Eros in *Eros* by Ye. Chentsov.

110. A scene from *Coppélia* by Lopukhov.

developed a special form of dance performance that incorporated singing, speaking, clowning, circus tricks, puppet theater, etc. Using this technique, he staged *Coppélia*, *Harlequinade*, *The Nutcracker* and *Pulcinella*. The history of the Soviet drama-ballet begins with his *Serf Ballerina*. Lopukhov addressed various subjects in his creative activities, including some very topical ones, in ballets such as *The Red Whirlwind* (*The Bolsheviks*), *The Bolt*, and *The Bright Stream*. He was always concerned about man's relations with nature, and this interest was reflected in *The Ice Maiden* and *The Spring Fairy Tale* (*The Snow Maiden*). He often used Slavic dance folklore and the old theater of Russian "skomorokhi" (wandering clowns): these elements are particularly evident in *Night on Bald Mountain*, *Christmas Eve*, *Le Renard*, and *Taras Bulba*. Lopukhov was an active figure in the theater. He helped form Byelorussian, Lithuanian, and Uzbek ballets. He organized the Leningrad Maly Opera Theater ballet company in 1931, and he was its art director until 1936. Later, he staged ballets there,

including *Harlequinade*, *Coppélia*, *La Fille Mal Gardée*, and *The Ballad of Love*. He was also an organizer and director of choreography courses at the Leningrad Ballet School from 1937 to 1941; in 1962, he headed the choreography department of the Leningrad Conservatory. Vladimir Varkovitsky, Boris Fenster, Konstantin Boyarsky, Georgy Alexidze, Nikolai Boyarchikov, and German Zamuel were among his students, but Lopukhov's influence on the Russian ballet was undoubtedly even greater because several generations of choreographers have been brought up on his creative work. Lopukhov wrote a number of books and articles on ballet theory, as well as his memoirs. His brother, Andrei Vasilyevich Lopukhov (1898-1947), was an excellent character dancer at the Mariinsky Theater and a creator of the teaching technique of folk character dance. His students included Yuri Grigorovich and Igor Belsky. His sister, Yevgenia Vasilyevna Lopukhova (1884-1943), was a character dancer at the Mariinsky Theater, and a participant in the

Russian Seasons. She was also active in musical comedies and drama theater. His younger sister, Lidia Vasilyevna Lopukhova (Lopokova) (1891-1981), was a classical dancer at the Mariinsky Theater and a participant in the Russian Seasons. She was in Diaghilev's Russian Ballet Company from 1916 to 1924. In 1925, she settled in the United Kingdom, where she performed in British companies and was active as a ballet critic.

## MUNGALOVA,
Olga Petrovna
(born December 11, 1905;
died August 26, 1942, in Perm).
*Ballerina.*
Mungalova was a student of Olga Preobrajenska and Agrippina Vaganova at the Petrograd Theater School and joined the Mariinsky Theater in 1923. She participated in the concerts of the Petrograd Young Ballet, where she performed in dances by Georgy Balanchivadze with her permanent partner Piotr Gusev. She became an ideal embodiment of many of Fedor Lopukhov's ideas. Taking into account Mungalova's unique

talents, Lopukhov created the main part in his *The Ice Maiden* (which turned out to be her greatest success), the role of Masha in *The Nutcracker*, Olga in *The Bolt*, and others. Mungalova's dance was precise and her performance manner was reserved, aloof, and austere. However, her athletic abilities and her virtuosity in swift movements and abrupt changes in rhythm gave her performance a distinctly modern flair. Mungalova liked acrobatics and easily combined elements of classical exercise and gymnastics; some exercises developed by her are still used in present-day training. Mungalova also participated in variety shows, demonstrating agility and incredible bravery in her athletic dances. Mungalova mastered the new repertoire of the 1930s: she danced the part of Maria in *The Fountain of Bakhchisarai*, Jacinta in *Laurencia*, and other parts. In the classical repertoire, Myrthe in *Giselle* was her favorite role; the Queen of Wilis resembled, in her interpretation, the Ice Maiden — cold, mysterious, and impassive. However, the actress was already beyond her artistic prime. She retired from the stage in 1942.

## TIKHOMIROV,

Vasily Dmitrievich
(born March 29, 1876, in Moscow; died there June 30, 1956).
*Dancer, choreographer, and teacher.*
Tikhomirov was a student of Ivan Yermolov at the Moscow Theater School from 1886: in 1891, he was transferred for advanced studies to the St. Petersburg Theater School, where he was tutored by Pavel Gerdt, Platon Karsavin, and Alexander Shiryaev. Having worked several months at the Mariinsky Theater after graduation, Tikhomirov returned to Moscow in 1893 and joined the Bolshoi Theater. Excellent stage qualities, an outstanding musical gift, and technical perfection soon made him a leading dancer of the company. After 1896, he worked as a teacher as well: he taught an advanced studies class at the theater and also at the Moscow Theater School. From 1917 to 1931, Tikhomirov headed the ballet department there.

Tikhomirov's long-term artistic contacts with Yekaterina Geltzer, who studied under him and was his partner in most of his performances, were of particular importance for him. Tikhomirov had a manly and heroic style combined with an academically rigid manner of performance. His noble characters were always knightly, proud and impeccably gallant. A consistent traditionalist who considered virtuoso classical dance to be the main expressive means of ballet and defended the inviolability of the academic canon, Tikhomirov openly opposed Alexander Gorsky's innovations and performed no principal parts in Gorsky's original ballets. Tikhomirov's best roles include Matteo in *L'Ondine, or la Nalade*, Jean de Brienne in *Raymonda*, Conrad in the *Le Corsaire*, Basil in *Don Quixote*, and Solor in *La Bayadère*. In 1903, Tikhomirov was appointed assistant director of the Moscow company. In 1909, he became director, and in 1913, ballet master. After the Revolution, he revived classical ballets at the Bolshoi Theater. Between 1925 and 1930, he headed the theater's ballet company. One of the landmarks of Tikhomirov's work was his production of *Esmeralda* in 1926; he also choreographed *The Red Poppy* in 1927 in cooperation with Lev Lashchilin. Tikhomirov left the stage in 1935. His students included Mikhail Mordkin, Alexander Volinin, Leonid Zhukov, Anastasia Abramova, Yelena Adamovich, Yelena Ilyushchenko, Maria Reisen, Margarita Kandaurova, Nina Podgoretskaya, and Viktorina Krieger.

111. Vasily Tikhomirov in *Dance Dreams*.

# THE DRAMA-BALLET
From the 1930s to the early 1950s

previous pages
112. The duel scene between Tybalt and Mercutio, with the principals surrounded by an exultant carnival crowd, is one of the most brilliant episodes in Leonid Lavrovsky's *Romeo and Juliet*.

113. Vladimir Dmitriev (1900-48) played a major role in the development of the choreographic drama. He wrote libretti and strove to establish new principles in stage design. As a stage designer, he underscored the concreteness of the libretto's situation by creating a concrete place for the action.

Here is a set for *The Flames of Paris*.

By the early 1930s, the principles of socialist realism had been firmly established for all Soviet arts. This concept demanded the "historically concrete depiction of reality in its revolutionary development." It denied the possibility of multiple artistic forms and styles and forced all individual expression into the common mold of the naturalistic depiction of reality. After a period of extensive searching, experimentation, and innovation during the twenties, the ballet theater of the 1930s moved toward the depiction of specific subject matter and toward dance dramatization. Demands for realistic expression, simplicity, and broad accessibility to an audience that was not always aesthetically prepared forced choreographers to use only the most simple forms. This effort eventually resulted in the domination of the so-called drama-ballet. The drama-ballet was a multiact performance that was usually based on a well-known literary work and followed the principles of conventional drama. As a rule, the plot concerned an individual's struggle against a specific social milieu and the relations of individuals to society in general; social and ideological motifs were highlighted in the drama-ballet, as in all Soviet art. A link between the choreographic art of the 1920s and the drama-ballet of the 1930s was formed by a ballet called *The Flames of Paris*, which was based on the trilogy *The Red of the South* (*Le Rouge du Mié jour*) by the French writer Felix Gras. *The Flames of Paris* was based on the events of the French Revolution and became quite popular in Russia. The ballet still retained some of the aesthetic features of the revolutionary pageants of the previous decade, such as the presentation of the tempest of revolution, the absence of individuated characters, and the crowd in the central role. The struggle between antagonistic social forces, i.e. aristocrats and revolutionaries, was unambiguously depicted. The climax of the performance was its third act, containing a

great variety of character dances that ranged from a slow, smooth Auvergne dance to an ecstatic, ardent Basque dance and a grand finale to the music of "Carmagnole." However, this ballet also clearly demonstrated some features of the future of ballet in that its script resembled a historical play with a number of

inserted stories and episodic characters. The performance was developed by the choreographer Vasily Vainonen in cooperation with the dramatic stage director Sergei Radlov. From that time on, this type of cooperation became the normal procedure for the drama-ballet: ballet began to take lessons from drama, and this had both positive and negative consequences. A serious attitude toward a ballet's script (which was normally based on a high-quality literary work), the

114. Nina Anisimova (1909-79) was the first to dance the role of Thérèse, who was a symbol of the feeling of a popular revolt. Anisimova was a character dancer with the Kirov Theater who was known for her fiery temperament. Oil painting by B. Sharapov.

115. The scene from *The Flames of Paris* in which the victory of the revolution is celebrated.

development of the director's concept resulting in the consistent movement of the action, and the requirement that each character's actions be inherently motivated elevated ballet to a higher level. On the other hand, the predominance of dramatized semi-dance and semi-mime performances that totally rejected traditional classical structures and classical ensembles, the undervaluation of musical dramaturgy (since music played only a secondary role in the drama-ballet) undermined ballet's position as a unique, independent form. From the 1930s to the early 1950s, the drama-ballet was the only trend in choreographic theater, and it eventually led to the impoverishment of ballet theater and an artificial uniformity. The repertoire was deprived of many dance genres, such as one-act performances and abstract and symphonic ballets. Dance forms and choreographic language also suffered: classical dance lost its symbolic power, and the search for metaphoric imagery came to an end. Since all experimentation beyond the scope of the drama-ballet was labeled formalism, many

choreographers were forced to abandon their most creative activities. Fedor Lopukhov, Kasyan Goleizovsky, Leonid Jakobson, and many others were deprived of the opportunity to stage ballets in the leading ballet companies, were compelled to leave Moscow and Leningrad, and were limited to the staging of variety shows. All representatives of those non-academic schools that adhered to free, plastic, or rhythmic dance ceased staging performances. The new genre of the drama-ballet demanded new expressive means, and expressive dance (dance subordinated to a dramatic image) was developed. "We view expressive dance primarily as narrative pantomime that, unlike simple dramatic pantomime, is not performed, but danced," wrote Ivan Sollertinsky, one of the most prominent critics of the period. Pure classical dance was used only when it was justified by the plot, for instance, in scenes depicting festivals, balls, or theatrical performances. Drama-ballets combined dance with dramatic acting, and this led to higher standards for dancers and contributed to the appearance of a

116. The first performers of *Romeo and Juliet*, Galina Ulanova and Konstantin Sergeyev, shown in the wedding scene.

Oil painting by A. Sokolov

117

host of dancers who combined lyric abilities and psychological depth with a heroic dance style, expressiveness, and dynamism. The drama-ballet also further developed Gorsky's ideas on the staging of mass scenes. Gorsky's ideas were based on ensemble episodes staged by the Moscow Academic Drama Theater, in which each character in the crowd had a specific task as an actor. These 92 scenes were particularly naturalistic in all regards, including scenery and costumes. In terms of both staging and dramatic performance, the Russian ballet achieved notable success and made a striking impression on spectators. The most important works in this style were *The Fountain of Bakhchisarai* and *Romeo and Juliet*. *The Fountain of Bakhchisarai* (produced by Rostislav Zakharov) was based on a narrative poem by Alexander Pushkin, which itself was based on a legend about a fountain in the Bakhchisarai palace in the Crimea. The main character of the ballet, Maria, the daughter of a Polish prince, was taken captive by Girey, the Crimean khan. She is lanquishing in a world that is alien to her and submerges herself in recollections of her home and of her murdered bridegroom. Girey's passion for Maria arouses jealousy and a desire for revenge in Zarema, the khan's favorite wife. Maria dies at the hand of the desperate Zarema, but her death transforms the savage Girey into a new, nobler man. The choreographic language of the ballet is not particularly rich. However, Galina Ulanova, who danced the part of Maria and whose artistic talent inspired the creation of the role, saturated the dance with inner meaning and made it so expressive that the paucity of the dance language was perceived as an intentional laconism on the part of the choreographer. Ulanova's name is associated with another great success, *Romeo and Juliet*, which was, perhaps, the most important ballet achievement of this period. Its creators, including choreographer Leonid Lavrovsky, stage director Radlov, and composer Sergei Prokofiev, tried to preserve all the complexity, diversity, and richness of Shakespeare's tragedy and all the dimensions of its plot. The ballet consisted of intertwined episodes of bitter duels and grand balls, picturesque folk festivals and mourning processions, solemn funerals and lyrical rendevous. Lavrovsky boldly combined refined lyrical scenes with colorful ensemble dances. He managed to evoke the image of a lively, motley crowd seething through the streets of Verona.

According to a foreign reviewer, it was indeed "a grandiose ballet fresco." The 1930s also saw the widespread introduction of national themes into dance. Folk talents and folk dances were put on display, and folk dance companies were established. This interest was not confined only to Russian art. On the other hand, Russian dancers and choreographers brought the art of classical dance to other

Soviet republics, this contributing to the development of national ballets. National ballets based on folk epics, legends, and tales (particularly those that depicted the heroic past) were produced. Vakhtang Chabukiani, a Georgian and a graduate of the Leningrad Ballet School who was to become a brilliant classical dancer, made his first productions during this period. In his works, he managed to combine the traditions of the Russian school of classical dance and national dance

traditions, such as the Spanish tradition in *Laurencia* (after *Fuente Ovejuna* by Lope de Vega) and the Georgian in *The Heart of the Mountains*. These productions, like drama-ballet, feature dawell-developed and multifaceted plot, and their main topic was a popular struggle against oppression. However, these ballets differed substantially from drama-ballet in that Chabukiani strove for

maximum dance action and in that their dramatic content was often expressed through dance based on the powerful dance language of nineteenth-century ballet. Ballet during this period truly became a popular art form. New ballet companies sprang up throughout Russia, both in the capital and in the provinces. The Moscow Art Ballet, which was a small dance company established in 1929 by the famous ballerina Viktorina Krieger, merged with the Nemirovich-Danchenko Musical Theater in Moscow. After Krieger, the Moscow Art Ballet was directed by Nikolai Kholfin, whose productions were imbued with humor and optimism. Kholfin was assisted by the Art Theater's stage directors, Boris Mordvinov and Pavel Markov. This alliance was instrumental in shaping the identity of the young company, and their productions attracted the attention of Vladimir Nemirovich-Danchenko, a famous stage director, writer, and comrade-in-arms of Konstantin Stanislavsky at the Art Theater. This theater also performed productions by Rostislav Zakharov and Fedor Lopukhov. In 1941, Vladimir Burmeister began his thirty-year association with this company, which was renamed the Stanislavsky and Nemirovich-Danchenko Musical Theater. The theater continued to develop its unique repertoire, in which ballets by Russian composers predominated. In the 1930s, the center of ballet was forcibly moved to Moscow, which had become the country's capital in 1918. In view of this, a number of leading dancers (such as Marina Semenova, Galina Ulanova, Alexei Yermolayev, and Sergei Koren) and choreographers (including Lopukhov, Gusev, Zakharov, and Lavrovsky) were transferred from Leningrad to the Bolshoi Theater. The best productions of the Leningrad stage were transferred to Moscow, and the best Leningrad professors began to teach at the Moscow School. Nonetheless, ballet activities continued in Leningrad. A new ballet company was established in 1932 under the

117. The theatrical work of Valentina Khodasevich (1894-1970) was distingushed by a historical and factual accuracy and a bright theatricality.

This sketch shows a set for the last scene of *The Fountain of Bakhchisarai*.

118. Act III from
Vladimir
Burmeister's *Swan
Lake*

auspices of the Maly Opera Theater. Lopukhov was one of its founders and original art directors. The main task of the new company was to develop a unique repertoire of predominantly lyrical and comic productions. Lopukhov, Lavrovsky, Vladimir Varkovitsky, Boris Fenster, Leonid Jakobson, and Piotr Gusev choreographed at this theater. During the post-revolutionary years, new ballet companies were formed under the auspices of pre-existing theaters in many Russian cities, including Sverdlovsk in 1922, Perm in 1926, Kuibyshev in 1931, Saratov in 1932, and Gorky in 1936. Later, during the Second World War, the leading dancer and choreographers of Moscow and Leningrad were evacuated to the provinces, where they greatly improved local dance companies. Actors from the Leningrad Kirov Theater performed a number of old and new ballets during their stay in Perm. The dance school, headed by Vaganova, enrolled local children and thus the famous Perm Dance School began operation. Its founder was Yekaterina Geidenreich from Leningrad, who was initially a dancer at the Kirov Theater and later became a teacher at the Leningrad Ballet School. The Perm School, one of the best ballet educational institutions in Russia is well-known throughout the world and still preserves the lofty traditions of the Leningrad school. In spite of famine, incessant bombing, and the other horrors of the blockade of Leningrad, ballet activities continued within the besieged city. Actors who chose to stay in the city, including Olga Jordan and Robert Gerbek (soloists from the Kirov Theater), performed on the front line, at industrial plants, and in hospitals. They also organized the Blockade Theater, which performed *Esmeralda*, *Chopiniana* (*Les Sylphides*), *The Little Humpbacked Horse*, and the third act of *The Fountain of Bakhchisarai*. On the day that war was declared against the Soviet Union, June 22, 1941, the graduating class of the Leningrad School performed *Bela*, based on a

119. Through the 1930s, the press and government decrees were full of calls to artists to "reflect socialist reality". One result was the ballet *The Bright Stream* about life on a collective farm. Despite its weak, naive libretto, this ballet was quite popular, thanks largely to the spectacular, witty music of Dmitry Shostakovich, the outstanding choreography of Fedor Lopukhov, and the bright sets of Mikhail Bobyshev. One of these sets is shown here.

overleaf
120. Peter Williams (1902-47), whose sets for *Romeo and Juliet* were historically accurate down to the smallest detail, created the designs for *Cinderella* and revealed himself to be a master at creating a fairy-tale setting. This production, which was staged amid the victory celebrations of 1945, was brilliant and spectacular, accurately reflecting the mood of its audience.

A set from *Cinderella*.

123

story by Mikhail Lermontov. The principal part was danced by Nonna Yastrebova, who was to survive the hardships of the siege and to return to artistic activity after the war. In spite of the famine, those teachers who stayed in the city continued to teach and to enroll new students. The Bolshoi Theater was evacuated to Kuibyshev, and the Ballet School was moved to Vasilsursk, a town on the Volga. Students there developed a program that was performed in nearby villages and hospitals. The stages on which they danced were tiny, and it was bitterly cold in the unheated halls; however, the ballets were choreographed by Kasyan Goleizovsky, the sets were designed by the stage designer Fedor Fedorovsky, and the parts were danced by senior students such as Raisa Struchkova, Violetta Bovt, and Lidia Krupenina, all of whom went on to become famous dancers. They were coached by Nikolai Tarasov, art director of the School, who was a gifted dancer and teacher and who developed his own method of teaching men's classical dance. In these difficult years, theaters staged bright, optimistic pieces and comedies that raised peoples' spirits and prevented them from falling into despair. Thus, the ballet

company of the Musical Theater, which remained in Moscow, performed Burmeister's joyful and bright production of *Straussiana* and his comedy *The Merry Wives of Windsor.* The Bolshoi Theater in Kuibyshev staged *Scarlet Sails*, a romantic ballet full of hope and faith; the part of the Bolshoi company that remained in Moscow under the direction of Mikhail Gabovich staged a flashy production of *Don Quixote*; and the Leningrad Kirov Theater in Perm presented *La Fille Mal Gardée.* Many actors actually performed on the front lines. They danced in light ballet garments in the most improbable locations, including snowy forest clearings and on open trucks, in any weather, and sometimes even under enemy fire. After the war, new ballets were rarely staged. Theater repertoires were dominated either by classical ballets that were instrumental in maintaining the high performance level of the Russian academic dancing school or revived productions from the 1920s and 1930s, such as *The Flames of Paris* and *The Red Poppy.* In the late 1940s and early 1950s, the drama-ballet began its decline, although it was still officially supported. The protest against its didactic naturalism reached a crescendo, and appeals to enrich dance were loud. Choreographers who supported the drama-

ballet took futile steps aimed at preserving it by trying to make performances more attractive for spectators through stage effects. For example, Zakharov transformed a romantic fairy tale about *Cinderella* (1945) into a pompous pageant. In a 1949 production of *The Bronze Horseman*, based on Pushkin's narrative poem, the complex philosophical conflict between the individual and the government was completely overshadowed by stage effects: in the flood scene, waves rolled across the stage carrying

123. The ballet *The Bronze Horseman* was the most significant creation of Mikhail Bobyshev. In this production, Bobyshev strove to accurately recreate St. Petersburg and to achieve maximum realism in his depiction of the flood.

This sketch shows a set from *The Bronze Horseman.*

household debris. However, the crushing blow to the drama-ballet was inflicted by the 1954 production of *The Tale of the Stone Flower*, based on a story by the Siberian writer Pavel Bazhov. Lavrovsky transformed Bazhov's meditation on creativity into a social drama denouncing the hardships of the past. The central themes of nature and creativity disappeared entirely from the ballet. Everyday life was reproduced on the stage in such detail that both poetry and dance were killed. This ballet marked the end of the drama-ballet.

# Great figures of Russian ballet

**BURMEISTER,**
Vladimir Pavlovich
(born July 15, 1904, in Vitebsk;
died March 5, 1971, in Moscow).
*Dancer and choreographer.*
Burmeister was born into the family
of a land surveyor. His mother, the
daughter of a cousin of Piotr
Tchaikovsky, inculcated in him a love
of music. Initially, Burmeister was
interested in painting; later, he
tried dramatic acting, and finally he
entered the Lunacharsky Moscow
Theater College to study choreography
at the age of twenty-one. In addition
to his studies, Burmeister performed
Hungarian, Spanish, and other
character dances in variety shows and
danced in the performances of the
Drama-Ballet Studio under the
direction of Nina Gremina. In
1930, he joined the Moscow Art Ballet
under the direction of Viktorina
Krieger. This theater was later merged
with the Nemirovich-Danchenko
Theater, which in turn was renamed
the Stanislavsky and Nemirovich-
Danchenko Musical Theater in
1941. Burmeister was a character
dancer, but he also played mime
roles. He made his debut as a
choreographer with this theater with
his stagings of dances in musical
comedies. Along with Fedor
Lopukhov and stage director Pavel
Markov, Burmeister produced the
ballet *Christmas Eve*, based on a story
by Nikolai Gogol. He was the chief
choreographer of the theater from
1941 to 1960 and from 1961 to
1971. Burmeister's temperament
and inventiveness as a choreographer
was manifested in his stagings of
folk heroic ballets such as *Lola*,
*The Shore of Happiness*, *Jeanne
d'Arc*, and *Little Red Devils*.
Burmeister was primarily a
choreographer with a talent for stage
direction. Burmeister's productions
of ballets based on literary subjects,
such as *The Merry Wives of Windsor*
(with Ivan Kurilov) and *The Snow
Maiden* (based on a play by
Alexander Ostrovsky), as well as his
own versions of classical ballets,
including *Esmeralda* and *Swan
Lake* (with Piotr Gusev), and his
interpretations of symphonic music,
such as *Straussiana* and *Shéhérazade*,
were characterized by dynamic
arrangements and logical plot
development. Burmeister's most
important production was *Swan
Lake*: in this ballet, he revived Lev
Ivanov's "swan" scenes, but
substantially reworked the third and
fourth acts, as well as the finale.
Burmeister also staged this ballet
at the Paris Opéra, and he presented
*The Snow Maiden* and the London
Festival Ballet.

124. A scene from
Vladimir
Burmeister's
*Snegourourotchka*

## DUDINSKAYA,
Natalia Mikhailovna
(born August 21, 1912,
in Kharkov).
*Ballerina and teacher.*
Dudinskaya was Konstantin Serge-yev's wife. Her first teacher was her mother, Natalia Tagliori, a student of Enrico Cecchetti and Yevgenia Sokolova, who had headed a private ballet school. Dudinskaya continued her studies at the Leningrad Ballet School under Agrippina Vaganova. While still at school, she attracted general attention in the part of Princess Florine in *The Sleeping Beauty*. After graduating in 1931, Dudinskaya joined the Leningrad Opera and Ballet Theater (which was later named the Kirov Theater), where she almost immediately began to dance in classical ballets: Odette-Odile, Aurora, Masha in *The Nutcracker*, *Kitri*, *Giselle*, and *Raymonda*. She also danced main parts in ballets by modern choreographers, such as Coralie in *Lost Illusions*, Gayane in *Gayane*, Cinderella in *Cinderella*, Maiden Bird in *Shurale* etc. With virtuoso dance technique and a vigorous spirit, Dudinskaya also performed heroic parts. One of her best works was the title role in *Laurencia*, based on Lope de Vega's play *Fuente Ovejuna*. Dudinskaya's performance in this role was saturated with heroic pathos and was noted for its energy, airiness, and its evocative Spanish rhythms. In her mature period, Dudinskaya was noted for the psychological profundity and emotional expressiveness of her performance. In the part of Sarie in *The Path of Thunder*, the ballerina exposed the development of her character's complex nature by means of a well-defined design, and a reserved expressiveness. From 1951 to 1970, she taught advanced study courses, and from 1965 to 1970, she was a coach at the Kirov Theater. She was appointed the senior professor of the Leningrad Ballet School in 1964. Dudinskaya appeared in a movie of *The Sleeping Beauty* in 1964 and in other films. Several television films, including *Dudinskaya's Class* (1973), *Dialogue with the Stage* (1988), and *The Birth of a Dance* 1991 have been devoted to Dudinskaya's artistic career.

## YERMOLAYEV,
Alexei Nikolayevich
(born February 23, 1910,
in St. Petersburg; died December 12, 1975, in Moscow).
*Dancer, choreographer and teacher.*
Having graduated from the Leningrad Ballet School in 1926 (where he had studied under Vladimir Ponomarev), Yermolayev danced in the Leningrad Opera and Ballet Theater from 1926 to 1930 and in the Bolshoi Theater from 1930 to 1958. His parts included the God of Wind in *The Talisman*, Basil in *Don Quixote*, Albert in *Giselle*, Siegfried in *Swan Lake*, and Ripafratta in *Mirandolina*. Yermolayev was one of the most outstanding representatives of the Russian ballet school between 1920 and 1950. He played an important role in the development of the Russian ballet. Yermolayev went further than others in demolishing the stereotype of the courteous and gallant cavalier dancer that had taken shape long ago at the Imperial Theatre. His interpretations of the classical repertoire were unexpected, keen, and profound, and his manner of dancing was particularly expressive. Yermolayev succeeded in changing many concepts of male dance: in some areas, such as tours en l'air and parterre, jumps, and, most importantly, speed, Yermolayev pushed male dance to a new level of virtuosity that became the standard for dancers of the following generations. However, some of Yermolayev's achievements, including his triple tours en l'air and double revoltades have not yet been duplicated. Yermolayev was well equipped to carry out this revolution in male dance: he had an experimenter's insatiable fanaticism combined with a keen, cold intellect; fearlessness; self-possession; a readiness to run any risk; and physical tirelessness. Yermolayev's prime lasted for more than ten years. However, extreme physical demands took their toll and, in 1937, he permanently injured his leg. Moreover, the artistic atmosphere was changing, becoming more decorous: Yermolayev's rebellious spirit seemed defiant and inappropriate. In addition, drama-ballet, which was a mime form of ballet theater, became predominant. Yermolayev's unique dancing gift could not find proper application and

125. Natalia Dudinskaya as Sarie in *The Path of Thunder*

126. Alexei Yermolayev as Vaya, the god of the wind, in *The Talisman*.

seemed a burden to many choreographers. Having returned to the stage of the Bolshoi Theater, Yermolayev continued to dance the leading parts. Though he could never achieve his former brilliance he did become a magnificent mime dancer. In the roles of Tybalt in *Romeo and Juliet*, Girey in *The Fountain of Bakhchisarai*, Abderâme in *Raymonda* and Severyan in *The Tale of the Stone Flower*, Yermolayev demonstrated effective, expressive gestures, as well as an unusual intensity of inner emotion. In terms of his impact on audiences Yermolayev could be compared with the most outstanding dramatic actors. Yermolayev began to work as a choreographer in the late 1930s. A born choreographer, he was unsuccessful as a librettist because of the influence of the vulgar sociological demands enforced in Soviet art. Regrettably, these demands also affected his productions. Yermolayev's activities as a teacher were more fruitful. Temperamentally unsuited to an everyday teaching routine, Yermolayev headed the Moscow Ballet School only from 1965 to 1972. However, he was successful and happy teaching at the Bolshoi Theater, working with talented dancers and devoting all his energy to the very best. Vladimir Vasilyev, Maris Liepa, and Alexander Godunov are much indebted to Yermolayev.

## GABOVICH,
Mikhail Markovich
(born December 7, 1905, in the village of Velikie Gulyaki (now Fastov district), near Kiev; died July 12, 1965, in Moscow).
*Dancer and teacher.*
As an adolescent, Gabovich began to study under Maria Gorshkova, and he joined the Moscow Ballet School on her recommendation. There he was a student of Alexander Gorsky and Vasily Tikhomirov. After graduating in 1924, he joined the Bolshoi Theater. Gabovich participated in Kasyan Goleizovsky's innovative staging of *Joseph the Beautiful* in 1925. He was among those adherents of Goleizovsky who were in conflict with the company's conservative directors. As a result of this conflict, Gabovich and a number of other performers were fired from the Bolshoi, but they were quickly reinstated. Later, Gabovich performed in Goleizovsky's concert programs. Gabovich became famous as a romantic dancer, performing the roles of princes and noble heroes in classical ballets such as Siegfried in *Swan Lake*, Désiré in *The Sleeping Beaty*, Solor in *La Bayadère*, Jean de Brienne in *Raymonda*, and others. Gabovich reached his artistic prime in the epoch of the drama-ballet in the 1930s and 1940s. He danced the leading parts in ballets staged by Rostislav Zakharov, including

127. Mikhail Gabovich as Jean de Brienne in *Raymonda*.

Vladimir in *The Prisoner of the Caucasus* and Andriy in *Taras Bulba*. His best roles include Romeo in *Romeo and Juliet* by Leonid Lavrovsky. Dancing in lyrical and dramatic parts, Gabovich strove for theatrical expressiveness in his gestures, sculpturelike poses, and sometimes even pathetics. He danced with Marina Semenova and Olga Lepeshinskaya and was a longstanding partner of Galina Ulanova. Gabovich's last part was that of Ma Lichen in the second Moscow version of *The Red Poppy* in 1949. He had to leave the stage at the age of forty-five as the result of an injury suffered during a dress rehearsal for *The Ruby Stars*. In the years of the Second World War, Gabovich directed an affiliate of the Bolshoi Theater that remained in Moscow. He taught at the Moscow Ballet School from 1951 and was its art director from 1954 to 1958. Vladimir Vasilyev was among his students. Gabovich was a brilliant ballet critic and theoretician, and he also wrote ballet libretti.

## KOREN,
Sergei Gavrilovich
(born September 6, 1907, in St. Petersburg; died June 6, 1969, in Moscow).
*Dancer and choreographer.*
Koren began to study ballet at the age of seventeen, first at the plastics studio of Natalia Natan-Gorskaya and, from 1924 to 1928, at the evening courses of the Leningrad

Ballet School. There he studied under Viktor Semenov, Vladimir Ponomarev, and Alexander Monakhov. After graduation, Koren danced at the Leningrad Maly Theater; from 1930 to 1942, he worked at the Kirov Theater. Remaining in Leningrad during the blockade, he participated in many concerts in 1941, and the revenues from these concerts were remitted to the Defense Fund. From 1942 to 1960, Koren performed at the Bolshoi Theater. Koren was a brilliant dancer. He performed the panaderos, a mazurka, a Spanish and a Hungarian dance in *Raymonda*; the flamenco and a dance with castanets in *Laurencia*. He had virtuoso technique and especially fine, subtle footwork. Moreover, he had a well-developed feeling of style and national identity, a keen graphical presentation of poses, and refined and elegant plastics. He combined a deep inner spirit with a reserved nobility of manners and an impeccably logical stage presence. In addition, Koren was a brilliant actor. One of his most important achievements was Mercutio in *Romeo and Juliet*: he conveyed the love of life, the keen brilliance, and wit of his character. The scene of Mercutio's death was depicted as a tragic duel with death. Koren's parts included Espada in *Don Quixote*, Florestan in the *Le Carnaval*, Amoun in *Egyptian Nights*, Cavalier Ripafratta in *Mirandolina*, Commander in *Laurencia*, and many others. He was active in concerts and often choreographed dances and programs for himself and his partners, including Nina Anisimova, Yadviga Sangovich, and Susanna Zvyagina. Between 1960 and 1969, he was a coach at the Bolshoi Theater. Koren was filmed in *Romeo and Juliet* in 1954, in the television film *Count Nulin* in 1959.

## LAVROVSKY (real name,
Ivanov), Leonid Mikhailovich
(born June 18, 1905, in St. Petersburg; died November 22, 1967, in Paris).
*Dancer, choreographer, and teacher.*
Having graduated from the Petrograd Ballet School (where he had been a student of Vladimir Ponomarev),

Lavrovsky performed at the Leningrad Opera and Ballet Theater from 1922 to 1935: there, he danced Amoun in *Egyptian Nights*, Albert in *Giselle*, Désiré in *The Sleeping Beauty*, Siegfried in *Swan Lake*, the Young Man in *Les Sylphides*, etc. He participated in the premiere of *The Greatness of the Universe*, Fedor Lopukhov's dance symphony. In addition to dancing, Lavrovsky began to work as a stage director. From 1935 to 1936, he was an art director at the Leningrad Maly Theater ballet company and, from 1938 to 1944, at the Kirov Ballet. During this period, he produced his most important ballets, including *The Prisoner of the Caucasus* and *Romeo and Juliet*. Lavrovsky was the chief choreographer of the Bolshoi Theater from 1944 to 1964, with short interruptions. There he staged *The Red Poppy*, *Fadette*, *The Tale of the Stone Flower*, *Paganini*, *Night City*, and *Pages from Life*, and he revived his version of *Romeo and Juliet*. Most of Lavrovsky's productions were drama-ballets with clearly delineated characters. He also worked closely with actors to develop the psychological justification of their actions. A connoisseur of classical dance, he paid much attention to the classical repertoire; among other things, he revived *Giselle*, *Raymonda*, and *Chopiniana* (*Les Sylphides*). Lavrovsky has gone down in the history of the Russian ballet as a choreographer whose career reflected the ups and downs of choreography from 1930 to 1960. A founder of the drama-ballet, he was also an eyewitness to the crisis of this trend. In his later works, such as *Paganini* and *The Classical Symphony*, he turned to more abstract forms. Lavrovsky's talent suffered from the government's strict control of the arts, and he sought an escape in constant artistic experimentation. His *Romeo and Juliet* was noted for its deep psychological penetration into the characters' motives and a highly artistic presentation of the ideas of Shakespeare's tragedy. Throughout his life, Lavrovsky worked at the Leningrad Ballet School, and he staged his first ballets there. From 1964 to 1967, he also worked at the Moscow Ballet School. While working at the Bolshoi Theater, Lavrovsky was also the art director of the Moscow Ballet School, where he produced a number of dances, including *The Classical Symphony*. He taught choreography at the Moscow Theater Institute from 1948 to 1967. He became a professor in 1952 and received many of the Soviet Union's top decorations. Lavrovsky's ballets were revived abroad in such countries as Finland, Hungary, and Yugoslavia,

128. Sergei Koren as Mercutio in *Romeo and Juliet*.

129. A scene from *Romeo and Juliet* by Leonid Lavrovsky.

occasionally by Lavrovsky himself. A film was made based on Lavrovsky's *Romeo and Juliet*, and a performance of this ballet was filmed by the BBC in 1973. In 1959, Lavrovsky organized the Soviet Union's first ice ballet company, and he served as its artistic director until 1964.

## LEPESHINSKAYA,
Olga Vasilyevna
(born September 28, 1916, in Kiev).
*Ballerina and teacher.*
Lepeshinskaya's father, a prominent civil engineer, did not approve of his daughter's dream of becoming a ballerina. However, having a strong character from early childhood, Lepeshinskaya enrolled in the Moscow Ballet School, which she graduated from in 1933 after studying with Alexander Chekrygin. She danced with the Bolshoi Theater until 1963. She debuted as Lise in the *La Fille Mal Gardée*. With brilliant technique, Lepeshinskaya was a virtuoso in all forms of classical dance. Her performance featured passion, elevation, and precision. Lepeshinskaya added dramatically motivated changes of mood to her treatment of such classical ballet characters as Kitri, Aurora, Odette-Odile, Swanilda, and others. Lepeshinskaya is also known for her Cinderella in *Cinderella* (1945). An innate sense of her times enabled her to bring to life the most important parts in ballets by Rostislav Zakharov, Leonid Lavrovsky, and Konstantin Sergeyev. These included Assol in *Scarlet Sails*, Jeanne in *The Flames of Paris*, Parasha in *The Bronze Horseman*, and Sarie in *The Path of Thunder*. Lepeshinskaya's unique talent was fully revealed in the part of Liza Muromskaya in *The Peasant Gentry Girl* (1949) and in the title role of *Mirandolina* (1949). She performed dances by Leonid Jakobson such as *The Hunter and the Bird* (1940) and *The Blind Girl* (1941). Lepeshinskaya's repertoire included three concert programs choreographed especially for her that she performed on the front line during the Second World War and in many cities in the USSR and abroad. Her partners included Piotr Gusev, Vladimir Preobrazhensky,

Alexei Yermolaev. She appeared in the television film *Count Nulin* in 1959. Since 1963, Lepeshinskaya has been teaching abroad at the Rome Dance Academy and at opera and ballet theaters in Budapest, Munich, Berlin, Stockholm, Vienna, Milan, and London. She chaired the Organizing Committee of the Moscow International Ballet Competition in the 1970s and 1980s. She also chaired the first Sergei Diaghilev Moscow International Competition of Young Ballet Dancers in 1992. She has been President of the Russian Choreographic Association since 1991.

## MESSERER, Asaf Mikhailovich
(born November 19, 1903, in Vilnius; died March 7, 1992, in Moscow).
*Dancer, choreographer, and teacher.*
After graduating from the Moscow Ballet School in 1921 (he had been a student of Alexander Gorsky),

Messerer danced in the Bolshoi Theater and was a leading solo dancer there until 1954. His parts included Petrushka and the Moor in *Petrushka*; Basil in *Don Quixote*; and Philippe in *The Flames of Paris*. He began to choreograph in 1925 and staged *The Footballer*, *Ballet School*, and dances in operas at the Bolshoi Theater. Messerer belonged to a big family of actors. His elder brother Azary was an actor at the Moscow Art Theater; his sister Rachel, Maya Plisetskaya's mother, was a film actress; his other sister Sulamith was a ballerina and teacher who danced leading parts at the Bolshoi Theater in the 1930s and 1940s, often in partnership with her brother; and his son Boris is currently one of the most outstanding stage designers in Russia. As a young man, Messerer was interested in sports rather than ballet. He began studying ballet at the unusually late age of sixteen, but his progress was so

130. Olga Lepeshinskaya. Oil paintiny by A. Gerasimov.

132

stunning that he graduated after only three years. He was open to all theatrical experiments. All of Messerer's activities, especially at the initial stage of his career, were closely connected with the avant garde. He worked with Vsevolod Meyerhold as a choreographer. Messerer soon became a classical virtuoso dancer with an unusual, original style. Messerer constantly invented ever more difficult movements and pas that had precise patterns, energy, and athletic power. When he performed his unconventional jumps, Messerer looked like a flying athlete. Moreover, he was endowed with a bright comedic gift and a unique sense of humor. He reinterpreted many parts from old ballets ironically, and one of his last parts, the Prince in *Cinderella*, was particularly noted for this quality. Having completed his dance career, Messerer concentrated all his energy on teaching. He began to coach leading dancers and ballerinas at the Bolshoi Theater in 1946, and it was here that Messerer found his second vocation and acquired international fame. He worked in Brussels in 1961-62, and later in Hungary, Poland, and other countries as a teacher and choreographer.

## ULANOVA,

Galina Sergeyevna
(born January 8, 1910,
in St. Petersburg).
*Ballerina and teacher.*
Ulanova's father, Sergei Ulanov, was a dancer and regisseur; her mother, Maria Romanova, was a dancer and teacher. When she was nine, Ulanova was enrolled in the Leningrad Ballet School; during her first four years, she was a student of her own mother. Later, she studied under Agrippina Vaganova. After graduating in 1928, she joined the Leningrad Opera and Ballet Theater (later renamed the Kirov Theater). She debuted as Princess Florine in *The Sleeping Beauty*. From 1944 to 1960, she was a ballerina of the Bolshoi Theater. Ulanova's performance was distinguished by a rare harmony of dance elements. Even at the beginning of Ulanova's career, the critics noted

a complete integration of dance technique, dramatic presentation, and rhythm in her performance. Without deviating from the strict purity of classical dance, Ulanova saturated her movements with anxious emotion. At the same time, even the most technically refined dance movements were as spontaneous and expressive as natural gestures. Ulanova's style is unique because her movements were neither interrupted nor completed, but instead they seemed to fade away into nothingness. This art of plastic ritardandi, fadings, and quietings created a special dance "touche" in her dance, a pianissimo, and delicacy. A modern classical dancer, Ulanova was an excellent performer of Odette-Odile in *Swan Lake*, Aurora in *The Sleeping Beauty*, Masha in *The Nutcracker*, and of *Giselle*. She was also an actress who proved that the works of great poets, full of philosophical content and human passions, could be translated into the language of dance. Her art reflected an inviolable faith in human dignity and perfection and in the ultimate triumph of the best spiritual qualities of humanity: this faith remained despite all the upheavals of her time. Ulanova's art moved gradually from the lyrical to the tragic. The fragile and defenseless Maria in *The Fountain of Bakhchisarai* became increasingly intransigent, while the tender Juliet of *Romeo and Juliet* became increasingly passionate and willful. The madness scene in *Giselle* was the pinnacle of Ulanova's mastery of tragedy. Ulanova's repertoire also

included Solveig in *The Ice Maiden*; the Firebird in *The Little Humpbacked Horse*; the Actress in *The Flames of Paris*; Diane in *Esmeralda*; Coralie in *Lost Illusions*; Raymonda in *Raymonda*; Cinderella in *Cinderella*; Parasha in *The Bronze Horseman*; Waltz, Nocturne, and Mazurka in *Les Sylphides*; as well as dances such as Fokine's *Dying Swan* and *Elegy*, created by Kasyan Goleizovsky especially for her.

Ulanova gained worldwide fame as she developed the principles and traditions of the Russian choreographic school. She has been working at the Bolshoi Theater as a coach since 1959. Nina Timofeyeva, Yekaterina Maximova, Vladimir Vasilyev, Ludmila Semenyaka, Nadezhda Gracheva, and other dancers had their advanced studies under her guidance. Ulanova's outstanding achievements were rewarded by many of the highest decorations and titles of Russia, as well as by the prize of the Paris Academy of Theater, the Anna Pavlova Prize (1958), Oscar Parcell Prize (1988: in Milan, Italy), and the Order of Merit in Art and Literature (France). Ulanova is a member honoris causa of the US Academy of Arts and Sciences. On November 16, 1981, a special event sponsored by UNESCO and dedicated to Ulanova was held in Paris, at which a ballet entitled *In Honor of Ulanova* was performed (choreographer, Vladimir Vasilyev). A sculpture of Ulanova by Yelena Jansson-Manizer has been erected in Stockholm, while a bronze bust by Mikhail Anikushin has been installed in St. Petersburg. Ulanova's dancing was

131. Asaf Messerer dances the concert number *The Soccer Player*.

132. Galina Ulanova dancing the title role in *Giselle*.

133

133. Galina Ulanova
as Maria in *The
Fountain of
Bakhchisarai.*

filmed many times, and several television films and books have been dedicated to her life and career.

## SEMENOVA,

Marina Timofeyevna
(born June 12,1908,in St. Petersburg).
*Ballerina and teacher.*
Semenova graduated from the Leningrad Ballet School in 1925, having studied under Agrippina Vaganova. From 1925 to 1929, she danced in the Leningrad Opera and Ballet Company; from 1930 to 1952, she was a leading ballerina at the Bolshoi Theater. Her roles included Princess Florine and Aurora in *The Sleeping Beauty*, Odette-Odile in *Swan Lake*, Nikia in *La Bayadère*, Aspiccia in *The Pharaoh's Daughter*, Raymonda in *Raymonda*, Giselle in *Giselle*, and the Queen of the Ball in *The Bronze Horseman*. Marina Semenova's name is not broadly known in the West, but it has become legendary in Russia. Many spectators who saw her perform in the 1920s, the 1930s, and the 1940s are convinced that they have seen the greatest ballerina of the epoch. Her contribution to the history of the Russian ballet is striking. With a nearly superhuman energy of movement and an equally fantastic sense of space, Semenova imbued classical dance with a new dimension and expanded it beyond the confines of virtuoso technique. At the same time, Semenova was particularly feminine in each scene, each pas, and each gesture. Parts in old ballets were the backbone of her repertoire, because it was there that she was especially brilliant and felt most at ease. Though she was by nature a gifted comic dancer, Semenova was more attracted to high tragedy, and she interpreted *Swan Lake* and *La Bayadère* as noble tragedies.

In 1937, Semenova's husband was arrested and executed, and her position in the theater was jeopardized. However, this ordeal did not break her. Her proud posture conveyed a moral power and a lofty artistic beauty that restored her audience's faith in humanity. She was called "a queen" in the theater milieu.
Semenova has been coaching the leading ballerinas of the Bolshoi Theater since 1953. Svetlana Adyrkhaeva, Natalia Bessmertnova, Marina Kondratyeva, Nadezhda Pavlova, Nina Timofeyeva, and Galina Stepanenko were among those who had advanced training in Semenova's class.

## SERGEYEV,
Konstantin Mikhailovich
(born March 5,1910,
in St. Petersburg; died there April 1,1992).
*Dancer, choreographer, and teacher.*

134

Sergeyev took evening courses at the Leningrad Ballet School under Yevgenia Snetkova, Maria Kozhukhova, and Viktor Semenov. He performed with the touring company of Josif Kchessinsky in 1928-29, dancing Siegfried in *Swan Lake* and Albert in *Giselle*. He then continued his education and, after graduating from the Leningrad Ballet School in 1930, Sergeyev became a leading classical dancer of the Kirov Theater and performed the basic classical repertoire. The nobility, elegance, and academic purity of his dance and his extraordinary acting talents combined to make Sergeyev an outstanding performer of lyrical and romantic parts. He imbued traditional characters with a new psychological depth and genuine feelings. The emphasis on social issues that predominated in the ballet of the 1930s and 1940s did not put an end to psychological interpretation, virtuoso technique, or exquisite performances. Sergeyev's interpretations of male roles in classical ballets had a strong influence on dancers of later generations. Sergeyev's lyrical gift was enhanced by his artistic fellowship with Galina Ulanova, his partner throughout the 1930s and 1940s: their partnership went down in the history of Russian ballet. In the postwar period, Sergeyev's artistic career was linked with that of Natalia Dudinskaya. Their partnership, which brought together two actors with very different gifts, helped expand the creativity of each and enriched the

range of their expressive means. Sergeyev's parts at that time included Ali Batyr in *Shurale*, Lenny in *The Path of Thunder*, Arbenin in *Masquerade*, Basil in *Don Quixote*, Colin in the *La Fille Mal Gardée*, and Philippe and Jérôme in *The Flames of Paris*. Sergeyev's well-developed sense of culture, his mastery of stage direction, and his knowledge of classical dance combined to make him an excellent choreographer. In 1946, he became a choreographer at the Kirov Theater and from 1951 to 1955 and between 1960 and 1970, he served as chief choreographer there. Though his productions always featured virtuoso dancing, Sergeyev was also concerned with the logic of plot development and the motivation of the action. Sergeyev's ballets, such as *The Path of Thunder* (after a novel by the South African writer Peter Abrahams), developed topical and publicistic themes. He also took up Shakespeare with his staging of *Hamlet*. His greatest success was *Cinderella*, in which his directorial and poetic visions combined perfectly. In his versions of classical ballets such as *Raymonda*, *Swan Lake*, *The Sleeping Beauty*, and *Le Corsaire*, Sergeyev abridged mime scenes and imbued mime characters with dance characteristics. Beginning in 1931, Sergeyev taught classical dance: from 1938 to 1940 and from 1973 to 1992, he was the art director of the Leningrad Ballet School. In 1991 he became president of the Vaganova Academy of Russian Ballet in St. Petersburg. Sergeyev also taught at the International Summer Seminar in Split, Yugoslavia from 1985 to 1988. He staged ballets in many countries, including Poland, Czechoslovakia, Japan, and the United States. He appeared in the film *The Masters of the Russian Ballet* in 1953. He also made a television series called *The Art of the Russian Ballet* and taped revivals of Michel Fokine's stagings of *Le Carnaval* (1986) and *Egyptian Nights* (1988). The film *Konstantin Sergeyev: Approaches to Choreography* (1976) explored Sergeyev's artistic career. In addition to titles,

134. Konstantin Sergeyev as the Prince in *Cinderella*.

decorations, and prizes from his own country, Sergeyev was awarded the prize of the Paris Academy of Dance in 1965.

## STRUCHKOVA
(married name, Lapauri), Raisa Stepanovna
(born October 5,1925, in Moscow). *Ballerina and teacher.*

In 1944, after graduating from the Moscow Ballet School where she had studied under Yelizaveta Gerdt, Struchkova began work at the Bolshoi Theater. Two years later, she danced her first major part as Lise in *La Fille Mal Gardée*. Her next roles were Maria in *The Fountain of Bakhchisarai*, and *Cinderella*, as well as parts in the classical repertoire such as Masha in *The Nutcracker*, Odette-Odile in *Swan Lake*, and Aurora in *The Sleeping Beauty*. Struchkova easily mastered the most complex dances. Her style was characterized by refined lines, remarkable plasticity, soft feminity, unconstrained grace, and emotionality. Kasyan Goleizovsky said that "the body of this charming ballerina is not just slender, graceful, and expressive; it is witty as well." Taking these qualities into account, her husband Alexander Lapauri (1926-75), a dancer and choreographer of the Bolshoi Theater, choreographed the part of the sly and coquettish lady-in-waiting in the ballet *Lieutenant Kizhe*, based on an ironic story by Yuri Tynyanov. Struchkova was also active in variety shows, dancing duets

135. Marina Semenova as Odette in *Swan Lake*.

with Lapauri. She appeared as Cinderella, one of her best roles in the film *The Crystal Slipper* and also danced in television versions of other ballets. She is a professor of choreography at the Theater Institute (GITIS) and has been Editor-in-Chief of the journal *Soviet Ballet* (*Sovetsky Balet*; *Balet* since 1992) since 1981.

## CHABUKIANI,

Vakhtang Mikhailovich
(born March 1910, in Tbilisi;
died there April 6,1992).
*Dancer, choreographer, and teacher.*
As a thirteen-year-old craftsman's apprentice, Chabukiani happened to visit Maria Perini's Children's Dance Studio. Perini (1873-1939) was an Italian dancer who worked at the Tbilisi Opera Theater from 1891 to 1907. This experience drew Chabukiani into ballet. After two years of study, he joined the ballet company of the Tbilisi Opera Theater in 1924. In the same year, he graduated from Perini's ballet studio and joined the Tbilisi Opera Theater (later renamed Paliashvili Theater). In 1926, Chabukiani went to Leningrad and was enrolled in the evening courses of the Leningrad Ballet School, where he studied under Viktor Semenov, Vladimir Ponomarev, and Alexander Shiryaev. He choreographed a work called *The Dance of Fire* for a school concert. He graduated from the courses and then worked at the Kirov Theater from 1929 to 1941. Chabukiani was a dancer of the heroic type in the ballet theater of the 1930s–1950s. As a performer and choreographer, he affirmed the theme of the heroic struggle against evil. He had virtuoso technique; his dance was energetic and carefully motivated by the demands of drama-ballet. He was able to capture all the energy, passion, and power of his leaps in sculptural poses. In classical ballets, he danced Siegfried in *Swan Lake*, Solor in *La Bayadère*, the Slave in *Le Corsaire*, Basil in *Don Quixote*, and Albert in *Giselle*. The following parts were choreographed especially for him: Jérôme in *The Flames of Paris*, Kerim in *Guerilla Days*, Acteon (of the pas de deux "Diane and Acteon"

in *Esmeralda*), and Andriy in *Taras Bulba*. In the 1930s, Chabukiani danced in heroic, romantic ballets that he choreographed himself, including *The Heart of the Mountains* and *Laurencia*, among others. He enhanced the dramatic conflict by choreographing particularly active dancing in these ballets. The characters of the highlander Djardji

in Hungary.

(*The Heart of the Mountains*) and the Spanish peasant Frondoso (*Laurencia*) confirmed Chabukiani's fame as a dancer and choreographer of heroic themes. Later, in 1957, he produced *Othello*; his rendition of the lead role was one of the most successful performances of the 1950s. As a

choreographer, Chabukiani combined the academic foundations of classical dance with folklore rhythms and motifs. Between 1941 and 1973, Chabukiani headed the ballet company of the Tbilisi Paliashvili Opera and Ballet Theater, where he staged many ballets. From 1950 to 1973, he headed the Tbilisi Ballet School, where he taught classical

dance for advanced students. From 1960 to 1970, he chaired the choreographic department of the Tbilisi Theater Institute. He was filmed as Othello in *The Moor of Venice* and in other ballet films. He also produced ballets in Japan, India, and Hungary.

136. Raisa Struchkova as the Maid of Honor in *Lieutenant Kizhe*. Pastel by V. Kosorukov.

## VAGANOVA,
Agrippina Yakovlevna
(born June 26, 1879,
in St. Petersburg; died November
5, 1951, in Leningrad).
*Ballerina, teacher, and choreographer.*
Born into the family of an usher,
Vaganova studied at the St. Petersburg
Theater School under Yekaterina
Vazem, Christian Johanson, and Pavel
Gerdt. After graduating in 1897, she
joined the corps de ballet of the
Mariinsky Theater and perfected
her skills with Olga Preobrajenska.
Vaganova's appearance was not
ideal: her body was strong and robust,
rather than frail. Her main advantages
were a keen intelligence and a
stubborn will. She had a swift and
soaring jump and stubbornly mastered
virtuoso dance technique. According
to Akim Volynsky, an outstanding
ballet critic, Vaganova's variations
will "remain forever among the
legends of ballet art." Indeed, she was
called "the queen of variation." She
danced the Queen of Waters in
*The Little Humpbacked Horse*, the Queen
of Dryads in *Don Quixote*, and
others. In 1911, not long before her
retirement, Vaganova received the
role of the fairy Naila in *The Brook*.
Later, she danced Odette-Odile in
*Swan Lake*, the Tsar-maiden in *The
Little Humpbacked Horse*, and the
title role in *Giselle*. In 1916, Vaganova
retired as a ballerina. She began her
teaching career at Volynsky's School
of Russian Ballet. Olga Spessivtseva,
a dancer at the Mariinsky Theater,
was Vaganova's student there. In 1921,
Vaganova joined the Petrograd
(after 1924, Leningrad) Ballet School,
where she became a professor in 1946.
Her teaching system gave new
impetus to the concepts of classical
dance performance. As a teacher,
Vaganova believed that the
foundation of dance is the proper
arrangement of the torso and
back, resulting in complete freedom
of movement and positioning of the
arms and legs. It was not by chance
that a number of the most
prominent dancers of our time were
among her students: they included
Marina Semenova, Olga Jordan,
Galina Ulanova, Tatiana Vecheslova,
Natalia Dudinskaya, Feya Balabina,
Alla Shelest, Alla Osipenko, and
Irina Kolpakova. From 1931 to
1937, Vaganova was the art director
of the Kirov Theater ballet company,
where she staged *Swan Lake* in 1933.
She treated Tchaikovsky's score as
"the story of a young man of the
nineteenth century," in the spirit of
German Romanticism. Vaganova
affirmed drama-ballet concepts in
her staging of *Esmeralda* in 1935.
Vaganova's school continues to
develop performance and teaching
techniques and exerts great influence
on ballet throughout the world.
Vaganova's methodology is
explained in her book *The
Fundamentals of Classical Dance*,
which has been translated into many
languages. The television film
*Agrippina Vaganova*, broadcast in
1988, and a number of books are
dedicated to Vaganova's artistic
career. In 1957, the Leningrad Ballet
School was renamed in Vaganova's
honor.

137. Vakhtang
Chabukiani in
*The Dance of Fire.*

## ZAKHAROV,
Rostislav Vladimirovich
(born September 7, 1907,
in Astrakhan; died January 15,
1984, in Moscow).
*Choreographer, stage director,
and professor.*
Having graduated from the
Leningrad Ballet School where he

*Gentry Girl* after works by Alexander Pushkin, and *Taras Bulba* after a story by Nikolai Gogol. However, it soon became clear that the concept of "dance in the dramatic character" was not versatile. In *Lost Illusions*, the mime and gestures merely elaborated the plot rather than conveying any meaning. Later, mime and dance became mere illustrations to a literary work, while the work itself became a pretext for staging a ballet. Zakharov found a way out by resorting to powerful scenes in the spirit of pageants that were designed to entertain the audience and inserted melodramatic episodes that had nothing to do with the main line of the plot. Zakharov also made use of exciting divertissements: for instance, he dramatized Bulba's death on the bonfire in *Taras Bulba* and created a flood for the centralepisodeof *The Bronze Horseman*, in which the stage of the Bolshoi seemed to be covered with crashing waves carrying debris. *Cinderella* was a particular success because it was staged in 1945 and was perceived as a victory celebration in honor of the end of the war. Zakharov also staged a number of operas, both at the Bolshoi Theater and abroad. In his ballets and operas, Zakharov demonstrated particular talent as a stage director. In the 1950s, Zakharov's ballets came under criticism for the poverty of the dance. For his part, Zakharov began to resist any innovations in the field of ballet, and he criticized such young choreographers as Yuri Grigorovich and Igor Belsky. Zakharov also spoke out sharply against the foreign companies that were beginning to tour the Soviet Union and against critics who were advocating reform in ballet. He was supported by official circles. From 1945 to 1947, Zakharov was the art director of the Moscow Ballet School; from 1946, he headed the choreography department at the State Institute of Theater Art, where he became a professor in 1951. Zakharov wrote a number of articles and books in which he developed his principles.

had studied under Vladimir Ponomarev, Zakharov was a solo dancer at the Kiev Opera Theater ballet company from 1926 until 1929. At the same time, he taught and staged small ballets in his own studio. In 1932, he graduated from the Directing Department of the Leningrad Theater College, where he studied under the famous director Sergei Radlov. While studying at the college, Zakharov produced dances for variety shows and for the theater. Between 1934 and 1936, he was a choreographer at the Kirov Theater. From 1936 to 1956, he was a choreographer and opera director at the Bolshoi Theater. In 1948, Zakharov received a degree from the Leningrad Theater Institute. Zakharov's first major work was *The Fountain of Bakhchisarai* in collaboration with Radlov at the Kirov

Theater. In his approach to this ballet, Zakharov drew heavily upon his experience as a stage director. While choreographing, he was guided by the concept of "dance in the dramatic character," as he described it. According to Zakharov, a dance beyond the confines of a literary plot is without meaning. The combination of mime and dance imbued with acting should be the basic means of expression in choreography. Of all the movements of classical dance, Zakharov selected only those that could be dramatized most easily. *The Fountain of Bakhchisarai* was an ideal drama-ballet because its plot was easily comprehensible. Zakharov also staged other ballets based on literary works: these included *Lost Illusions* after a novel by Balzac, *The Prisoner of the Caucasus* and *The Peasant*

# REBIRTH
From 1956 to the early 1990s

previous pages
140. A scene from
*Raymonda* at the
Bolshoi.

141. The finale from
*The Stone Flower* is the
wedding of Katerina
and Danila. Here.
Katerina is
Yekaterina Maximova
and Danila is
Vladimir Vasilyev in
the Bolshoi Theater's
production.

After Stalin's death, Nikita Khrushchev, the new head of the Soviet Union, delivered an important speech in 1956, in which he began to expose the harsh totalitarian regime that had dominated the country for more than thirty years and heralded changes in government policy. As a result of these changes, the isolation of the country from the rest of the world was broken, and cultural exchanges between the USSR and western countries were finally made possible. The first tour of the Bolshoi Theater in the United Kingdom in 1956 was an unbelievable success: the British capital was again overwhelmed by the art of Russian choreographers, as it had been during Diaghilev's Russian Seasons in London at the beginning of the century. Marie Rambert, an outstanding figure of the British ballet. noted that the Russians "have bella danza, a thing which nobody else has." Galina Ulanova's performances in the parts of Juliet and Giselle became a real sensation. *Romeo and Juliet* by Leonid Lavrovsky was also a great success. British critics wrote that the Russians had managed to elevate the ballet to the level of one of Shakespeare's greatest tragedies. They also noted the strong continuity of the stage narration, which was not interrupted by striking dances or virtuoso pas having nothing to do with the plot. The best aspects of the drama-ballet influenced foreign ballet theater, and Lavrovsky's followers appeared in the west. Foreign companies began to tour Russia at the same time, and Russian dancers discovered many novelties and rediscovered things that had been forgotten long before. First, they were exposed to a great variety of ballet genres and styles. This familiarization with other performing trends and with the work of important western choreographers and dancers was especially fruitful because the new social climate in the country fomented freedom of artistic expression. This period, which was called "the thaw" in the USSR in contrast with "the winter" of Stalin's

totalitarianism, was imbued with a longing for rebirth. For the first time, after many years of severe ideological control, one could affirm the development of many trends in art, including ballet. Experimentation and the search for new forms and manifestations of one's artistic indentity were now possible. A struggle was unleashed against the clichés and dogmas that had shaped ballet during the

142. Alla Osipenko The Mistress of the Copper Mountain in the ballet *The Stone Flower* staged by Yuri Grigorovich

previous period. The choreography of the 1950s and 1960s reinforced its position in the polemics with the negative aspects of the drama-ballet, particularly with the underestimation of the expressive means of dance. After decades of drama-ballet, with its emphasis on the literary plot, music came to

143. In *The Legend of
Love*, classical dance
was colored with the
motifs of eastern
movements.

This scene shows the
young Princess Shirin
(Natalia
Bessmertnova) with
her maids in the
Bolshoi's production

the forefront. Discoveries made in ballet in the years to come were largely based on music. The development of symphonic dance, which had been cut short in the late 1920s, was resumed. The symphonic ballet was considered far from ambiguous. It could master the broadest range of figurative expression. Its characters could have strong traits of individuality or could be treated as multifaceted, generalized figures. Leningrad choreographers were the first to begin

Furthermore, in opposition to the well-established canons of drama-ballet, Leonid Jakobson tried to recover the poetry and meaning of classical dance in his ballet Shurale in the mid-1950s. Grigorovich closely followed both of them with his main theme, which was the complex interdependence of man and nature, and with his forms of expression, which included the interrelation of music and dance and the development of symphonic choreography. However, Grigo-

144. The collaboration of choreographer Oleg Vinogradov and the director Yuri Lyubimov led to the creation of bright stage metaphors in the ballet *Yaroslavna*.

Here, *"Prince Igor's Army Sets Off"*. Leningrad Maly Opera Theater.

innovating. Ironically, it was *The Stone Flower*, which had marked the end of the drama-ballet when it had been staged by Lavrovsky, that heralded the dawn of a new epoch in the Russian ballet when it was restaged by the young Yuri Grigorovich. However, Grigorovich's innovative activities were not entirely new. His *The Stone Flower* was based on forms created by Fedor Lopukhov in *The Ice Maiden* in the 1920s and further developed in *The Spring Fairy Tale* in the 1940s.

rovich also built upon the best achievements of the previous decades, including meaningful dramaturgy, a specific plot, and attention to psychology and his characters' inner life. In *The Stone Flower*, Pavel Bazhov narrated the story of Danila, a stonecutter from the Urals who abandons his bride Katerina and goes forever to the subterranean mine kingdom (as the Mistress of the Copper Mountain had ordered him) in search of the Stone Flower, the symbol of perfect beauty. However, Katerina

145. Igor Belsky (born 1925) followed the program of Dmitri Shostakovich's music for his ballet *The Eleventh Symphony*, but in developing the theme of the 1905 revolution, he elevated it to a commentary on revolution in general.

This scene is from the fourth part of the performance ("The Alarm"). Kirov Theater.

147

146. A scene from *Ivan the Terrible*. Tsar Ivan, his wife Anastasia, and the entire Russian nation celebrate victory over the Kazan Khan. Anastasia: Natalia Bessmertnova; Ivan: Yuri Vladimirov. Bolshoi Theater.

searches for Danila everywhere, and she is not afraid to descend into the Mistress's underground abode and to confront the enchantress. The love between Katerina and Danila touches the Mistress, and she sets the stonecutter free, even though he has learned the innermost secret of creativity. Bazhov's tale, with its truthfulness and fairy-tale qualities, as well as Sergei Prokofiev's profound, expressive music, enabled Grigorovich to develop a lyrical dance poem about the artist and the unending search of the secret of perfection in art. The images of the plot and the main idea of the production were explored only by means of dance.

Grigorovich's next ballet was *The Legend of Love*, based on a narrative poem by Nazym Hikmet about the beautiful queen Mehmene Bahnu, who sacrifices her beauty in order to save her young sister Shirin despite her tragic

147. According to one legend, Boris Godunov, in order to become Tsar of Russia, murdered the young heir Dmitry, Ivan the Terrible's son. In his choreographic tragedy *Tsar Boris*, Nikolai Boyarchikov presented a clever, powerful figure whose sense of guilt drove him to confusion and death.

Tsar Boris: Nikita Dolgushin. Leningrad Maly Opera Theater.

148. The roles of the Polovtsy soldiers in Yuri Grigorovich's *Spartacus* depicted a white-hot conflict between good and evil, between two spiritually and morally incompatible camps and two powerful, but antipathetic personalities. The luxurious and gloomy world of patriarchal Rome is depicted in the scene "Crassus' Feast".

love for the painter Ferkhad, Shirin's lover. This ballet became one of the most important works in Grigorovich's career and in the whole Russian choreographic theater of the 1960s. Grigorovich demonstrated his unique talent in ballet production and his ability to arrange mass ensembles using laconic means, but achieving a powerful emotional impact. His ability to develop his characters' inner transformations through changes in plastic expressions was especially noteworthy in this production. The productions of Igor Belsky stand in complete contrast to Grigorovich's. While Grigorovich was focused on the

complex and often contradictory inner worlds of his characters, Belsky tried to embody a single and deliberately exaggerated quality in each of his characters, sometimes developing it into a symbol. Hence, his characters did not have proper names but were called the Fisherman, the Beloved One, the One Who Lost Her Lover, etc. In the footsteps of Lopukhov's dance symphony *The Greatness of the Universe*, Belsky moved from a detailed plot in his choreography and replaced it with a vague outline of a situation. His productions were based on his understanding, and sometimes even his "feeling," of music.

Belsky's desire to reach the maximum generalization drew him to the genre of the ballet symphony.

In addition to Grigorovich and Belsky, the 1960s saw the return of Fedor Lopukhov, Kasyan Goleizovsky, and Leonid Jakobson to active artistic activity. Moreover, young choreographers such as Oleg Vinogradov, Natalia Kasatkina and Vladimir Vasilyev, Nikolai Boyarchikov, Igor Chernyshov, and Georgy Alexidze began working during this period. Each of them developed their own themes and possessed specific artistic features; however, all of them were similar in searching for enhanced dance expressiveness. The long-forgotten genres of the one-act ballet, the "poster ballet," the satirical ballet, the ballet symphony, and the choreographic miniature were revived. The language of classical dance was enriched: with all due respect to the classics, which have always been the foundation of Russian ballet, new dance trends were actively developed. The range of ballet topics was also expanded. The 1970s saw ballets on apparently non-ballet historical themes, in which a real historical figure was the central character. Russian choreographers turned their attention to the highlights of the

149. The tragic culmination of the ballet *Spartacus'* is Sparticus' death when he is impaled on sharp lances.

151

previous pages
150. Dmitry
Bryantsev's entry into
Moscow's
Stanislavsky and
Nemirovich-
Danchenko Musical
Theater led to a
considerable
renovation of the
repertoire. Bryantsev
brought with him
the spirit of
experimentation and
creative daring.

Here, the dancers of
the Leningrad
Ensemble Ballet
perform a scene from
Dmitry Briantsev's
ballet *The Scythians*.

151. Maya
Plisetskaya's first
attempt at
choreography was
*Anna Karenina,* based
on the novel by Lev
Tolstoy.

155

history of their homeland. Oleg Vinogradov's ballet *Yaroslavna* was the first production of this kind. It was based on the epic poem *The Lay of Igor's Campaign*, an outstanding work of ancient Russian culture that was written in the late twelfth century by an unknown author. It narrated the tragic campaign of Prince Igor of Novgorod-Seversky against the nomadic Polovtsy tribes, who periodically raided the Russian land. In developing the parts of the Russian characters, including Prince Igor, his wife Yaroslavna, and the soldiers of his army, Vinogradov turned to the movements of ancient Russian rites and to "free" dance. Bare-footed and clad in white

linen robes according to Russian traditions about warriors who were about to meet certain death, they moved in a smooth, but somewhat awkward, manner. In contrast, the Polovtsy, a dangerous and merciless enemy, moved with a unique boldness, originality, and expressiveness. The role of the Polovtsy's soldiers were danced by women using toe technique. The keen, sharp form of their movements, which was based on straight, oblong lines, and the concentration of the dancers in small groups created the image of an incomprehensible and hideous monster. *Yaroslavna* was soon followed by Grigorovich's *Ivan the Terrible*, which was about one of the most controversial figures in Russian history,

and Nikolai Boyarchikov's *Tsar Boris*, based on a tragedy by Alexander Pushkin about an episode from seventeen-century Russian history. In general, Russian ballet became more multi-colored, varied, and intense. However, dancers and choreographers were not completely satisfied. The structure of permanent theaters in Russia, with big (sometimes, enormous) ballet companies of over 250 members, could survive only by means of state subsidies, and they developed a tradition of big, expensive productions that demanded many rehearsals and prevented the quick development of their repertoires. A dancer had to wait a long time for new roles (even for minor parts) in the existing repertoire of major theaters such as the Bolshoi and Kirov Theaters, where there were many prominent dancers. Moreover, these companies were headed by chief choreographers who were appointed by the government and who did not like to invite guest choreographers. This contributed to the stagnation of these companies, which could merely develop the particular style of their art directors. Dancers, whose artistic careers are very short, were naturally unhappy about this situation. As a result of a conflict with the management of the Kirov, Rudolf Nureyev, one of the most brilliant dancers of the Leningrad school, left Russia and settled in Paris in 1961. He was followed by Natalia Makarova, Mikhail Baryshnikov, Alexander Godunov, and others. At that time, emigration meant the loss of all family links, of Soviet citizenship, and of the possibility of ever returning to Russia. On the other hand, Vladimir Vasilyev, Maya Plisetskaya, and Nikita Dolgushin responded to the situation differently. They began to stage ballets by themselves. Leonid Jakobson and Igor Moiseyev established new, independent ballet companies and staged choreographic miniatures. Later, at the end of the 1970s, this process was intensified. The number of these companies began to grow dramatically during

the period of Mikhail Gorbachev's perestroika. These small groups, with a specially chosen repertoire, toured the country and familiarized the inhabitants of distant towns with ballet. Among these companies, the State Classical Ballet Theater (headed by Natalia Kasatkina and Vladimir Vasilyev) and Boris Eifman's Modern Ballet Leningrad Company are especially noteworthy. The late

1980s also saw the formation of studios for free dance and modern dance, which developed entirely new dance languages composed by their art directors. As a result, the situation of Russian ballet today is complex and multidimensional. Since the 1970s, Russian choreographers have been working abroad more and more often. Grigorovich, Vinogradov, Plisetskaya,

Vasilyev, and others began to produce ballets, and head ballet companies, in the United States and Europe. Russian ballet teachers now work in all parts of the world. Russian dancers of the younger generation perform in many foreign ballet companies. All of this indicates the profound nature of the influence that Russian ballet had on world ballet in the 1980s and 1990s.

155. A scene from *The Magic Camisole*, a ballet based on a story by E. T. A. Hoffmann, at the Theater of Classical Ballet.

156. Vladimir
Malakhov (born
1968), a graduate of
the Moscow Ballet
School, performs the
miniature *Narcissus*
by Kasyan
Goleizovsky.

157. Stanislav Isayev (born 1956) was also a graduate of the Perm Ballet School. He combines a penetrating dramatic talent with high, free leaps, pure lines, soft movements, and native virtuosity. Here, he performs a pas de deux from *Le Corsaire.*

158. Among the new ballets of the 1980s, *Twelfth Night*, or *What You Will*, based on Shakespeare's comedy, by Boris Eifman was noted for its gay mischief.

# Great figures of Russian ballet

**BARYSHNIKOV,**
Mikhail Nikolayevich
(born January 27, 1948, in Riga).
*Dancer.*
Born into the family of an officer and a peasant's daughter. He began his professional studies at the Riga Ballet School, and in 1967 he graduated from the Leningrad Ballet School, where he had been a student of Alexander Pushkin. As an undergraduate, he won First Prize at the International Ballet Competition in Varna in 1966 by demonstrating the impeccable qualities of a classical dancer, a natural expressiveness of movement, and perfect technique in his pirouettes and jumps. At the beginning of his career, Baryshnikov seemed doomed to character parts by virtue of his appearance. However, he stubbornly rejected the comic parts that were predetermined by his height (5ft 4 1/2in) and youthful appearance.

159. Mikhail Baryshnikov in Leonid Jakobson's dance *Vestris*.

A strict regime and constant training enabled him to take on romantic parts. Later, his performance of Albert in *Giselle* became renowned. Baryshnikov was a soloist at the Kirov Theater from 1967 to 1974. His dance (which was bright, festive, unconstrained, bold, and unpredictable) imbued traditional parts with brilliance and novelty. Baryshnikov demonstrated his talent as an improvisor, parodist, and comedian in *Vestris*, which brought him the Gold Medal at the International Ballet Competition in Moscow in 1969. He affirmed an optimistic and joyful world outlook by means of irony. Baryshnikov participated in virtually all new theater productions of this period, dancing as Mercutio in *Romeo and Juliet*, Hamlet in *Hamlet*, Adam in *The Creation of the World*, and the Prince in *The Prince of Pagodas*. In 1974, after the Kirov Theater had toured in Canada, Baryshnikov chose

not to return to Russia; he explained that he wanted to control his artistic destiny himself. Baryshnikov was a soloist at the American Ballet Theater from 1974 to 1978. He was active both as a dancer of the classical repertoire and as a choreographer of *The Nutcracker*. Working there gave Baryshnikov access to modern ballet with its great variety of styles. He danced the principal parts in a number of ballets, including *Le Jeune Homme et la Mort*, *Les Patineurs*, *Medea*, *Le Sacre du Printemps*, *Hamlet*, *Connotations*, *Shadowplay*, and *Awakening*. While mastering this repertoire, Baryshnikov met the world's best choreographers, including George Balanchine, Roland Petit, Frederick Ashton, John Neumeier, Kenneth McMillan, and Jerome Robbins. In 1978-79, Baryshnikov was a soloist at the New York City Ballet, where he performed in Balanchine's ballets *Apollo*, *The Prodigal Son*, *Rubies*, *A Midsummer-Night's Dream*, *Orpheus*, *Harlequinade*, *La Somnambula*, etc. Baryshnikov toured broadly, danced in various companies and theaters, and acquired popularity throughout the world in those years. He was later appointed art director and leading dancer of the American Ballet Theater.

160. Mikhail Baryshnikov as the Young Man in *Gorianka*.

There he staged *Don Quixote*, *Cinderella*, and *Swan Lake*. At the age of 44, having undergone four leg operations, Baryshnikov began to master modern dance. As far back as 1976, the choreographer Twyla Tharp produced a ballet specially for Baryshnikov called *Push Comes to Shove*, which brought Baryshnikov his first success as a modern dancer. In 1990, Baryshnikov gathered a group of sixteen dancers into a company called The White Oak Dance Project. He continues to work with this group in the South of the United States. Baryshnikov has been filmed many times, including *The Turning Point*, *White Nights*, *Dancers*, and *The Cabinet of Dr. Ramirez*. He has also participated in a number of television programs, including *Baryshnikov on Broadway*, *Baryshnikov in Hollywood*, *Baryshnikov: The Dance and the Dancer* (a show with Liza Minelli and other stars), and *Metamorphosis*, a dramatic production on Broadway.

### BESSMERTNOVA,
Natalia Igorevna
(born July 19,1941, in Moscow).
*Ballerina, wife of Yuri Grigorovich.*
Bessmertnova has been working in the Bolshoi Theater ballet company since she graduated from the Moscow Ballet School in 1961, after studying under Maria Kozhukhova and Sophia Golovkina. Bessmertnova's debut in *Chopiniana* (*Les Sylphides*) shaped her career as a Romantic dancer. She seemed to be specially designed for Romantic ballet with her delicate figure; pensive and pathetic expression; and weightless, refined movements. Her Russian beauty was combined with a mysterious oriental charm. Moreover, her dance was refined and ornate in the oriental manner. That's why Bessmertnova was so attractive in *The Legend of Love*, *Leili and Medjnun*, and in Kasyan Goleizovsky's miniatures. Bessmertnova's special concentration on the spiritual aspect of dance enabled her to revive Romantic ballet traditions as she danced *Giselle* in 1963. This kind of lofty inspiration is typical of Bessmertnova's other parts as well. Despite some contrasts, her roles were united by their Romantic nature: Masha in *The Nutcracker*, Odette-Odile in *Swan Lake* (staged by

161. Natalia Bessmertnova as *Raymonda*.

Grigorovich), as well as parts having nothing to do with Romanticism, including Phrygia in *Spartacus*, Kitri in *Don Quixote* and Valentina in *Angara*. The ballerina's great musical gift is not limited to merely following music: instead, she perceives dance as a form of musical performance. Her manner (which is richly profound and even daring) seems like improvisation and is saturated with a great variety of expressive hues. Bessmertnova danced all of Grigorovich's ballets: *The Legend of Love*, *Spartacus*, *Romeo and Juliet*, and *The Golden Age*. Her repertoire also includes Maria in *The Fountain of Bakhchisarai* and the Girl in *Le Spectre de la Rose*. Bessmertnova's performance at the International Ballet competition in Varna in 1965 brought her the First Prize, and she was awarded the Anna Pavlova Prize in Paris in 1970. She has many state decorations and awards.

### BOYARCHIKOV,
Nikolai Nikolayevich
(born September 27,1935,
in Leningrad).
*Dancer and choreographer.*
Having graduated from the Leningrad Ballet School in 1954, where he had studied under Boris Shavrov, Boyarchikov began dancing at the Leningrad Maly Opera Theater. An interesting dancer with a great acting gift, Boyarchikov danced both classical and character parts. From the beginning of his performing career, he was interested in choreography. He graduated from the choreography department of the Leningrad Conservatory in 1967, after studying under Fedor Lopukhov and Igor Belsky. While still a student, Boyarchikov staged an optimistic and witty ballet entitled *The Three Musketeers*, after the novel by Alexandre Dumas. Boyarchikov was the chief

choreographer of the Perm Theater from 1971 to 1977, and, having developed a unique repertoire, he transformed this theater into one of the best ballet companies in the country. There he staged his version of *Romeo and Juliet* and *The Miraculous Mandarin*, produced the ballet *Tsar Boris* after a tragedy by Alexander Pushkin, staged a comic production of *A Servant of Two Masters* after Carlo Goldoni's play, and the rock ballet *Orpheus and Euridice*. As far back as Perm, Boyarchikov proved to be one of the most interesting new choreographers. He imbued each production with a unique artistic concept and a richness of expressive forms. Having been appointed the director of the ballet company of the Leningrad Maly Opera Theater (now, the Modest Mussorgsky Leningrad Opera and Ballet Theater) in 1977, Boyarchikov formulated the final concepts of his art. His work, like that of many of his predecessors, is based on classical literary works, and he strives to present the main idea and the essence of a literary work, rather than merely follow the plot. He focuses on his characters' inner world and on human psychology. The main theme of his ballets is the search for harmony in a world out of balance. Among these

works are *The Robbers*, based on the play by Friedrich Schiller; *A Marriage*, based on the comedy by Nikolai Gogol; *Macbeth*, based on the tragedy by William Shakespeare; *The Quiet Don* after the novel by Mikhail Sholokhov; and *Petersburg*, after the novel by Andrei Biely. Boyarchikov's position as one of the most consistent psychological choreographers of the Russian Ballet has been firmly established in the 1980s and 1990s.

**BRYANTSEV,**
Dmitry Alexandrovich

(born February 18, 1947, in Leningrad).
*Dancer and choreographer.*
After graduating from the Leningrad Ballet School (where he had been a student of Nikolai Zubkovsky), Bryantsev became a soloist of the dance company Young Ballet (since 1971, the Classical Ballet) and danced there from 1966 to 1976. However, after graduating from the choreographic department of the Moscow Institute of Theater Art (GITIS) in 1976, he devoted all his time and energy to producing dances. Bryantsev became famous through his television ballets *Galatea* (after *My Fair Lady*, a musical by Frederick Low) and *The Old Tango* (based on *Peter*, a film comedy that was popular in the 1940s). Yekaterina Maximova danced in both of these ballets. With these productions, Bryantsev demonstrated his talent for comedy and a real feeling for the genre and style of television ballet, which favors action dance and the development of garish and, even, grotesque characters. He continued to work in comedy with his next ballet at the Kirov Theater: *The Hussar Ballad*, staged after a play about Nadezhda Durova, a historical figure who disguised herself as a hussar and

162. A scene from Nikolai Boyarchikov's production of Petersburg. Gali Abaidulov as Apollon Ableukhov.

163. A scene from Nikolai Boyarchikov's production of *Macbeth*.

participated in the war against Napoleon. Between 1981 and 1985, Bryantsev was a choreographer at the Kirov Theater. There he staged his versions of *The Little Humpbacked Horse*; *The Passions of Seville*, or *Bravo, Figaro!*, a ballet paraphrase of Gioacchino Rossini's opera *The Barber of Seville*; and *Nine Tangos and... Bach*. Bryantsev has been the chief choreographer of the Stanislavsky and Nemirovich-Danchenko Musical Theater in Moscow since 1985. He strives here for diversity in the repertoire, staging comedies (such as *The Cowboys*), lyrical productions (including *The Swan's Song*, *Cranes*, and *The Lone Human Voice*), and even tragedies (like *An Optimistic Tragedy*). He also choreographs dances on the music of various composers. A leading choreographer of our time, Bryantsev has a fertile imagination and incessantly enriches the forms of ballet with elements of popular and variety show dances, free dance, and folklore. He has been teaching at the choreographic department of GITIS since 1986.

## SHELEST,
Alla Yakovlevna
(born February 26, 1919, in Smolensk).
*Ballerina and teacher.*
Shelest studied at the Leningrad Ballet School under Yelizaveta Gerdt until she was 15; later, she studied under Agrippina Vaganova. After graduating in 1937, she joined the Kirov Theater. However, Shelest's life was particularly unlucky. In the words of the choreographer Fedor Lopukhov, "for sixteen years, she was doomed to understudy" Natalia Dudinskaya, who reigned supremely at the theater. Occasionally, however, she was able to attain real perfection in secondary roles such as a wicked stepsister in Konstantin Sergeyev's *Cinderella*. However, Shelest eventually became one of the most outstanding dancers of the twentieth century. With her gift for tragedy, highly developed intellect, and audacity, Shelest created psychologically complex characters. Her heroines (such as Laurencia, Zarema, and Baroness Strahl in *The Masquerade*) are generally strong personalities, passionate, strong-willed,

rebellious, and torn apart by inner contradictions. She was attracted by Leonid Jakobson's ballets, and the part of Aegina in his *Spartacus* was one of her chefs-d'œuvre. Shelest saw in this insidious and seductive courtesan, who disposes lightly of other people's destinies, a symbol of Rome's power and its tragic emptiness. The lack of pointe technique in this ballet gave the performer a chance to concentrate on expressive movements and postures and to develop the psychological content of each gesture. Yakobson created *The Eternal Idol* specially for Shelest. She also performed in Yuri Grigorovich's ballets: Katerina and the Mistress of the Copper Mountain in *The Stone Flower* and Mekhmene Bahnu in *The Legend of Love*. She worked on her parts as would a stage director, going into every detail in order to reach

a perfection of pattern. Shelest began to teach in 1952, initially at the Leningrad Ballet School and later at the Kirov Theater and the Leningrad Conservatory. She also taught in Hungary and Italy. In 1981, she was a coach at the Estonian Theater Vanemuine in Tartu and, in 1989, at the Leningrad Ballet Theater under Boris Blankov. She has worked as a choreographer and stage director in many companies, in particular as chief choreographer of the Kuibyshev Theater from 1970 to 1973. In 1989, Shelest danced in the feature film *Prishvin's Paper Eyes*.

## DOLGUSHIN,
Nikita Alexandrovich
(born November 8,1938, in Leningrad).
*Dancer, choreographer, and teacher.*
Born into an artistic family, Dolgushin inherited a striking musical gift from his mother, who was an opera singer. Against his parents' wishes, he decided to become a dancer and was enrolled in the Leningrad Ballet School at the age of twelve. There he was a student of Valentin Shelkov, Boris Shavrov, and Alexander Pushkin. After graduation. Dolgushin worked at the Kirov Theater from 1959 to 1961. He performed his first solo part as a Satyr in *Spartacus* while still a student. During his two years at the

164. A scene from Dmitry Bryantsev's revival of *Le Corsaire*.

165. A scene from Dmitry Bryantsev's *The Little Humpbacked Horse*.

Kirov, Dolgushin danced Albert in
*Giselle*, the Prince in *The Nutcracker*,
Smith in *The Path of Thunder*, and
the Poet in *Chopiniana* (*Les Sylphides*).
His career seemed to be progressing
successfully; however, a longing for
something new motivated Dolgushin
to leave the country's best ballet
company and go to the provincial
city of Novosibirsk, where the young
choreographer Oleg Vinogradov was
beginning his work. Dolgushin created
the parts of the Prince in *Cinderella*
and Romeo in *Romeo and Juliet* in
Vinogradov's productions; he also
danced leading parts in classical ballets.
In 1964, Dolgushin won first prize
at the International Ballet Competition
in Varna, in 1966, he was awarded a
prize at the Festival "Quartier du
Marais" in Paris and a Diploma of
Honor by the Paris Dance University.
He worked at the newly formed
Moscow Young Ballet Company
from 1966 to 1968, and many talented
choreographers produced their ballets
there. Dolgushin worked at the
Leningrad Maly Opera Theater from
1968 to 1982. There he danced Colin,
Franz, and Prince Igor in Vinogradov's
new versions of *La Fille Mal Gardée*,
*Coppélia*, and *Yaroslavna*, respectively. He also danced the Tutor in *A
Pedagogical Poem* by Leonid Lebedev,
Karl Moor in *The Robbers* by Nikolai
Boyarchikov, as well as other roles. He
also danced with other ballet companies
and had a great number of recitals.
Dolgushin is a refined and elegant
performer. His dancing style is
noble; his technique impeccable; and

his interpretation demonstrates a lofty,
inner culture and, according to one
critic, "intellectual charm." Dolgushin's
incessant quest for innovation led him
to develop his own choreography,
and he dances in his own productions.
An adherent of academic ballet and a
choreographer endowed with a keen
sense of style, Dolgushin successfully
revives classical ballets. Dolgushin has
been teaching at the Chair of
Choreography at the Leningrad
Conservatory since 1983. He is also
the art director of the ballet company
of the Conservatory Opera Studio,
renamed the Music Theater of the St.
Petersburg Conservatory in 1991,
where he sometimes produces ballets
and dances. Several films by the
Leningrad Television Company have
been dedicated to his career.

## EIFMAN,
Boris Yakovlevich
(born July 22, 1945, in Rubuevsk,
Altai Region).
*Dancer and choreographer.*
Eifman graduated from the Kishinev
Ballet School in 1964 and from the
choreographic department of the
Leningrad Conservatory in 1972. At
the Conservatory, he had been a student
of Georgy Alexidze. As a dancer,
Eifman did not perform much because
he was more attracted to choreography.
He produced ballets at the Leningrad
Ballet School from 1970 to 1977.
During this period, Eifman was a
choreographer with the ballet company
of the Opera Studio under the

Leningrad Conservatory. There he
staged his versions of *Gayane* and
*Firebird*. Eifman has been the art
director and a choreographer of the
Leningrad New Ballet (now, the St.
Petersburg Ballet Theater) since 1977;
there he built an original repertoire.
According to Eifman's approach, when
transferring literary works to the stage,
a choreographer must focus on the
characters' relations and need not
merely allude to the plot of the work
in question. The characters' features
and, thus, the meaning of the work,
are explored by a complex dance
polyphony. Eifman staged *The
Boomerang* (after works by Berthold
Brecht), *The Idiot* (after Fedor
Dostoyevsky), *Twelfth Night* (after
William Shakespeare), *The Master
and Margarita* (after Mikhail Bulgakov),
*The Murderers* (after Emile Zola's *Thérèse
Raquin*), and *The Legend* and *Junior
Lieutenant Romashov* (after Alexander
Kuprin). A belief in the transforming
power of love is a major theme in
Eifman's artistic activities. Eifman's
productions always have a solid
structure; he exploits the forms and
expressive means proper to modern
ballet. His ballets (whether in one or
many acts) and his dances are always
brilliant theater, and this requires both
dance technique and dramatic skill
from his dancers. Using classical dance
as a basis, Eifman mixes in elements
of modern and jazz dance, folk and
historical dances and also mime in
the spirit of the German "Tanztheater."
He also uses grotesque, slapstick
techniques from folk street theater and
acrobatics. Eifman has a keen sense
of musical structure and the means
of music's emotional and philosophical
character. He generally uses music that
was not originally intended for
ballet.

## GODUNOV,
Alexander Borisovich
(born November 28,1949, in
Yuzhno-Sakhalinsk).
*Dancer.*
Godunov graduated from the Riga
Ballet School in 1968. A tall young
man in blue jeans with a careless mane
of blond hair and an unapproachable
look, he seemed to be a proud and
reserved person. However, he

transfigured himself on stage into a classic prince with knightly elegance, a dancer with a unique magnificence of lines, an enormous developpé, and a light leap. He was soon noticed by Igor Moiseyev, who invited him to join the newly formed Young Ballet Company. Godunov danced there from 1967 to 1971. Then Grigorovich invited him to work at the Bolshoi Theater, where he danced from 1971 to 1979. From the first days of his work at the theater, Godunov was trained by Alexei Yermolayev, who coached many Russian ballet stars. Godunov has a unique style, dance technique, and feeling for his partner. He maintains the expressive impulses and refined classical canons of harmony. His dance, which combines traits of the St. Petersburg and Moscow schools, is characterized by a perfection of form accompanied by virtuoso technique. His repertoire included the main characters of *Swan Lake* and the tragedy *Ivan the Terrible*. He also danced an elegy of poetic dreams in *Chopiniana* (*Les Sylphides*) and dramatic passions in *Carmen Suite*, as well as the rigid classics of the "Act of Shadows" from *La Bayadère* and the spontaneous power of *The Rite of Spring*. He offered a profound interpretation of his part in *La Rose Malade*, which he danced with Maya Plisetskaya. He was awarded the Gold Medal at the International Ballet Competition in Moscow in 1973 and was awarded the Vaslav Nijinsky Prize in Paris. In 1979, Godunov visited the United States with the Bolshoi Theater and decided to remain there. His last part at the Bolshoi was Tybalt in *Romeo and Juliet*, choreographed by Grigorovich specially for Godunov. Godunov was the first Bolshoi dancer to emigrate, which required tremendous courage at that time and led to many troubles for his family. The poet Joseph Brodsky helped him greatly during that period. During his first years in emigration, Godunov was a guest artist in various European, Australian, and Argentinian companies. His partner was Eva Yevdokimova. From 1980 to 1982, he was a soloist at the American Ballet Theater Company on the invitation of Mikhail Baryshnikov. His meeting with the Hollywood star Jacqueline Bisset utterly changed his life. He appeared in the Hollywood film *Die Hard*. Godunov lives in Los Angeles and continues to act in films.

### GOLOVKINA,
Sofia Nikolayevna
(born October 13, 1915, in Moscow).
*Ballerina and teacher.*
After graduating from the Moscow Ballet School (where she had been a

168. A scene from Boris Eifman's *The Master and Margarita*.

169. Alexander Godunov in *La Rose Malade*.

student of Alexander Chekrygin), Golovkina worked at the Bolshoi Theater from 1933 to 1959. There she danced parts from the classical repertoire, including Odette-Odile in *Swan Lake*, Aurora in *The Sleeping Beauty*, the Tsar-maiden in *The Little Humpbacked Horse*, and Kitri in *Don Quixote*. She also appeared in modern ballets, dancing Tao Hoa in *The Red Poppy* and Zarema in *The Fountain of Bakhchisarai*. Golovkina's dance style featured passion and a swift tempo. She has been a director and a teacher of classical dance at the Moscow Ballet School since 1960. Natalia Bessmertnova, Nina Sorokina, Alla Mikhalchenko, Galina Stepanenko, and Nadezhda Gracheva were among her students. Golovkina established a ballet school in Tokyo in 1985. She has been director of the Moscow Choreographic Institute, which she founded, since 1988. She revived *Coppélia* and *La Fille Mal Gardée* (both in cooperation with Maxim Martirosyan and Alexander Radunsky), *A Small Symphony*, and *Ballet Class* on the stage of the Bolshoi Theater. Golovkina also wrote scripts for ballet training films, including *The Basics of Classical Dance* and *Stage Practice*.

170. Vyacheslav Gordeyev as Romeo in *Romeo and Juliet*.

**GORDEYEV**
Vyacheslav Mikhailovich
(born August 3, 1948, in Moscow).
*Dancer and choreographer.*
Since his graduation from the Moscow Ballet School (where he was a student of Piotr Pestov) in 1968, Gordeyev has worked at the Bolshoi Theater. A classical dancer, Gordeyev possesses a broad range of expressive means, an impeccable technique, and an outstanding musical gift. He thoroughly polishes each pas until it attains maximal expressiveness. As a result, the garishness of his movements is overwhelming. Like an arrow shot from a bow by a mighty hand, Gordeyev rushes onto the stage as Désiré in *The Sleeping Beauty*. He excelled in *Swan Lake*, *The Nutcracker*, *Don Quixote*, *Spartacus*, *The Legend of Love*, and other ballets. He was a permanent partner of Nadezhda Pavlova from the mid-1970s until the mid-1980s. Their duet was extremely popular. Gordeyev began to choreograph in 1981 at the Ensemble of the Russian Ballet (later, the Russian Ballet Company) and became its art director in 1984. This small, mobile company tours many cities and countries, performing on different stages and giving preference to programs of dances and choreographic miniatures, sometimes presenting

abridged versions of popular ballets. Gordeyev occasionally dances with this company. He won the first prize at the International Ballet Competition in Moscow in 1973.

**GRIGOROVICH,**
Yuri Nikolayevich
(born January 2, 1927, in Leningrad).
*Choreographer.*
After graduating from the Leningrad Ballet School (where he had been a student of Boris Shavrov and Alexei Pisarev), Grigorovich became a soloist at the Kirov Theater, where he danced such character parts as Nurali in *The Fountain of Bakhchisarai*, Shurale

171. Sofia Golovkina in class at the Moscow Ballet School.

in *Shurale*, Severyan in *The Stone Flower*, and others. He staged his first productions in 1948 at a children's amateur dance studio, presenting *A Storkling* and *Seven Brothers*. Grigorovich's productions of *The Stone Flower* in 1957 and *The Legend of Love* in 1961 at the Kirov Theater were outstanding events. Though both were story ballets with strongly built plots and a strictly psychological presentation of the characters, they were very different from the drama-ballets of the previous period because the choreographer turned to dance structures and revived complex ballet forms in order to achieve a deeper union of choreography and music. Classical dance, enriched with elements of other dance systems including folk dance, was the basis of Grigorovich's choreography. Mime was absent as an independent phenomenon, and its elements were organically incorporated into dance. The complex forms of symphonic dance reached a high level of development (for instance, the fair in *The Stone Flower* and the

procession and the vision of Mehmene Bahnu in *The Legend of Love*). From 1962 to 1964, Grigorovich worked as a choreographer at the Kirov Theater. In 1964, he was appointed chief choreographer of the Bolshoi Theater. Grigorovich reached new heights in his artistic achievements with *Spartacus*, staged in 1968. He based his production on ensemble dance scenes that expressed the highlights of the plot (such as the invasion or uprising) and that were combined with dance monologues by the principal characters. *Ivan the Terrible*, a ballet about a difficult period in Russian history, was also based on these artistic concepts. *Angara*, about the country's present-day young generation, featured classical dance enriched with elements of folk and popular dances, free plastics, mime, and movements borrowed from calisthenics. These were forged into a single choreographic unit. Grigorovich also staged *The Golden Age*, in which he used ballroom dances such as the tango, foxtrot, and

Charleston, to recreate the atmosphere of the 1920s. Grigorovich's stagings of classical ballets, including *The Sleeping Beauty*, *Swan Lake*, and *Raymonda*, are also important: he modernized them to meet the requirements of our time but still kept most of the original choreography intact. However, Grigorovich produced a completely new *The Nutcracker*, based on Tchaikovsky's unabridged and unaltered score. Using the same aesthetic concepts, Grigorovich produced *Romeo and Juliet* for the Opéra de Paris in 1978, incorporating into Sergei Prokofiev's score some hitherto unknown music from the composer's archives. Grigorovich produced ballets on many other Russian and foreign stages. Grigorovich has been a professor of choreography of the Leningrad Conservatory since 1973. He was President of the Dance Committee of the International Theater Institute from 1975 to 1985. He was appointed head of the Choreography Department of the Moscow Choreographic

172. A scene from Yuri Grigorovich's *The Golden Age*

previous pages
173. A scene from
*Nutcraker* by Youri
Grigorovitch

Institute in 1988. He has been President of the Dance Association since 1989 and President of the Russian Ballet Foundation since 1990. He became the artistic director of the Yuri Grigorovich Ballet Company in 1991.

## JACOBSON,

Leonid Veniaminovich
(born January I 5, 1904, in St. Petersburg; died October 17,1975, in Moscow and buried in St. Petersburg).
*Dancer and choreographer.*
After graduating from the Leningrad Ballet School (where he had been a student of Vladimir Ponomarev), Jacobson was a dancer at the Leningrad Opera and Ballet Theater from 1926 to 1933. There he performed small classical grotesque parts. He started composing dances as a student and staged the second act of *The Golden Age* at the theater in 1930. He then created ballets for various companies, including *Till Eulenspiegel* after Charles De Coster, *Lost Illusions* after Honoré de Balzac, *Shurale* after a Tatar fairy-tale, *Solveig* after *Peer Gynt* by Henrik Ibsen, *Spartacus*, *The Bedbug* after a play by Vladimir Mayakovsky, *The Country of Wonders*, etc. A follower of Michel Fokine, Jacobson also "went against the current." As a young man, he rejected classical dance. He affirmed the drama-ballet, but, in contrast to the dominant principles of the time, he turned to dance to develop the plots of his ballets. Having returned to classical dance in his maturity, Jacobson modernized it in order to convey contemporary ideas. Evil and social vices as objects of ridicule and condemnation were to become Jacobson's lifelong theme. On the other hand, his positive characters were often presented as fairy-tale knights or were exaggerated. Jacobson's preferred artistic form is what we call the "choreographic miniature" (dance or short ballet). The content of his dances is varied: scenes from Russian fairy-tales (*The Snow Maiden*, *Firebird*, or *Baba Yaga*); sculptures by Auguste Rodin (*Eternal Spring*, *The Kiss*, or *The Eternal Idol*), genre scenes (*Merry Wives*, *Troika*, and *A Village Don Juan*); and lyrical scenes – *A Dream*

174. A scene from
Leonid Jakobson's
*Mozartiana.*

172

or *Meeting*). The best dances were combined to form a program called *Choreographic Miniatures*, which was staged at the Kirov Theater and was awarded the Gold Nymph Prize in Monte Carlo in 1961. The author himself was conferred a Diploma of the Paris University of Dance.

In 1969, Jacobson was instrumental in establishing the Leningrad Choreographic Miniatures Company, and he became its first art director. Here his old dances were revived, and he produced new ones especially for this company, including *Taglioni's Flight*, *The Minotaur and the Nymph*, *Paolo and Francesca*, *A Travelling Circus*, *An Exercise of the Twentieth Century*, *A Wedding Cortege*, *Mozartiana*, *Hiroshima*, and *A Crazy Dictator*. After Jacobson's death, this company was directed by Askold Makarov, an outstanding dancer from the Kirov Theater. The Jacobson Foundation has established the Kirov Theater Young Ballet Company within the Kirov Theater, and it is devoted to reviving and presenting the choreographer's heritage.

### KASATKINA,
Natalia Dmitrievna
(born June 7, 1934, in Moscow).
*Ballerina and choreographer.*
Having graduated from the Moscow Ballet School in 1953, Kasatkina was a character dancer at the Bolshoi Theater from 1954 to 1976. However, she began to choreograph in 1960 with her husband, Vladimir Vasilyev, who was born February 8, 1931 and was a dancer at the Bolshoi Theater from 1949 to 1970. Their first ballets, *Vanina Vanini* (after a short story by Stendhal), *A Heroic Poem* (*Geologists*), and *The Rite of Spring*, were staged at the Bolshoi Theater. Later, they produced *The Creation of the World*, after satirical drawings by the French painter Jean Effel, and the vocal and choreographic symphony *Pushkin: Reflections on the Poet* at the Kirov Theater and worked in other theaters around the country. But their artistic activities are connected mostly with the Classical Ballet Company (today called the State Classical Ballet Theater), which they have headed since 1977. They revive their former productions, such as *The Tale of*

175. Natalia Kasatkina as the Possessed One in *The Rite of Spring*.

*Romeo and Juliet*, and stage new ones specially for the company, including *Gayane*, *The Magic Camisole*, (after Ernst Hoffmann's tale *Klein Zaches gennaut Zinnober*), a ballet comedy *Terpsichore's Pranks*, and their own version of *Le Baiser de la Fée*. The productions of Kasatkina and Vasilyev are solidly built. Their choreography is based upon a combination of the classical and modern dance. For their company, they also staged new versions of classical ballets such as *Swan Lake*, *Don Quixote*, and *Giselle*. Pierre Lacotte, a guest choreographer from France, revived for them *Natalie, ou La Laitière Suisse* by Filippo Taglioni. In this touring company, a lot of attention is paid to individual dancers. It is here that many talents have developed, such as that of Irek Mukhamedov, Stanislav Isayev, Galina Shlyapina, and Vladimir Malakhov.

### KOLPAKOVA,
Irina Alexandrovna
(born May 22, 1933, in Leningrad).
*Ballerina and teacher.*
Kolpakova graduated from the Leningrad Ballet School in 1951, where she had been the last student of Agrippina Vaganova. While still a student, she danced the part of the Fairy Fleur de Farine in *The Sleeping Beauty* at the Kirov Theater. In her graduation performance, she demonstrated an elegant dancing style and confident technique. Kolpakova's beauty and excellent training, her elevation, the grace of her poses, and her brilliant footwork quickly enabled her to dance solos and principal roles in the classical repertoire. She soon starred in *Chopiniana* (*Les Sylphides*), *The Nutcracker*, and *Cinderella*, where she could manifest the lyrical nature of her gift. Kolpakova was outstanding as Aurora in *The Sleeping*

176. A scene from *The Creation of the World*, produced by Natalia Kasatkina and Vladimir Vasilyov.

*Beauty*, Raymonda, Giselle, and Sylphide. She had a keen feeling for poetry and style, as well as noble simplicity. Although Kolpakova was brought up on the academic traditions of Marius Petipa's ballet aesthetics, she also excelled in modern choreography. She danced lyrical parts in ballets by Yuri Grigorovich (Katerina in *The Stone Flower* and Shyrin in *The Legend of Love*), Igor Chernyshov (Juliet in *Romeo and Juliet*), and Oleg Vinogradov (the Fairy in *The Fairy of the Rondo Mountains*). She also danced Desdemona in *Othello* by Vakhtang Chabukiani, His Beloved One in Igor Belsky's *The Coast of Hope*, and other roles in ballets by choreographers belonging to a number of trends and styles. They were attracted to Kolpakova because of the harmony of her dance and her sensitivity and refined taste. Kolpakova has been filmed in several television ballets. She has been a coach at the American Ballet Theater since 1989. In addition to a number of top decorations and titles from her own country, she won the Grand Prix of the Vienna Dance Festival in 1959, the Gold Star of the International Dance Festival in Paris in 1965, and the Anna Pavlova Prize of the Paris Dance Academy in 1982.

**KOMLEVA,**
Gabriela Trofimovna
(born December 27,1938, in Leningrad).
*Ballerina and teacher.*
Komleva graduated in 1957 from the Leningrad Ballet School, where she had been a student of Vera Kostrovitskaya and Varvara Mei, and began working at the Kirov Theater. She continued to dance there until 1988. Having absorbed the best traditions of the Leningrad academic school, Komleva acquired a serene self-confidence: her dance was pure and technically perfect. With an infallible sense of style and music, Komleva became an ideal performer of the classical repertoire. Her dramatic quality was initially brought out only in modern productions, including ballets by Igor Belsky, Yuri Grigorovich, and Oleg Vinogradov. She created several dramatic parts, including The One Who Lost Her Beloved in *The Coast of Hope*, Mehkmene Bahnu in *The Legend of Love*, and Asiyat in *The Girl from the Mountains*. She also danced character parts. Gradually building up her repertoire, Komleva attained a harmony between technical perfection and

artistic interpretation, combining academic style with romantic passion. The part of Nikia in *La Bayadère* became a highlight of her artistic career. She danced Giselle, Sylphide, Aurora, and Odette-Odile while also participating in ballet experiments and working with contemporary choreographers including Georgy Alexidze, Mai Murdmaa, and Boris Eifman. She performed in ballets by Jose Limon, George Balanchine, and Roland Petit. She also had a broad repertoire of recital dances. Komleva's artistic career has been the subject of the television films *Images of Dance* (1974) and *Gabriela Komleva Dances* (1971). She also participated in television versions of *La Bayadère*, *Cinderella*, *The Moor's Pavane*, Eifman's *Firebird* and others. Komleva has been teaching since 1971, initially at the Leningrad Ballet School and Kirov Theater and later at the Leningrad Conservatory. She produced a series of programs under the title *Terpsichore's Teachings* for the Leningrad television company between 1985 and 1989.

**LAVROVSKY,**
Mikhail Leonidovich
(born October 29,1941, in Tbilisi).

177. Irina Kolpakova as Aurora and Sergei Berezhnoy as Prince Désiré in *The Sleeping Beauty*.

*Dancer and choreographer.*

A son of the famous choreographer Leonid Lavrovsky and of Yelena Chikvaidze, a ballerina of the Bolshoi Theater. Lavrovsky was raised in an atmosphere imbued with ballet, music, and theater. In 1961, he graduated from the Moscow Ballet School, where he had been a student of Nikolai Tarasov, one of the best Moscow teachers. He was invited to join the Bolshoi Theater, where he danced under the guidance of Alexei Yermolayev. Lavrovsky's first major part was Philippe in *The Flames of Paris*. He won the Gold Medal at the Dance Competition in Varna in 1965, and in 1972, he won the Vaslav Nijinsky Prize of the Paris Dance Academy. A classical dancer with an inclination for romantic and tragic roles, Lavrovsky danced many classical roles: Blue Bird in *The Sleeping Beauty*, Albert in *Giselle*, Basil in *Don Quixote*, and Siegfried in *Swan Lake*. He also appeared in modern ballets: Kais in *Leili and Medjnun*, Ferkhad in *The Legend of Love*, and the title roles of *Spartacus* and *Ivan the Terrible*. He danced Romeo in *Romeo and Juliet* and Paganini in *Paganini*, both of which were choreographed by his father. Lavrovsky created the parts of Viktor

in *Angara* and Artynov in *Anyuta*. Courteous and attentive in duets and unrestrained in variations, Lavrovsky embodied the best traditions of the Russian school. His dynamic dance was imbued with heroic intonations, inner expressiveness, and a sincerity of

feeling. In his dance, Lavrovsky reckoned with existing traditions but rejected clichés and often shocked the public with his innovative interpretations. In many of his roles, he stressed inner disharmony (Albert, Spartacus, Ivan the Terrible, and Ferkhad). Lavrovsky graduated from the choreographic department of GITIS in 1979 and was the art director of the Paliashvili Theater ballet company in Tbilisi from 1981 to 1985. There, he produced *Romeo and Juliet* and a jazz ballet called *Porgy and Bess*, based on the well-known opera by Benjamin Britten. Lavrovsky also appeared in and produced many television ballets. Lavrovsky was invited to the United States in 1987, where he staged *Bach's Second Suite for Flute* at the Arizona Ballet (Phoenix) and *Variations on the Theme of Casanova* in Atlanta in 1989.

## LIEPA,

Maris (Maris-Rudolf)
(Born July 27,1936, in Riga; died March 26, 1989, in Moscow).
*Dancer, choreographer, and teacher.*

Liepa's father was an opera singer in Riga, and Liepa was enrolled in a children's choir because he had a good voice. However, his mother was fond

178. A scene from The Story of *Romeo and Juliet*, produced by Natalia Kasatkina and Vladimir Vasilyev.

of ballet and insisted that he enter the Riga Ballet School. He performed a pas de trois from *The Nutcracker* in 1950 at a school recital. Liepa's slender body and well-developed torso, his blond hair and expressive blue eyes made him perfectly suited for the stage. Agrippina Vaganova, a well-known teacher who attended the concert, noticed him, and this was a turning point in his life. He was transferred to the Moscow Ballet School, where he was tutored by Nikolai Tarasov and from which he graduated in 1955. Liepa was a soloist at the Moscow Stanislavsky and Nemirovich-Danchenko Musical Theater from 1956 to 1960 and at the Bolshoi Theater from 1960 to 1984. One of the best classical dancers, Liepa built a repertoire of romantic roles including Siegfried in *Swan Lake*, Albert in *Giselle*, Jean de Brienne in *Raymonda*, Vaslav in *The Fountain of Bakhchisarai*, and the male part in *Le Spectre de la Rose*. While performing these parts, Liepa stressed their psychology and drama. His acting, a careful study of every detail of the part, made Liepa one of the most exciting "dancing actors" of the ballet theater. Liepa was an excellent partner and a real knight to his lady. He was strong, sensitive, and attentive. Liepa had dreamed of dancing Siegfried since he was ten years old, and he danced it for the first time in 1961 with Maya Plisetskaya. Liepa was awarded the Vaslav Nijinsky Prize in 1971 by the Dance Academy in Paris for his

performance as Albert. The climax of Liepa's artistic career was Crassus in *Spartacus*. This is one of the greatest male characters ever created. Crassus was merciless in his malice and hatred. The Dance Academy in Paris conferred the Marius Petipa Prize to Liepa for this role. Having retired from the Bolshoi Theater, Liepa headed the People's Opera in Sofia in 1984-85 and staged productions in Moscow, Riga, Leningrad, and Dnepropetrovsk. He participated in the television ballets *Hamlet* and *Galatea* and in feature films as a dramatic actor. He made plans to create a rock opera theater. Richly endowed by nature, Liepa was a good painter and sculptor and was the champion of Latvia in swimming several times. He taught at the Moscow Ballet School from 1963 to 1989. He published a book entitled *Ballet Today and Tomorrow*, in which he reflected on the future of choreography. In 1971, Liepa was proclaimed the best dancer in the world by the Dance Academy in Paris. He won all the most prestigious national decorations. His children, Ilse and Andris Liepa, have become famous solo dancers of the Bolshoi Theater. Liepa often published articles in the mass media and gave many interviews, sometimes using the title "I want to dance for one hundred years." However, this was not his fate: he died at the age of fifty-three.

**MAKAROVA,**

Natalia Romanovna (born November 21,1940, in Leningrad).
*Ballerina.*
Having graduated from the Leningrad Ballet School in 1959 after studying with Yevgenia Shiripina, Makarova began working at the Kirov Theater. After a triumphant performance as Giselle, she was promoted to leading dancer. She was awarded the Gold Medal at the International Ballet Competition in

179. Gabriela Komleva in *Firebird*.

180. Maris Liepa as Bacchus in the ballet scene "Walpurgisnacht" in the opera *Faust* by Gounod.

Varna in 1965. Her unique dancing quality and perfect technique shaped Makarova's artistic style. Her dancing surprised audiences by its unusual nuances and unexpected movements. Ballet critics compared her with Giulietta Masina. Roles from the classical repertoire looked strangely new in Makarova's performance. She gave a very personal interpretation to Romantic characters such as Giselle, Odette-Odile in *Swan Lake*, and Sylphide. In modern ballets danced by Makarova, there is often bitterness and tragic foreboding. In 1970, when the theater was touring London, Makarova decided to stay in the West. She danced there with the best companies of Europe and America, including the Royal Ballet in London, the American Ballet Theater, Le Ballet du XXme Siècle, and the Stuttgart Ballet; she worked with choreographers Jerome Robbins, Maurice Béjart, John Neumeier, John Cranko, and others. She danced in

181. Mikhail Lavrovsky as Ferkhad in *The Legend of Love*.

*Romeo and Juliet*, *Manon Lescaut*, *Onegin*, *Epilogue*, *A Month in the Country*, and *Le Jeune Homme et la Mort*. In 1980, Makarova revived *La Bayadère* for the American Ballet Theater using Marius Petipa's choreography. This production was subsequently included in the repertoire of the Swedish Royal Ballet and La Scala. She also revived *Swan Lake* for the London Festival Ballet Company in 1986 and the third act of *Paquita* for the American Ballet Theater and the National Canadian Ballet in 1984 and 1991, respectively. In 1983, Makarova participated in the Broadway musical *On the Toes* by George Abbott: she was awarded a Tony Award as the Best Actress in a Musical in 1983. Makarova left the ballet stage in 1989 but continued to dance in concerts. She debuted as a dramatic actress in 1991 at the London Piccadilly Theater in the comedy *Tovarich* by Jacques Deval. She performed in Moscow in 1992 with Roman Viktiuk's company in *Two for the Seesaw* by William Gibson. A number of BBC television films have been devoted to Makarova, including *Assoluta*, *Makarova Returns*, and *The Legend of Leningrad*. She wrote the script and narrated the four-part BBC program *Ballerina* in 1987.

Makarova described her difficult life in her autobiography, which was published in New York in 1979.

## MAXIMOVA,
Yekaterina Sergeyevna
(born February 1, 1939, in Moscow).
*Ballerina and teacher.*
Maximova wa still a little girl when Vasily Tikhomirov predicted her bright future in the theater. She was enrolled in the Moscow Ballet School and while still in the second grade, she danced on the stage of the Bolshoi Theater as the Squirrel in *Morozko* and was noticed by both the public and the critics. A year before graduating, she successfully performed Masha in *The Nutcracker*. After graduating from the school in 1958 (she had studied under Yelizaveta Gerdt), Maximova began working at the Bolshoi Theater. Her first major part was Katerina in *The Stone Flower* in 1959. At this time, the golden duet of Maximova and her husband Vladimir Vasilyev was formed. In the same year, having toured abroad for the first time, Maximova gained world renown: American newspapers called her "a baby of the Bolshoi Ballet" and "a lovely little elf." It was also in this

same year that she was awarded First Prize at the Ballet Competition in Vienna. In 1964, she won First Prize in Varna. Her repertoire includes Giselle (which she has danced all her life), the Sylphide in *Chopiniana* (*Les Sylphides*), Jeanne in *The Flames of Paris*, Masha in *The Nutcracker*, Maria in *The Fountain of Bakhchisarai*, Cinderella in *Cinderella*, Princess Florine and Aurora in *The Sleeping Beauty*, the Ballerina in *Petrushka*, Phrygia in *Spartacus*, Juliet in *Romeo and Juliet*, and Kitri in *Don Quixote*. Raised in the best traditions of the academic school, an ideally built miniature ballerina, Maximova dances with refined elegance, joy, and technical perfection. She delights audiences with her virtuoso footwork. Her surprisingly feminine heroines enter into real life and everything becomes a discovery for them. Maximova brings to life the process of the growth of a human soul from naive childhood dreams and a timid conception of love to the triumph of its maturity. She has danced in comic, dramatic, and lyrical ballets. Maximova's heroines never lose their charm: nevertheless, they matured with time, and their cloudless inner world became more profound and complex. Her performing style changed as well: it acquired dramatic expressiveness and graphic sharpness while retaining its harmony. Seeking freedom of expression and being aware of the existence of many dance styles, Maximova successfully danced in

created complex characters such as Eliza Doolittle in *Galatea*, Peter in *The Old Tango*, and Anyuta in *Anyuta*. Vladimir Varkovitsky and Kasyan Goleizovsky choreographed dances (*The Nightingale* and *Mazurka*, respectively) especially for Maximova. Maximova graduated from the State Institute of Theater Art in 1980 after studying to become a teacher and choreographer. She has been teaching at the chair of choreography since 1982. She was appointed a coach of the Kremlin Ballet Theater in 1990. She played dramatic roles in the television film *Gigolo and Gigolette* and in the film *Fouetté*. She also acted in the monoplay *The Song of Songs*. In addition to high national decorations and titles, Maximova was awarded the Anna Pavlova Prize in 1969 and the Marius Petipa Prize in 1972 by the Paris Dance Academy. She won the prize of the Simba International Academy in 1984 and the UNESCO Pablo Picasso Prize in 1990.

**MEZENTSEVA,**
Galina Sergeyevna
(born November 8,1952, in Stavropol, which is now Togliatti).
*Ballerina.*

Mezentseva began to dance as a member of a children's amateur group in the town of Kerch in the Crimea. Thereafter, she was enrolled in the Leningrad Ballet School, where she studied with Nina Belikova and from which she graduated in 1970. In the same year, she joined the corps de ballet of the Kirov Theater. Olga Moiseyeva, a leading ballerina of the theater who initially offered Mezentseva shelter at her home and later became her tutor and coach, trained her for the parts of Raymonda, Nikia in *La Bayadère*, Aurora and the Lilac Fairy in *The Sleeping Beauty*, Giselle, Sylphide, and other roles from the classical repertoire, as well as Mekhmene Bahnu in *The Legend of Love*, the Mistress of the Copper Mountain in *The Stone Flower*, and Zarema in *The Fountain of Bakhchisarai*. Mezentseva has an expressive body with long legs and arms; she is lithe and fragile. She is especially gifted in tragic parts, is very musical, and is inclined to improvise. Her best parts include the Lilac Fairy, Odette, and Nikia. Giselle and Esmeralda also occupy special places in Mezentseva's repertoire. Mezentseva has worked at the Scottish National Ballet in Glasgow since 1990. She played the

productions by the most outstanding foreign choreographers, including Maurice Béjart (Juliet in *Romeo and Juliet*), Roland Petit (Rose in *The Blue Angel*), and John Cranko (Tatiana in *Onegin*). Vasilyev created the following parts in his ballets especially for her: Aeola in *Icarus*, the Ballerina in *These Charming Sounds*, the Solo Dancer in *I Want to Dance* and *Fragments of a Biography*, Anyuta in *Anyuta*, and Cinderella in *Cinderella*. Due to her unique acting gift, which reflects the traditions of the Russian psychological theater, Maximova

184. Natalia Makarova as the Planet in *A Distant Planet*.

185. Yekaterina Maximova as *Anyuta*.

main role in the television film *A Stranger* (after Alexander Blok) and a documentary film about her career was produced. Mezentseva was a prize winner at international ballet competitions in Moscow in 1977 and Osaka in 1980.

### MUKHAMEDOV,
Irek
(born March 8, 1960, in Kazan, Tatarstan).
*Dancer.*
Mukhamedov graduated from the Moscow Ballet School, where he had been a student of Alexander Prokofiev, and worked at the Classical

Ballet Company from 1978 to 1981. He took part in ballets by Natalia Kasatkina and Vladimir Vasilyev, dancing the Shepherd in *The Rite of Spring*, Armen in *Cayane*, and Tybalt in *Romeo and Juliet*. The company's magnificent coach, Naum Azarin, trained Mukhamedov for the International Ballet Competition in Moscow in 1981, and he was awarded the Grand Prix and was invited to work at the Bolshoi Theater. Affirming himself as a heroic and romantic dancer, Mukhamedov danced the main parts in all of Yuri Grigorovich's ballets: he appeared in the title roles in *Spartacus* and *Ivan*

*the Terrible*, Romeo in *Romeo and Juliet*, the Prince in *The Nutcracker*, and Ferkhad in *The Legend of Love*. He also created the part of Boris in *The Golden Age*. A manly, flamboyant dancer with outstanding energy, Mukhamedov continued the heroic traditions of the Russian ballet into the 1980s. He also danced classical roles: Basil in *Don Quixote*, Jean de Brienne in *Raymonda*, Siegfried in *Swan Lake*, and Albert in *Giselle*. He danced the part of Désiré in *The Sleeping Beauty* produced by Rudolf Nureyev at the Vienna Opera and the Opera de Paris. Mukhamedov has been a soloist of the Royal Ballet in London

since 1990. He appeared with the company before the British public for the first time at a concert in honor of the ninetieth birthday of the Queen Mother. However, his offlcial debut was in November, 1990, in *La Bayadère*. Later, Mukhamedov danced in *The Prince of Pagodas* by John Cranko and in *Manon Lescaut*, *Three Sisters*, *The Judas Tree*, and *Winter Dreams* by Kenneth McMillan. The BBC made a documentary film about him and he also won the Laurence Olivier Award.

**NUREYEV,**
Rudolf Khametovich
(born March 17, 1938, on a train near the station of Razdolnoe, Irkutsk area; died January 6, 1993, in Paris).
*Dancer and choreographer.*
When he was five, Nureyev saw a ballet for the first time in his life and decided to become a dancer despite his family's reservations. He began dancing in an amateur group and later participated in the productions of the Opera Theater in Ufa. At the age of seventeen, Nureyev entered the Leningrad Ballet School and, after studying from 1955 to 1958 in Alexander Pushkin's class, he began working at the Kirov Theater. Even while he was at school, it became clear that Nureyev was extraordinarily gifted. In only three seasons, he danced Albert in *Giselle*, Frondoso in *Laurencia*, Désiré and Blue Bird in *The Sleeping Beauty*, Solor in *La Bayadère*, and Basil in *Don Quixote*. He immediately attracted everyone's

attention by the virtuosity of his dance and his unique expressiveness. In 1961, while he was touring Paris, he refused a sudden request that he return to the USSR and decided to remain in the West. Initially, he worked at the Grand Ballet du Marquis de Cuevas and, from 1962, at the Royal Ballet in London. There he danced with Margot Fonteyn. He also appeared with other companies, both in ballets from their repertoires and in productions staged specially for him. He toured regularly in many countries beginning in the mid-1970s with programs called *Nureyev and Friends*. Even though he remained abroad, Nureyev continued to draw on the Russian School that he was brought up in, while simultaneously mastering the various other schools of ballet and modern dance that he encountered in Europe and America. He was the first to combine various traditions of the nineteenth and twentieth centuries so completely. It made him an idol of ballet audiences in many countries for many years and greatly influenced the emerging generation of ballet dancers, especially male dancers, in the West. Many choreographers created works for Nureyev, including

Frederick Ashton (*Marguerite and Armand*), Roland Petit (*Paradise Lost*, *L'Estasi*, and *Pelléas et Mé- lisande*), Rudi van Danzig (*The Ropes of Time* and *Ulysses*), Maurice Béjart (*Song of a Wayfarer*), Glen Tetley (*Tristan*), Martha Graham (*Lucifer*), Murray Louis (*Moments*), George Balanchine (*Le Bourgeois Gentilhomme*), and Pierre Lacotte (*Marco Spada*).

As a choreographer, Nureyev began by reviving Russian ballets, but later he staged his own ballets. His original productions include *The Tempest* at the Royal Ballet (London), *Tancredi* in Vienna, *The Nutcraker* in Stockholm, *Romeo and Juliet* at the Festival Ballet in London, and *Manfred* at Opéra de Paris. Most of his productions have been reproduced in other theaters. He was the art director of the Opéra de Paris ballet company from 1983 to 1989. In 1987, for the first time in twenty-six years, Nureyev appeared on the stage of the Kirov Theater as James in *La Sylphide* as the partner of Yanna Ayupova. One of the greatest dancers of the twentieth century, Nureyev danced over one hundred parts. He also appeared in several feature films (*I am a Dancer* and *Valentino*), participated in the musical *The*

187. Yekaterina Maximova in the title role of *Cinderella*.

188. Galina Mezentseva as Odette in *Swan Lake*.

*King and I*, wrote an autobiographical book (*Nureyev*), and began to appear as a conductor in 1991. The premiere of Nureyev's revival of *La Bayadère* took place on the stage of the Opéra de Paris in October, 1992. After the performance, he was named Commandeur de l'Ordre des Arts et des Lettres. This was the last time that the public saw him alive.

## OSIPENKO,
Alla
(June 16, 1932, in Leningrad). *Ballerina and teacher.*

Osipenko began dancing in a school amateur group. Just before the war began, on the last peaceful day of 1941, she entered the Leningrad Ballet School. Having studied under Agrippina Vaganova, Osipenko graduated in 1950 and was a leading ballerina of the Kirov Theater from 1950 to 1971. Her talent became

apparent even while she was still in school. She had a beautiful body of exquisite proportions and a unique fluency of movement that generated clear, "singing" lines and light, oblong proportions. One could sense strong emotions in Osipenko's dance despite an outward appearance of reserve. Though Osipenko danced in many classical ballets and was even awarded the Anna Pavlova Prize by the Dance Academy of Paris, she preferred modern dance. The only classical roles that she liked were Odette-Odile in *Swan Lake*, the Lilac Fairy in *The Sleeping Beauty*, and Gamzatti in *La Bayadère*. However, she was especially versatile in contemporary ballets.

The highlight of Ospenko's artistic career was the role of the Mistress of the Copper Mountain in *The Stone Flower*, which was created especially to display her talents. In this part, her talent for tragedy was

revealed. While apparently aloof and frigid, Osipenko was really intensely passionate.

Howere, she did not let her emotions come to the surface. Osipenko's dance was based on contrasts that went to the heart of her heroines' psychological dilemmas. This opened new opportunities in ballet interpretation. After the Mistress of the Copper Mountain, Osipenko danced The Beloved One in *The Coast of Hope*, Desdemona in *Othello*, and Mekhmene Bahnu .in *The Legend of Love*. She also worked with Georgy Alexidze in the Chamber Ballet in 1966-67 and danced the main part in *Antonius and Cleopatra* by Igor Chernyshov at the Leningrad Maly Theater in 1968. After retiring from the Kirov Theater, Osipenko worked at the Choreographic Miniatures Company with Leonid Jakobson from 1971 to 1973 and with Boris Eifman from 1973 to 1977. She was fascinated with the novel choregraphy and unique talents of these choreographers.

Osipenko appeared in several television ballet films and in feature films as a dramatic actress. She has been teaching abroad since 1988.

## PAVLOVA,
Nadezhda Vasilyevna

189. Rudolf Nureyev as Frondoso in *Laurencia*.

190. Irek Mukhamedov as Boris in *The Golden Age*.

(born May 15, 1956, in Cheboksary).
*Ballerina.*
Pavlova graduated from the Perm Ballet School in 1974 after studying with Ludlila Sakharova.
While a student, she danced on the stage of the Perm Opera and Ballet Theater in *Coppélia*, *Giselle*, *Don Quixote*, and *Romeo and Juliet*. While still in school, she won the first prize at the All-Union Ballet Competition in Moscow.

This sixteen-years-old girl from Chuvashia, who looked like a child, effortlessly outperformed experienced dancers. She became famous even before she finished school. The same thing happened again the next year at the Moscow International Ballet Competition, where she won the Grand Prix and a Gold Medal. Her pas de chat amazed everyone with its perfection, and she performed the 32 fouettés on a single spot near the footlights. Pavlova's dance delighted spectators with its astounding grace, purity, freshness, and joy. She joined the Bolshoi Theater company in 1975, and Galina Ulanova and Marina Semenova became her coaches. Pavlova's repertoire includes Masha in *The Nutcracker*, Shirin in *The Legend of Love*, Princess Florine in *The Sleeping Beauty*, and Katerina in *The Stone Flower*. She is best in the parts of lighthearted, gay heroines, but she can also express strong emotions. From 1975 to 1985, she danced with Vyacheslav Gordeyev in a duet that was a great success with the public. Pavlova has been decorated with several state orders.

**PLISETSKAYA,**
Maya Mikhailovna
(born November 20,1925, in Moscow).
*Ballerina.*
Plisetskaya was born into an artistic family on her mother's side. When the eight-year-old, red-headed girl was brought for examinations to the Moscow Ballet School, her talent was evident. She worked with great

191. Rudolph Nureyev as James in *La Sylphide.*

192. Alla Osipenko as Mekhmene Bahnu in *The Legend of Love.*

assiduity. Plisetskaya studied under Yelizaveta Gerdt and Maria Leontyeva and graduated in 1943. She joined the Bolshoi Theater and gained wide renown almost immediately. Plisetskaya is one of the most outstanding ballerinas of the second half of the twentieth century. Her name has become legendary. Her long career is seemingly a mystery. But there are reasons for it: her extraordinary career was made possible both by her natural gifts (energy, a strong will, and a unique suppleness of her muscles) and, primarily, by her remarkable perseverance. From the beginning,

Plisetskaya developed her own style, and she ended by creating her own type of ballet theater. Her style is graphic and graceful, but sharp. Every gesture, pose, and separate pas is complete in itself and falls into a perfect whole. Endowed with a great imagination and an inexhaustible interest in every new trend, Plisetskaya nevertheless consistently and laboriously built up her unique artistic image. Thus, she became a great tragic actress of the ballet theater. Tragedy has attracted her since adolescence. The first embryo of a tragedy was demonstrated by Plisetskaya in

1945, when *Cinderella* was produced. Due to her extraordinary elevation, expressive movements, and keen feeling of rhythm, she imbued the dance "Autumn", a mere divertissement in the episode in which Cinderella travels to the palace, with poignant drama. The contrast with the atmosphere of fairy entertainment that prevailed in the ballet was striking. The same contrast with the style of the "grand ballet" of the 1950s and 1960s was later evident in nearly all of Plisetskaya's stage performances. Her emotions were intense, and her dance was striking both in the lighthearted *Don Quixote* and in the academic ballet *Raymonda*. This brilliance was coupled with tragedy in the part of Carmen (*Carmen Suite*), which was to become one of Plisetskaya's most important creations at the Bolshoi. In this ballet, Plisetskaya achieved her goal: the ballet was modern in its choreography, and its theme was tragic. In the 1970s, Plisetskaya began staging ballets herself: *Anna Karenina*, *The Sea Gull*, and *The Lady with a Dog*. Plisetskaya left the Bolshoi Theater in 1988. She was offered an opportunity to dance in a genuinely classical tragedy (*Phèdre*) by the Ballet Company of Nancy in France and in *Mary Stuart* by the Madrid Ballet Company. Plisetskaya has performed Fokine's solo dance *The Dying Swan*, which represents the very essence of her tragic art. Plisetskaya danced in productions by foreign companies, including *La Rose Malade* (Ballet du Marseille), *Boléro*, *Isadora*, and *Léda* (Le Ballet du XX$^e$ Siècle, Brussels), *Phèdre* (The Ballet Company of the Nancy Theater, the Odéon in Paris, and the Rome Opera), and *El Renedero* (Theatro Colon, Buenos Aires). She was the art director of the Rome Opera Ballet Company in 1983-84 and of the Theatro Lirico Nacional in Madrid from 1988 to 1990. There, she revived *La Fille Mal Gardée* and danced in *Carmen Suite* and *Mary Stuart*. A ballet after the play by Jean Giraudoux, *La Folle de Chaillot*, was first staged in 1992 at Espace Pierre Cardin, with Plisetskaya dancing the main role. She appeared in the ballet films *Master of the Russian Ballet*, *Swan Lake*, *The Little Humpbacked Horse*, and *Anna Karenina*, and in feature films

193. Nadezhda Pavlova as Kitri in *Don Quixote*

184

such as *Anna Karenina* and *Tchaikovsky* as a dramatic actress. She also appeared in the television film *Fantasy*. Plisetskaya was awarded the Anna Pavlova Prize in 1962 and the French title of Commandeur de la Légion d'Honneur in 1984 and 1986. She has also been decorated with a number of prestigious national orders. She was conferred the title of Doctor of the Sorbonne, Honoris Causa. She has participated in recital programs abroad and has given master classes since 1990. She is married to the composer Rodion Shchedrin, who has written the music for several of her ballets.

### SEMENYAKA,
Ludmila Ivanovna
(born January, 16, 1952, in Leningrad).
*Ballerina.*
Born into a family that had no interest in either the theater or the ballet, Semenyaka herself applied to a dance studio in a Young Pioneers' Palace and immediately attracted everyone's attention with her grace and musical gift. She was recommended as a candidate student to the Leningrad Ballet School, where she was enrolled and became a student of Nina

Belikova. After graduating in 1970, she danced at the Kirov Theater and, from 1979 to 1991, at the Bolshoi Theater. At the Bolshoi, Semenyaka was coached by Galina Ulanova and Marina Semenova. While still a student she entered the Moscow International Ballet Competition in 1969 with a dance called *We*. She amazed everyone with her technique in representing a mischievous teenager and won over audiences with her youthful ardor and amusing dancing. Semenyaka combines the strict academism of the St. Petersburg school and the emotional manner of the Moscow School. She demonstrates perfect correctness in executing pas while simultaneously conveying absolute sincerity. Her refined and virtuoso dance is correct but unrestrained and filled with natural emotions. Semenyaka is both an ideal classical dancer and an actress who is able to develop characters with the full range of longings, impulses, and feelings. Her artistic manner was greatly influenced by Leonid Jakobson. Semenyaka's repertoire includes *Swan Lake*, *The Sleeping Beauty*, *Raymonda*, *Giselle*, and all of

Yuri Grigorovich's ballets at the Bolshoi. She gained international renown after touring the United States with the Bolshoi Theater. Semenyaka danced three times at the Teatro Colon in Buenos Aires, and each time she was awarded a laurel wreath. She also danced with the Opéra de Paris, the Swedish Royal Ballet, and the Royal Ballet in London on a contract basis and as a touring dancer in 1991-92. She had great success at international ballet competitions in Moscow in 1969, in Varna in 1972, and in Tokyo in 1976. She was awarded the Anna Pavlova Prize in Paris in 1976.

### SIZOVA,
Alla Ivanovna
(born September 22 1939, in Moscow).
*Ballerina and teacher.*
A graduate of the Leningrad Ballet School (where she studied with Natalia Kamkova), Sizova danced the Queen of Dryads in *Don Quixote* with great success at the Kirov Theater while still a student. She joined the Kirov in 1958 and, two years later (during a tour of France, the United

195. Maya Plisetskaya in the title role of *Isadora*.

196. Maya
Plisetskaya in the
title role of *Anna
Karenina*

197. Ludmila
Semenyaka as Aurora
in *The Sleeping Beauty*.

Kingdom, the United States, and Canada), she captivated the public with her performance in *The Sleeping Beauty*. Sizova's Aurora seemed to embody charming and carefree youth itself; her triumphant and weightless flight drew the audience into her happiness. Sizova won the Anna Pavlova Prize in Paris in 1964 for her role in the film *The Sleeping Beauty*. This was followed by a whole series of victories at various festivals and competitions. Sizova danced Giselle, Juliet, Katerina in *The Stone Flower*, and Maria in *The Fountain of Bakhchisarai*, creating lyric characters of great charm. The part of the Girl in *The Leningrad Symphony* by Igor

Belsky was created especially for her in 1961. The 1960s saw many of Sizova's triumphs. However, her career was so demanding that it resulted in several traumas. She managed to overcome her first serious illness within a relatively short time, but the second one threatened to end her career. When Sizova returned to the stage in 1968, after an absence of about three years, the public found that her characters had become more mature. Her performances were full of spirit and harmony, but now lyrical and dramatic parts were closer to her heart. Konstantin Sergeyev created the part of Ophelia in *Hamlet* and Oleg Vinogradov the part of

Princess Rose in *The Prince of the Pagodas* for Sizova in the early 1970s. She appeared in the ballet film *Encounter with Terpsichore*. Sizova retired from the stage in 1988 and has been teaching at the Leningrad Ballet School since then.

**SOLOVYOV,**
Yuri Vladimirovich
(born August 10, 1940,
in Leningrad; died there January
12,1977).
*Dancer.*
In 1958 Solovyov graduated from the Leningrad Ballet School, where he studied under Boris Shavrov, and joined the Kirov Theater. Because

198. Alla Sizova as Princess Florina in *The Sleeping Beauty*.

**TIMOFEYEVA,**
Nina Vladimirovna
(born June 11, 1935, in Leningrad).
*Ballerina and teacher.*
Timofeyeva graduated from the Leningrad Ballet School, where she had been a student of Natalia Kamkova. She made her debut at the Kirov Theater in 1952 as Masha in *The Nutcracker* and, after graduating in 1953, she joined this company. During her first two seasons, Timofeyeva attracted attention as Odette-Odile in *Swan Lake* and Myrtha in *Giselle*. She moved to the Bolshoi Theater in 1956 and danced there for more than thirty years. Timofeyeva is regarded as one of the greatest tragic actresses of the twentieth-century ballet. Her virtuoso and academically pure dance was characterized by expressiveness and overwhelming power. Her heroines were torn by inner contradictions: because they were suppressing passionate impulses, they could find no peace. Timofeyeva danced many roles in the classical repertoire, as well as Mireille de Poitiers in *The Flames of Paris* and Laurencia in *Laurencia*. Her best performances were in ballets by modern choreographers: she was the first to dance Aegina in *Spartacus* by Yuri Grigorovich and was unforgettable as Mekhmene Bahnu in his *Legend of Love*. She created Lady Macbeth in Vladimir Vasilyev's *Macbeth*, which was staged especially for her. She danced in several original television ballets,

of his outstanding talent, Solovyov was immediately noticed by the critics. He had a fabulous elevation, easily performed double tours in the air, and successfully danced parts that required virtuoso classical dance technique and impeccable style, such as Siegfried, Désiré, Albert; the Poet in *Chopiniana* (*Les Sylphides*), and the Genie of the Waters in *The Little Humpbacked Horse*. Performing the Blue Bird in *The Sleeping Beauty*, Solovyov soared over the stage, softly descended, and shot upwards again as if the air were his natural element. In 1963, the French Academy of Dance conferred on Solovyov the title of the world's best dancer, and he won the Gold Star Prize in 1965 at the International Dance Festival. Among his best roles were Ferkhad in *The Legend of Love*, the Fisherman in *The Coast of Hope*, and Danila in *The Stone Flower* (by Yuri Grigorovich). This last role became a landmark in

his career: his dance animated the poetry of the Russian fairy tale and the Russian soul. A lyrical dancer, Solovyov did not confine himself to one type of ballet. His dance reached a heroic climax and was imbued with dramatic pathetics in Belsky's *The Leningrad Symphony*, in which the Young Man was created especially for Solovyov. Dancing the part of God in *The Creation of the World* by Natalia Kasatkina and Vladimir Vasilyev, Solovyov unexpectedly demonstrated a gift for comedy. He worked with many choreographers, including Konstantin Sergeyev, Konstantin Boyarsky, Leonid Jakobson, and Georgy Alexidze. He was filmed as Désiré in the film *The Sleeping Beauty* in 1964 and appeared in several television concerts. Solovyov died suddenly and tragically in the prime of his career. His image has merged with those of the characters that he created.

199. Yuri Solovyov as Danila in *The Stone Flower*.

188

including Phèdra in the ballet of the same name (1972) and the Old Countess and the Queen of Spades in *Three Cards* after Pushkin's story *The Queen of Spades* (1983). She was filmed in *Spartacus* (1976) and in some television dance programs, including a film called *How Can the Heart Express Itself?*, which was dedicated to her career (1973). She also appeared in a film called *Solo Dancers of the Bolshoi Theater* (1978), which included two miniatures that she choreographed herself. She also appeared as the ballerina Tropinina in the television film *Grand Pas*, which she choreographed as well. After retiring from the stage in 1988, Timofeyeva coached at the Bolshoi Theater from 1989 to 1991. She has lived and worked in Israel since 1991 and has written a book entitled *The World of Dance*, which was published in Moscow in 1993.

## VASILYEV,
Vladimir Viktorovich
(born April 18,1940, in Moscow).
*Dancer and choreographer.*
In 1958, he graduated from the Moscow Ballet School, where he studied under Mikhail Gabovich. A blond man of medium height with a round face and brown eyes, Vasilyev stood out for his unique beauty of movement and, more importantly, for his selfless love of dancing. After graduating, he was immediately accepted by the Bolshoi Theater as a soloist. He danced the lighthearted,

mischievous Ivanushka in *The Little Humpbacked Horse*, a role characterized by humor and elements of buffoonery. At the same time, he danced the poetic part of Danila in *The Stone Flower* in 1959. Easily changing his appearance and way of moving, Vasilyev subordinated the dance to the character, thus combining the best traditions of the classical Russian ballet with the subtleties of modern choreography. He danced the love-possessed Medjnun in *Leili and Medjnun*, creating on the ballet stage a real oriental prince. In the part of Fokine's Petrushka, Vasilyev used grotesque puppet movements to reveal a profound human tragedy. He was irresistible as Basil (*Don Quixote*), with virtuoso technique and an unusual combination of movements. The Prince Nutcracker was Vasilyev's greatest success. While he was still a toy nutcracker, his movements were mechanical, sharp, abrupt – then, when he was transformed into the Prince, they acquired elegance, romantic beauty and boldness. The purity of the dance pattern conveyed the character's purity of heart. As Romeo in *Romeo and Juliet*, Vasilyev gave the part new meaning by demonstrating the inner development of the young man from his initial light-heartedness to the tragic revelations of the end of the ballet. As Désiré in *The Sleeping Beauty*, Vasilyev tried to get insight into a poetic character by treating him as a Romantic hero. The role of Spartacus, which was meant to be a symbol of heroic longing and action, is the dancer's most outstanding achievement. Many of these roles he danced with Yekaterina Maximova, his wife. In addition to his brilliant dancing gifts and dramatic talent, Vasilyev has knowledge and intuition that enable him to understand the philosophy and the structure of the music that he works with. In 1964, Vasilyev won First Prize at the International Ballet competition in Varna and the Vaslav Nijinsky Prize in Paris: he was proclaimed the best dancer in the world. Vasilyev performed in Maurice Béjart's Ballet du XXe Siècle and Roland Petit's Ballet de Marseille,

usually in duet with Maximova. Vasilyev graduated from the choreographic department of the State Institute of Theater Art in 1982 and started teaching the same year at the chair of choreography. He headed that department from 1985 and became a professor in 1989. He staged a number of ballets, including *Icarus* (1971), *These Charming Sounds* (1973), *Macbeth* (1980), *Anyuta* (1986), *Romeo and Juliet* (1990), and *Cinderella* (1991). Vasilyev is an accomplished painter as well, specializing in Russian landscapes. The Ballet and Music Festival was held in Moscow in May 1993 in his honor. He has won a number of prestigous national prizes and decorations.

## VINOGRADOV,
Oleg Mikhailovich
(born August 1,1937, in Leningrad).
*Dancer and choreographer.*
After graduating from the Leningrad Ballet School (where he had been a student of Alexander Pushkin), Vinogradov worked at the Novosibirsk Theater from 1958 to 1965. There he danced his first character parts and made his debut as a choreographer. Initially, he staged

200. Nina Timofeyeva as Lady Macbeth in *Macbeth*.

201. Vladimir Vasilyev as Basil in *Don Quixote*.

202. A scene from
Vladimir Vasilyev's
production of *Icarus*

203. Vladimir
Vasilyev as Piotr
Leontievich and
boldness. The purity
of the dance in
*Anyuta*.

190

204. A scene from
Oleg Vinogradov's
staging of *The Knight
in the Tiger Skin*.

205. The *Revizor* from
Oleg Vinogradov

dances in ballets; however, in 1964 he produced his first full ballet *Cinderella*, and in 1965, he produced *Romeo and Juliet*. In his first productions, Vinogradov displayed a startling artistic independence and created a new choreography that attracted great interest. He extended the ideas of the innovative choreographers of the late 1950s and 1960s, who believed strongly in dance and expressed their ideas through it exclusively. Vinogradov worked as a choreographer at the Kirov Theater from 1968 to 1972. There, he staged several ballets: *Gorianka* (*The Girl of the Mountains*), which used Dagestan's dance folklore; *Alexander Nevsky*; *The Two*; and *The Enchanted Prince*. He was chief choreographer of the Leningrad Maly Theater from 1973 to 1979 and produced new versions of classical ballets there: *La Fille Mal Gardée* and *Coppélia*. *Yaroslavna* was one of his most important ballets: it was produced with the help of stage director Yuri Lyubimov. Vinogradov has been the art director and chief choreographer of the Kirov (now, Mariinsky) Theater since 1977. Today, Vinogradov is one of the most prominent Russian choreographers. His interests are varied: he draws inspiration from fairy-tales, such as *The Fairy from the Rondo Mountains*; tragedies, such as *Battleship "Potemkin"*; and satyrical comedies, including *The Inspector General*, after the comedy by Nikolai Gogol. He boldly experiments in developing new dance forms. Graphic sharpness is typical of Vinogradov's choreographic style. Vinogradov also staged *Asel*, based on a story by the Kirghiz writer Chingiz Aitmatov that was popular in the 1960s; *The Knight in the Tiger Skin*, after a narrative poem by the great twelveth-century Georgian writer Shota Rustaveli

(Vinogradov won the international prize The Golden Dancing Girl of Picasso for this ballet at the Chicago Festival in 1987); and his own version of *Petrushka*. As the art director of the Mariinsky theater, Vinogradov pays great attention to the revival and preservation of the best classical ballets. He often invites western choreographers to Russia. In 1990, he founded the Universal Ballet Academy in Washington D.C., and he has established the St. Petersburg school as the educational basis there. He also organized the Mariinsky Theater Small Ballet Company. In addition to the highest titles and decorations of Russia, Vinogradov has won the Marius Petipa Prize in France, the Laurence Olivier Award in the United Kingdom, and has been conferred the title of Chevalier in France.

**VLADIMIROV,**
Yuri Kuzmich
(born January 1, 1942, in Moscow).
*Dancer.*
Vladimirov studied at the Moscow Ballet School under Alexei Yermolayev, and after graduating, he worked at the Bolshoi Theater from 1962 to 1988. Although he did not meet all the standards of a classical dancer, Vladimirov was endowed with indomitable energy, unreserved audacity, and powerful elevation. Thus, he was able to excel in modern choreography. This extraordinary dancer was first discovered by the choreographers Natalia Kasatkina and Vladimir Vasilyev, both beginners at that time. They staged a ballet called *A Heroic Poem (Geologists)* with Vladimirov's unique qualities in mind.
His dancing gifts, infused with spontaneous power, were demonstrated even more clearly in the part

of the Shepherd in *The Rite of Spring*, which was also staged by Kasatkina and Vasilyev. At this time, a remarkable duet between Vladimirov and Nina Sorokina formed, and it soon won international recognition, first at the Ballet Competition in Varna, Bulgaria, in 1966, and then at the first International Ballet Competition in Moscow in 1969. In 1969, they also won the Gold Medal as the Best Ballet Duet at the International Festival in Paris, and Vladimirov himself won the Vaslav Nijinsky Prize of the Paris Academy of Dance. Consequently many roles were created especially for Vladimirov: the Peasant at the Station in *Anna Karenina*, Benedict in *Love for Love*, and Don Quixote in *The Knight of the Sad Image*. The part of Tsar Ivan the Terrible in the ballet by Yuri Grigorovich was to become Vladimirov's most important achievement.
Vladimirov has been a coach at the Bolshoi Theater since 1989. He has appeared in several television ballet films and in the ballet feature film *The Terrible Age*, based on *Ivan the Terrible*. His wife, Nina Ivanovna Sorokina (born May 13, 1942), was a student of Sofia Golovkina at Moscow Choreographic School. After she graduated from the School, she worked at the Bolshoi Theater in 1961-88 where she perfected her skills under Marina Timofeevna Semenova. Sorokina's dance imbued with immaculate technique was clear and tender and her movements were perfect. Her behavior on the stage featured spontaneity, naturalness, and sincerity. Sorokina's characters were lyrical, feminine, defenseless, and self-denying. These features excellently complemented and emphasized the quality of Yuri Vladimirov, a courageous, spontaneous, and unexpectedly emotional dancer.

206. Oleg Vinogradov's sketch for *Asel*

207. Yuri Vladimirov
in the title role *Ivan
the Terrible.*

THE IMMORTAL RUSSIAN BALLET

Ballet is an art for the young: generational changes take place here much faster than in any other art. Dancers enter the theater when they are quite young, and the best of them quickly become famous. Altynai Asylmuratova, Farukh Ruzimatov, Nina Ananiashvili, and Andris Liepa seem to have appeared on the stage just recently, but they are already world-class stars. In turn, they have been followed by new dancers, who are still not very widely known. However, it is worth while for admirers of Terpsichore to memorize their names.

Two Nikias in *La Bayadère*. 209 a. The dance of Yulia Makhalina (born 1968; since 1985, at the Mariinsky Theater) is graphically precise and expressive, with strong jetés that seem to dissect the air. It is natural, therefore, that strong-willed characters are her forte.

previous pages 208. The apex of classical Russian ballet was Marius Petipa's *The Sleeping Beauty*, shown here in a revival on the stage of the Mariinsky Theater.

209 b. Nadezhda Gracheva (born 1969; since 1987, at the Bolshoi Theater). Her main advantage is neither a broad, beautiful developpé , nor her elevation but rather a touching fluidity of lines and a tense inner life. These qualities are nurtured in the ballerina by the great Galina Ulanova, her tutor at the Bolshoi.

210. Galina Stepanenko (born 1966: first appeared on stage in 1984; since 1989, at the Bolshoi Theater) is noted for unique pirouettes, heated dance bravura, and high jumps. Andrei Uvarov (born 1971; since 1989, at the Bolshoi Theater) is a lyrical and romantic dancer with a lofty performance style and expressive arms. He is one of the few to have been awarded the Benois Prize. Stepanenko as Odette and Uvarov in the role of Siegfried in *Swan Lake*.

211. Alla Mikhalchenko (born 1957; since 1976, at the Bolshoi Theater). Tall and shapely, Mikhalchenko is refined and striking, and her dance is smooth and harmonious. Mikhalchenko dances Shirin in Yuri Grigorovich's ballet *The Legend of Love*.

212. Inna Petrova (born 1967; since 1985, at the Bolshoi Theater) has a special smoothness of movements and a perfection of body lines. The dance of Mark Peretokin (born 1964; since 1983, at the Bolshoi Theater) is picturesque and harmonious especially in duets. Petrova as Juliet and Peretokin as Romeo in Grigorovich's *Romeo and Juliet*.

213. Nina Ananiashvili (born 1963; since 1981, at the Bolshoi Theater). Ananiashvili captivates spectators with her fine, plastic pattern and refined reserve. Among her numerous decorations and awards, she cherishes most highly a pearl brooch that was presented to her as a gift by the great Tamara Toumanova: this brooch once belonged to Anna Pavlova. Andris Liepa (born 1962; at the Bolshoi Theater from 1981 to 1990). Maris Liepa's son. The expressiveness of his dance and the sincerity of his stage presence enable Liepa to perform parts of many styles and forms. Ananiashvili and Liepa in Fokine's ballet *Le Spectre de la Rose*.

214. Inna Chistyakova (born 1957; since 1975, at the Mariinsky Theater). A precision of dance presentation, a thorough refinement of each movement make even the most virtuoso passages look strictly academic for this ballerina.

Chistyakova in The Grand Pas from *Paquila.*

215. Ulyana Lopatkina (born 1973; since 1991, at the Mariinsky Theater). St. Petersburg critics believe that Lopatkina is the first ballerina in the last twenty years to graduate from the Ballet School with such a charming and refined gift.

Lopatkina in Michel Fokine's *The Dying Swan.*

216. Tatiana Chernobrovkina (born 1965; first appeared on stage in 1983). Having mastered virtuoso technique and being endowed with an expressive manner, Chernobrovkina feels at home with many different styles of dance. Chernobrovkina dances in Dmitry Bryantsev's *The Swan Song*. Her partner is Vladimir Kirillov.

217. Maria Bylova
(born 1956; since
1975, at the Bolshoi
Theater) combines an
academic performing
style with a genuine
stage presence.
Alexander Vetrov
(born 1961; since
1979, at the Bolshoi
Theater) has excellent
choreographic
qualities: elevation,
swift pirouettes, and
an extraordinary
temperament.

Bylova is shown as
Aegina and Vetrov as
Crassus in
Grigorovich's ballet
*Spartacus*.

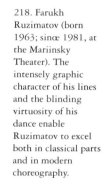

218. Farukh Ruzimatov (born 1963; since 1981, at the Mariinsky Theater). The intensely graphic character of his lines and the blinding virtuosity of his dance enable Ruzimatov to excel both in classical parts and in modern choreography.

Ruzimatov dances with Natalia Bolshakova in *Heliogabale* by Maurice Béjart.

219. Altynai Asylmuratova (born 1961; since 1978, at the Mariinsky Theater). She is regarded as "the pearl of the company." A classic dancer of lyrico-dramatic style, Asylmuratova unites in her performance the best principles established by the Academic School of St. Petersburg: purity and lyricism of dance, accuracy and beauty of lines, lightness and inspiration.

Asylmuratova dances the part of Kitry in *Don Quixote*. Basil is danced by Konstantin Zaklinsky.

# Great figures of Russian Ballet
# Index

ACKNOWLEDGEMENTS

Ballet scholars and critics whose works have been used in this book:

E. Belova, E. Bocharnikova, G. Brodskaya, N. Chernova, V. Chistyakova, A. Chizhova, S. Davlekamova, G. Dobrovolskaya, N. Dunaeva, E. Dyukina, V. Gaevsky, T. Gorina, B. Illarionov, M. Ilyicheva, G. Inozemtseva, P. Karp, V. Krasovskaya, F. Krymko, T. Kuzovleva, B. Lvov-Anokhin, V. Majniece, O. Martynova, E. Nadezhdina, T. Orlova, V. Pappe, N. Sadovskaya, A. Sokolov-Kaminsky, I. Stupnikov, E. Surits, V. Zarubin, N. Zozulina.

**Photographers:**

V. Baranovsky, A. Brazhnikov, E. Fetisova, D. Kulikov, G. Larionova, A. Nevezhin, V. Perelmuter, L. Sherstennikova, S. Shevelchinskaya, G. Solovyev, A. Stepanov, E. Umnov.

**Illustrations** have been supplied by collections of the A. A. Bakhrushin State Central Theater Museum, St. Petersburg Theater and Musical Art Museum, Diaghilev Center Moscow Association (by courtesy), Ceramics Museum at Kuskovo 18th century estate, State Russian Museum, State Tretyakov Art Gallery, S. Sorokin's private collection, and other collections of Russia.

The scientific editor of the book is Doctor of Fine Arts E. Surits, a well-known ballet scholar. Contributors are also prominent modern Russian ballet scholars.

*Edition director:* Paul André

*Scholarly compilers:* G. Andreevskaya, A. Smirina.

*Scholarly editors:* Dr. N. Gadzhinskaya, B. Khudyakova.

*Reviewing editors:* Dr. N. Landa, E. Rodina, V. Sinyukov, Dr. G. Yakusheva. Artwork designer: B. Miroshin. Art editor: L. Mushtakova.

*Translated into English by* V. Arkadyev, I. Bershadsky, and F. Kreynin.

*English Translation editor:* R. Coalson, United States.

*Project coordinators:* E. Beglyarova, I. Smirnova, and E. Talalaeva.

*Layout:* Parkstone Press

*Computersetting:* Gabriela Wachter/Marie Pleyber

*Coordination:* Chantal Jameux

*Assistant:* Céline Gallot

Printed and bound in Europe
ISBN 1 85995 175 9
© Parkstone Publishers, Bournemouth, England 1998
© The Great Encyclopedia of Russia, Publishing House